AF394567

BETWEEN THE LINES

Published by:
National Library Board, Singapore
100 Victoria Street
#14-01 National Library Building
Singapore 188064
www.nlb.gov.sg
For enquiries, please contact ref@nlb.gov.sg

Designed by Marshall Cavendish International Asia Pte Ltd
Printed in Singapore

National Library Board, Singapore Cataloguing in Publication Data
Name(s): Singapore. National Library Board, publisher.
Title: Between the lines : early print advertising in Singapore, 1830s–1960s.
Description: Singapore : National Library Board, Singapore, [2018]
Identifier(s): OCN 1039215383 | ISBN 978-981-47-9467-1 (hardcover)
Subject(s): LCSH: Advertising–Singapore–History–19th century–Pictorial works. | Advertising–Singapore–History–20th century–Pictorial works.
Classification: DDC 659.1095957–dc23

BETWEEN THE LINES

Early Print Advertising in Singapore
1830s–1960s

Advertisement by local company F&N marketing its aerated waters with an exoticised image of Malaya, brought to life by dramatic copywriting.
Source: *The Straits Times Annual*, 1952, p. 112. Retrieved from PublicationSG.

Contents

Advertisement for Raleigh bicycles, a British brand, riding on the recent coronation of Queen Elizabeth II to launch its "New Elizabethan" model.
Source: *The Straits Times Annual*, 1954, p. 131. Retrieved from PublicationSG.

Foreword

This volume presents nearly 400 advertisements – from the 1830s to 1960s – from the collection of the National Library, Singapore. They are selected from a variety of print materials, including newspapers, books, periodicals and ephemera.

Written by our own librarians and curators, the eight chapters in this book provide an overview of print advertisements for a range of goods or services: automobiles, entertainment, fashion, food, hospitality, household goods, medical and travel. Beyond offering a glimpse into the material world of a particular period, advertisements may also reveal certain cultural conditions of the day, such as racial prejudices and gender stereotypes. By situating advertisements within a socio-historical context, we can understand better why and how companies peddled certain products – and ideals – as well as why consumers might have been drawn to them.

The introductory essay by writer Yu-Mei Balasingamchow sets the backdrop for subsequent chapters as she explores the history of newspaper advertising, the rise of the consumer class as well as the cultural history of shopping in Singapore. Put together, this book paints a vivid picture of the wealthy and middle class in colonial Singapore, shedding light on some of their anxieties, aspirations and manufactured desires.

The National Library is delighted to present this volume of advertisements from our past. We hope it will interest not only advertising professionals, but also history buffs and researchers, in fact, anyone who seeks a deeper understanding of the material lives of a privileged class in old Singapore.

Wai Yin Pryke
Director, National Library
National Library Board

Advertisement for Daks flannels sold at Whiteaway's. (1940)

INTRODUCTION

How many advertisements have you seen today? Probably more than you realise. Our world is saturated with them, from print ads in magazines and newspapers, to commercials on radio and television, to pop-up ads on websites, and all manner of posters, banners and billboards dotting the urban landscape. We are surrounded by more advertisements than we can make sense of, selling us things we might need, things we never knew we needed, and things we clearly will never need – and yet we sometimes fall prey to them anyway.

Cast your mind back to 55 years ago, to a time before the introduction of television broadcasting in Singapore. Advertisements then played a rather different role within the information ecosystem. Newspapers and magazines were the cheapest, most accessible way of finding out what was going on, and advertisements were an essential component of these publications. How else would you know when the latest fashion, music or movies had arrived in town, or which department store was having a sale that weekend?

Cast your mind back another half a century earlier: Print advertisements were then strikingly simpler in design and predominantly text-based, without the large illustrations or photographs that we have become accustomed to. Despite being less arresting visually, they were packed with information and persuasive claims – the best accommodation to be had in town, the advantages of buying a gas stove for the home, the need for insect repellents to prevent "tropical diseases", the latest and most fashionable brands of perfumes and soaps from Europe. These advertisements paint a captivating picture of everyday life at the time, the things people needed, and the comforts and pleasures they desired.

This book presents an overview of print advertisements in Singapore publications that are held in the collection of the National Library Board,[1] spanning the 1830s up to the 1960s, when the introduction of television broadcasting and advertising profoundly changed the economic, social and media environment. Like voices from the past, these print advertisements are lively and expressive, at times straight-talking and at times oblique, rewarding our close attention with surprising details about life in Singapore, particularly its consumer culture, over a century and a half of change.

NEWSPAPER ADVERTISING, FROM EUROPE TO SINGAPORE

Of the many types of publications that carried print advertisements in Singapore, newspapers are likely the oldest, the longest-running and widest in reach, making them one of the richest and most diverse sources of such historical material. Singapore published its first newspapers soon after it became a British colony: the first was the English-language *Singapore Chronicle and Commercial Register,* which published its inaugural edition on 1 January 1824.[2] Singapore's main English-language broadsheet today, *The Straits Times*, dates back to 15 July 1845, while the first newspapers in Asian languages appeared in the late 19th century: the Malay *Jawi Peranakkan* (1876), several Tamil newspapers (1870s), the Chinese *Lat Pau* (1881) and the Baba Malay *Bintang Timor* (1894).[3]

All these newspapers grew largely out of the European model. After the invention of the mechanised printing press by Johannes Gutenberg in 1439, printed materials could be produced far more quickly and in far greater quantities than before. By the 17th century, many towns and cities in Europe had publications resembling what we now think of as a newspaper: a regularly printed publication containing news and information, targeted at the masses and openly available for sale to anyone who could afford it.[4]

From the start, newspapers relied on advertising revenue to cover their cost of production and perhaps even to turn a profit. As historian Kevin Williams notes, "[A]s early as 1705 one of the leading newspaper figures of the period, Daniel Defoe, could comment that 'the principal support of all the public papers now on foot depends on advertisements'."[5] By the 18th century, the word "advertisement" was being used as we know it today, and Samuel Johnson's seminal *Dictionary of the English Language* (1755) defined the term "advertiser" as a "paper in which advertisements appear".[6]

The role of advertising agents had emerged – they worked for newspapers to sell advertising space in exchange for a cut of 10 to 15 percent – and newspaper advertising space grew in demand. As newspaper historian Bob Clarke writes, "No other medium could offer such wide circulation, instant publication, regular appearance and extensive distribution."[7]

By the early 19th century, further technological developments such as mechanised paper-making and the invention of more powerful presses allowed newspapers and other publications to be produced even more cheaply and quickly. With new typefaces, improved print types and the ability to reproduce drawings, publications became more readable and attractive.[8] In England, printing blocks for advertisements could be centrally produced and sent to different publications all over the country; this enabled advertisers to run national campaigns for products as diverse as cocoa, tobacco, soap and medicines.[9]

It was at this time that the printing press and the newspaper medium arrived in Singapore.

SINGAPORE GOES TO PRINT

The first printing press in Singapore was run by the London Missionary Society and began operating in 1823, just four years after the British flag was hoisted on Singapore soil.[10] Although the press focused on printing translations of the Bible and Christian materials, it was also

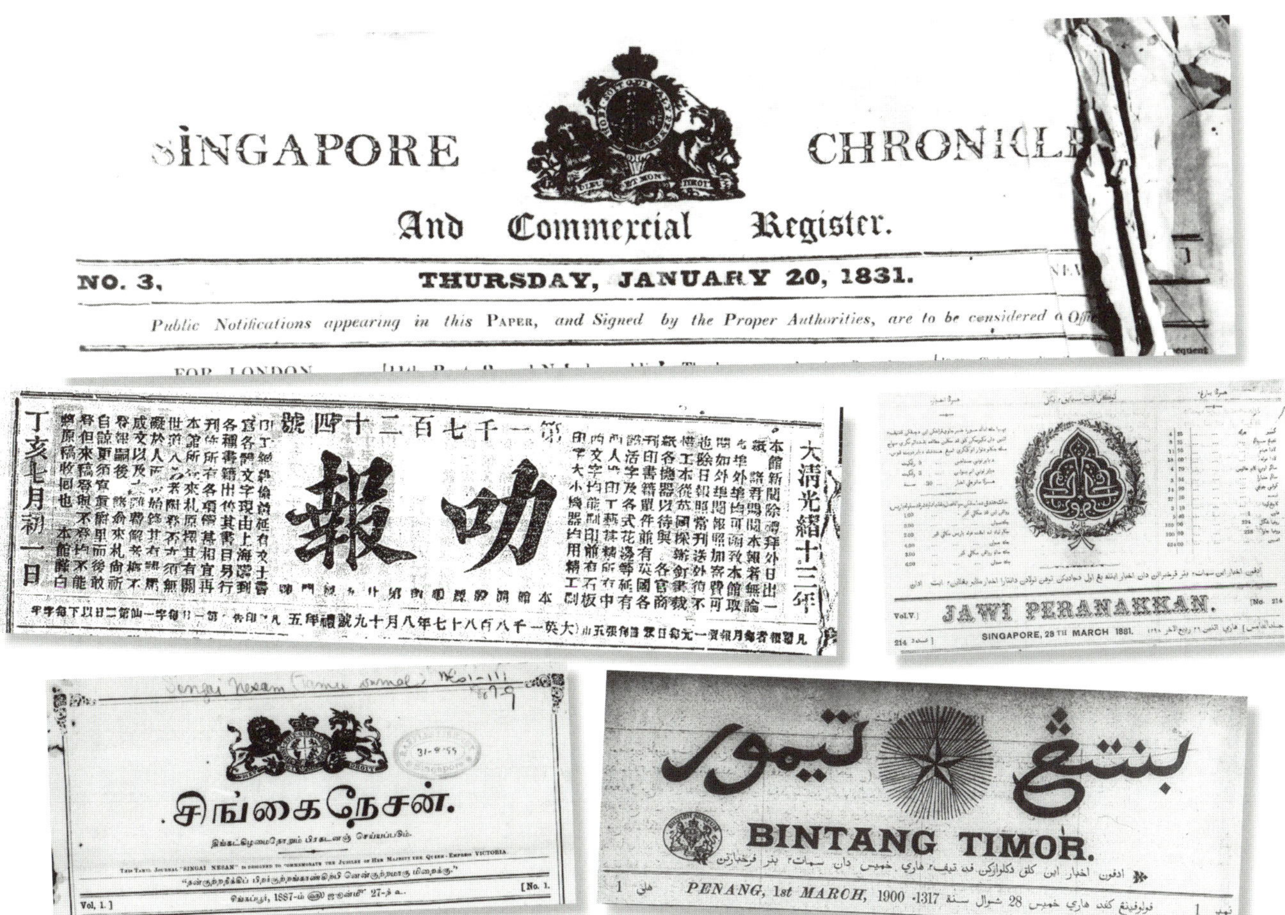

Mastheads of some of Singapore's earliest newspapers for each language (anticlockwise from top): *Singapore Chronicle and Commercial Register*, 20 January 1831; *Lat Pau*, 19 August 1887; *Singai Nesan*, 27 June 1887; *Bintang Timor*, 1 March 1900; and *Jawi Peranakkan*, 28 March 1881.

used for commercial printing, such as the *Singapore Chronicle* from 1824 to 1830.[11] The *Chronicle* began as a four-page newspaper, published once a fortnight, with information about Singapore shipping and news reports taken from newspapers in Melaka, Penang, Bengal and England.[12] Given its language medium and content, the *Chronicle* was clearly targeted at a readership of British traders and East India Company officials who wanted to keep up with news from home as well as from other company possessions in which they had commercial interests.

The *Singapore Chronicle* also carried "occasional commercial announcements" – what we might call advertisements – and did well enough to expand its coverage of local affairs and become a weekly newspaper by around 1830. No doubt some of its success was due to the fact that it was the only newspaper in Singapore until 1835, not to mention the only English-language newspaper in the British East Indies from 1830 to 1835 (the Melaka and Penang publications had closed down). This in effect gave it a monopoly on local advertising.

Tellingly, historian Carl Alexander Gibson-Hill points out that the *Chronicle*'s fortunes changed after a second English-language newspaper, *The Singapore Free Press and Mercantile Advertiser*, appeared on 8 October 1835. The better-quality *Free Press* drew advertisers away from the *Chronicle*, even though the *Free Press* charged higher advertising rates. Within two years the *Chronicle* lost the fight, ceasing publication after 30 September 1837.[13]

Thus, competition for advertising revenue has been the lifeblood of newspapers in Singapore from the beginning. Unlike today,

Advertising and Subscription Rates in *Singapore Chronicle* and *The Singapore Free Press* in the 1830s			
Newspaper	**Cost of advertisement**	**Cost of additional line of advertising**	**Subscription rates**
Singapore Chronicle (1 September 1831)	$4.00 per advertisement of not more than eight lines, to be inserted in three issues of the newspaper	20 cents per additional line	50 cents per copy, or $18/year, or $4.50/quarter
Singapore Free Press (8 October 1835)	$2.50 per advertisement of not more than 15 lines, or $4.00 per advertisement of 16 to 25 lines, to be inserted in four issues of the newspaper	10 cents per additional line	36 cents per copy, or $16/year, or $4.50/quarter
Singapore Chronicle (January 1836)	$2.50 per advertisement "not exceeding half a column" (50 lines), to be inserted in four issues of the newspaper	10 cents per additional line	50 cents per copy for non-subscribers, or 25 cents for subscribers, or $12/year

Source: Gibson-Hill, C.A. (1953, July). The Singapore Chronicle (1824–37). *Journal of the Malayan Branch of the Royal Asiatic Society*, 26(1)(161), pp. 192–193, 195–196.

the earliest advertisements typically appeared on the front page, at the top or in the middle columns – the most prominent positions – and they usually contained only text, rarely illustrations; this was true of newspapers in all languages. The same advertisements sometimes appeared over days, weeks or even months. This perhaps reflected the nature of a port-city: people and goods came and went with great frequency, and businesses needed to keep the transient and mobile population informed of their latest offerings.

ADVERTISING TO THE UPPER CLASS

It is worth remembering that publications of the 19th and early 20th centuries were meant for a much more selective audience than the newspapers of today. English was the lingua franca of British officials and some of their trading partners, but this group made up only a small proportion of Singapore society.

In the 1880s and 1890s, the English-language *Singapore Daily Times* and *The Singapore Free Press* each had a circulation of only 300 to 400 copies, while *The Straits Times*' circulation was fewer than 200.[14] According to the government census, in 1921 fewer than 20,000 people (only 5.6 percent of the population) were literate in English.[15]

Newspapers and publications in other languages were probably started only when literacy in those languages became sufficient to generate potential readership; this readership would have included an illiterate but interested audience who would listen to newspapers being read aloud at settings such as a coffee shop or by street storytellers. Even so, journalism scholar Marina Samad observes that when the *Jawi Peranakkan* was published in the late 19th century, its official circulation was only 250 copies, and "[a]t least three-quarters of the Malay population of Singapore at the time were unable to read or write Malay".[16]

Likewise, researchers of early Chinese and Tamil newspapers in Singapore suggest that these publications were often short-lived and had a limited impact because the majority of the Chinese and Tamil communities were illiterate and, moreover, employed in poorly paid jobs where they could not have afforded to buy a newspaper even if they had wanted to.[17] For instance, *Lat Pau*'s circulation was a promising 350 copies in its early years, but fell to 200 in less than a decade.[18] In terms of general literacy, even by 1921 less than a third of the Singapore population was literate in a non-English language.[19]

It is unsurprising, therefore, that early print advertisements were focused on products, shops and services that only wealthy or well-connected Europeans and Asians could afford. From products such as soda water and watches, to establishments that we now call department stores selling European food and fashion, to Western-style pharmacies, hotels and restaurants, the contents of these advertisements created the impression that the bounty of the British Empire could be found in Singapore – but, of course, this was only for those who had the means to pay for them.

The horse races at what is now Farrer Park, and later Bukit Timah, were important social events for the wealthy. Spectators dressed in their finest to attend the "spring" races (held in May) and the "autumn" races (held in October).[20] (1926)

Fashion advertisements were often targeted at upper-class, status-conscious customers. This 1933 ad by Maison Vogue boutique boasted of dressmaking departments that were "entirely under European supervision by an experienced French couturiere".

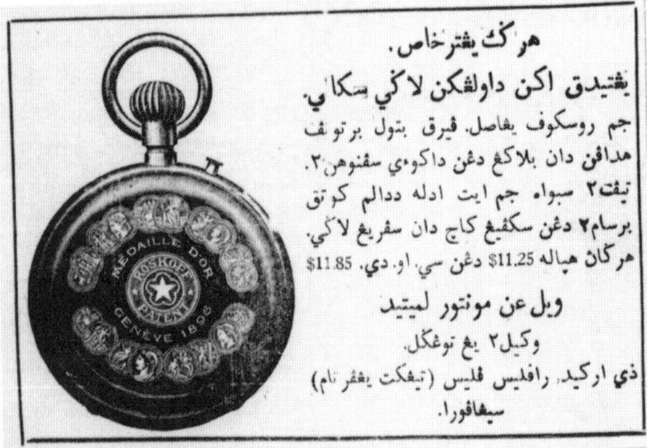

This Roskopf pocket watch was advertised as being "guaranteed real silver with front and back cover". Its retail price in Singapore was $11.25 – a tidy sum in 1933, when this ad was published.

Underwood typewriters were advertised as the "best performing" in their field and suitable for business use. They were imported by Paterson Simons, a trading company with diverse business interests in Singapore, and could be paid for in instalments. (1937)

Similarly, in the first half of the 20th century, we see print advertisements that tried to wow readers with the latest technological innovations – automobiles, gramophones, refrigerators, radios, electric fans and other cooling mechanisms, lamps and lightbulbs – as well as the new urban comforts and conveniences offered by cinemas, amusement parks and shops like Cold Storage (named literally for its ultramodern cold storage facilities, which imported perishable food, such as fresh butter and milk as well as frozen meat from Australia, into Singapore for the first time).

Many of these products and technologies became available in Singapore following the development of mass manufacturing in the industrial West and the transformation of European and North American nations into industrial market societies.[21] Again, however, given the cost of shipping and importation, combined with the relative poverty of the Singapore population, these products were by no means goods for mass consumption. Things that today seem as ordinary as an electric fan or an ice-cream cone, were priced – and thus prized – as luxury items a century ago.

For example, refrigerators were marketed as "a kitchen servant that more than pays its own salary" – such advertisements were clearly targeted at the class of consumer who could afford to keep servants in the first place.[22] Fashion advertisements in English-language publications focused on European fashion and accessories: men's patent leather Oxford shoes or dress pumps, various styles of men's ties, rubber raincoats, wool sweaters and mufflers, women's voile or polished crêpe dresses, and "smart clothes for the races" (the horse races at what is now Farrer Park and later Bukit Timah were important social events for the wealthy).

Strikingly, some of these items would have been extremely uncomfortable to wear in Singapore's tropical climate. European products were also promoted as markers of modernity and status in non-English publications, which carried advertisements for everything from fountain pens and Swiss watches to Raleigh bicycles and Western-style shoes.

Another global phenomenon of the early 20th century that was reflected in English-language print advertisements was the growth of mass tourism and leisure travel from the West. Travel agencies such as Thomas Cook & Son in England had pioneered the organised tour as a mode of international travel, and such travellers – arriving by steamship, train or later airplane – typically stopped over in Singapore for a few days on their tour of the "Far East".

Publications such as the *Malayan Traveller's Gazette* (published by Thomas Cook), *Willis's Singapore Guide* and *Souvenir of Singapore* were targeted at this small but highly lucrative market, and were chock-full of advertisements for jewellers, camera retailers, and shops selling antiques, curios and other orientalised souvenirs such as Asian silk and embroidery. There were also regular newspaper advertisements placed by department stores for travel goods such as

A WEEK IN ADS, 15–21 FEBRUARY 1937

By 1937, Singapore was a bustling imperial port, home to a modern railway, daring Modernist architecture and the brand-new Kallang Airport, while the world's largest dry dock was being constructed at the British naval base in Sembawang.[23] At the same time, the port-city was marked by social inequality; as an American observer wrote in 1937, while the bulk of the population lived in "sordid poverty", the country was "run by a small group of insiders living a life [with] comforts and luxuries".[24] Looking at the newspaper advertisements that appeared in the week of 15 to 21 February 1937, we can get a glimpse of what the comforts, lifestyle and concerns of this group of "insiders" might have been like.

In the English-language *Straits Times* and *Malaya Tribune*, large advertisements appeared almost daily for alcohol; cigarettes; consumer goods such as radios, refrigerators, typewriters and cars; convenience foods such as tinned fruit, milk powder and baby food; and women's beauty products such as perfumes and cosmetics. Advertisements for certain modern products – such as pens, typewriters and watches – also appeared in non-English newspapers, perhaps appealing to business owners in these language communities who would need such accoutrements to enhance their business and social dealings.

The wealthy, as well as a newly emerging "consumer class", were also the targets of advertisements for cinema and public entertainment that appeared regularly across the various newspapers. The English press had listings for not only Western movies, but also Tamil-language ones from India, while the Chinese-language *Nanyang Siang Pau* carried advertisements for English-language movies as well as films in Mandarin and Cantonese from China. Other mainstays in the English and Chinese press were advertisements for the daily cabaret shows and other performances at the Great World and New World amusement parks (Happy World would not open until May that year), as well as ads by bookstores and music stores announcing the arrival of new titles.

Across all newspapers, however, the most common advertisements by far were for health-related products: all manner of tonics, remedies, pills, tablets, laxatives, syrups and all-purpose "cures" that claimed to heal the consumer or act as a preventative against every conceivable ailment, from a cough or a cold, to indigestion, general fatigue, aches, pains and "tropical diseases". Many of these advertisements also mentioned the dispensary or medical hall where the products could be purchased. While some products advertised in the English newspapers promised to induce weight loss (for women) or reduce hair loss (for men), others in *Tamil Murasu*, *Nanyang Siang Pau* and the Malay-language *Warta Malaya* purported to ease women's menstrual and reproductive health difficulties, or overcome male impotence. The English and Chinese press also had advertisements, graced by drawings of bonny babies and happy mothers, for new-fangled products such as powdered milk and processed baby food.

Some advertisements were, understandably, community-specific. *Tamil Murasu* had advertisements for restaurants in the Serangoon Road area, *Warta Malaya* and *Tamil Murasu* frequently carried advertisements for hair oil, including brands imported from Europe, while *Nanyang Siang Pau* published advertisements for products to help consumers quit smoking (possibly opium). As the 15-day Chinese New Year celebrations had just begun, some advertisements in *Nanyang Siang Pau* mentioned festive promotions or events such as fireworks displays at the Great World amusement park. Meanwhile, some advertisements in *The Straits Times* were anticipating the coronation of King George VI in May that year, promoting products and services with celebratory messages.

various styles of trunks, valises and ladies' hat boxes – no doubt catering to Europeans moving back to Europe and the small group of wealthy Asians who could afford to travel.

ADVERTISING FOR THE MASSES

It's in the postwar decades that we finally see a much wider range of publications in Singapore. Published in English and local languages, these catered to a bona fide *mass* audience. Besides the sustained publication of newspapers in several languages, there were also magazines, journals and other periodicals that capitalised on the burgeoning interest in popular culture. Unlike their predecessors in earlier decades, these publications could survive – and some even thrived – because of Singapore's rapidly increasing literacy rate (from 52.3 percent in 1952 to 72.2 percent in 1970) and its improving economic situation, which meant that more people could afford to buy reading materials.[25]

While some publications focused on literary culture and sociopolitical issues of the day, what was new in the postwar era were popular magazines catering to a local-born population that was young, increasingly urban, and clued in to fashion, music and other cultural trends, particularly those from the West. This was an era when teenagers mobbed Asian and Western movie stars and pop musicians arriving at the airport, when Singapore had one of the highest annual rates of cinema attendance in the world, and when young people of every ethnicity began to favour Western-style fashion instead of traditional Asian attire.[26]

Advertisements that relied on conspicuous consumption would focus on the glamorous associations or purported intangible qualities of a product. The objective was to make a product desirable, regardless of its functional qualities. This 1962 ad used Cathay-Keris film star Mary Lim to lend glamour to Gordon's dry gin.

More broadly, Singapore was becoming a consumer society, that is, one where "the act of consumption, and the commodities themselves, came to take on meanings far wider than those of satisfying basic needs".[27] While many print advertisements were still product-oriented and informative – educating readers about the merits of new-fangled household items such as rice-cookers and televisions – the tone and approach in advertising gradually became

This 1958 advertisement depicts a "blissful matrimony" between an Ikoflex camera (the bride) and Gevaert photographic film (the groom). Both products were imported by The Scientific Instrument Company and sold at major camera shops.

more persuasive, selling intangible, imagined qualities such as style and symbolic value.[28]

Taking the cue from advertising strategies in the West, print advertisements in Singapore increasingly sought to create *desire* and promote "conspicuous consumption" – introducing readers to products and services that had just been invented or brought to Singapore, that no one *needed* but, the advertisements claimed, could bring the buyer immense personal satisfaction and a better standing in society if they espoused these fashions or indulged in these new experiences.[29]

This manufacturing of desire, combined with the continued colonial characterisation of Singapore as a "shopping paradise", gave rise in the postwar years to the emergence of shopping as a leisure activity for the masses.[30] This refers not to the purchase of food, provisions and other necessities per se, but to the act of shopping for "fun" – the intrinsic pleasure derived from the act of browsing, comparing and consuming, and finally purchasing the product or service not only for its utility, but for the image and prestige associated with it. Even going to the supermarket (instead of to the "wet" market or a neighbourhood provision shop) became an indicator of social status and the efficient, modern way of life.[31]

As in other capitalist consumer societies around the world, the act of shopping became enshrined as a worthwhile pursuit in and of itself, and places where one could shop – or be seen shopping – became focal points of cultural importance.

SHOPPING HOTSPOTS, 1830s–1960s

While Singapore's prime shopping district today is firmly entrenched in the Orchard Road area, this is a relatively recent development. From the 19th century until the 1970s, shops that catered to different social groups were found all over what we now consider downtown Singapore. Some of the earliest general stores catering to Europeans were set up at Commercial Square (later renamed Raffles Place) – for example, Little, Cursetjee & Co. (established in 1845 and later reconstituted as John Little & Co.) and Robinson & Co. (established in 1858).[32]

The earliest newspaper advertisement for Little, Cursetjee & Co. listed the various types of gentlemen's coats, trouser fabrics and caps on offer, while that for Robinson's advertised "first

Whiteaway, Laidlaw & Co. was a department store founded in Calcutta in 1882. In its heyday, there were Whiteaway's stores in British India, East Africa, Southeast Asia and China.[33] The first Whiteaway's store in Singapore opened in 1900, and in 1905 it relocated to the brand-new Oranje Building (renamed Stamford House in 1963). (1905)

class cabin stores" such as preserved meats and vegetables, liquors and spirits, pickles, jams and jellies.[34]

One of the oldest shopping thoroughfares in Singapore used to be High Street and North Bridge Road, which – together with Hill Street – were the first roads to be built after the British arrived.[35] By the late 19th century, Sindhi traders, who had emigrated from the Indian subcontinent, had set up shop in this area, beginning with Wassiamull Assomull & Co. in 1873 and followed soon after by Chotirmall & Co. and J.T. Chanrai.

These stores catered to European tastes, importing quality European and Indian textiles, and selling curios obtained from all over Asia. They regularly advertised their wares in the English-language newspapers.[36] Sinhalese jewellers, from Ceylon (now Sri Lanka), also had retail outlets here and on Orchard Road, notably B. P. de Silva Jewellers on High Street. By the early 20th century, High Street and North Bridge Road had become a hub for businesses owned by

Gujaratis, Tamil Muslims and Sikhs, and the area grew into a lively shopping strip for the wealthy European and Asian elites of Singapore.[37]

South Asian importers and retailers were such a significant presence in the prewar years that their businesses stretched from High Street all the way northeast to Kampong Glam. As Rajabali Jumabhoy described it in an oral history interview:

... there were many Indian merchants also in North Bridge Road right up to Middle Road and Arab Street, Haji Lane, Bali Lane, Kandahar Street, Bussorah Street. The textile merchants and the *sarong* merchants were mostly in Arab Street, Beach Road, Kandahar Street and Bussorah and the surrounding areas; whilst North Bridge Road from Arab Street, right up to High Street, say about 30 percent were Indians, dealing in consumer goods and textiles, shirts and so on.[38]

By the 1920s, High Street and the area around it were home to businesses owned by Sindhi, Gujarati, Tamil Muslim, Sikh and Sinhalese traders, selling textiles, jewellery and curios from India. (1920s)

In Kampong Glam, the Indian enterprises sat cheek by jowl with Arab- and Malay-owned businesses that catered to the needs of their communities. Many of the latter shops sold everyday necessities such as food, *songkok*, textiles and housewares, while some – such as the still-operating V.S.S. Varusai Mohamed & Sons – catered to the thousands of Muslim pilgrims from all over Southeast Asia who came through Singapore en route to Mecca for the *haj*, supplying them with the food, blankets, shawls, perfumes and money belts needed for their long journey.[39]

Importantly, from the late 19th century onwards, printers and booksellers set up shop in Lorong Masjid Sultan (now Bussorah Street), where they published and sold newspapers and religious texts, as well as modern texts about society and politics.[40]

Other early shopping areas were likewise located in ethnic enclaves. Before the Second World War, Circular Road and South Bridge Road were the centre of Chinese textile trading.

People would come here to buy fabrics to tailor-make into clothes as well as bedlinen and other household items.[41] In the 1910s, branches of the two earliest Chinese-owned department store chains from Hong Kong opened in Singapore: Wing On on High Street and Sincere Co. on South Bridge Road.[42] In the Serangoon Road area, there were numerous shops run by South Indians selling food, spices, clothing, ornaments, flowers and gold to their fellow immigrants.[43] In particular, the general stores owned by P. Govindasamy Pillai (popularly known as "PGP") became a household name in the 1930s; his businesses later expanded to include textile shops and flour mills.[44]

Even Singapore's small prewar Japanese community had its own shopping district at Middle Road. A number of Japanese businesses selling textiles and garments arrived in the late 19th century, catering primarily to the Japanese prostitutes (*karayuki-san*) who lived and worked in the brothels nearby. One of the most successful draperies here was Echigoya, which opened

Aurora department store was at the corner of High Street and North Bridge Road (where the present-day Supreme Court now stands). It was the Singapore branch of a department store chain from Java and opened for business in 1938. (c. 1940)

in 1907 on Middle Road and later became popular with European customers. As colonial municipal commissioner Roland Braddell wrote in 1934, Echigoya was to him "a real Japanese shop, where you can get a proper Japanese kimono tailored to measure, and have your pick of the latest Japanese fashions".[45] After the Second World War, Echigoya was the first Japanese business to return to Singapore, this time on Coleman Street, and the store was often mentioned in tourist shopping guides in the postwar decades.[46]

As mentioned previously, shopping as a leisure activity for the masses only emerged in the postwar era, largely centred on two main areas: Raffles Place/Battery Road and High Street/North Bridge Road.[47] Both shopping enclaves had been popular with Singapore's elite before the Second World War, but after the war, thanks to a growing middle class, shopping in these areas became more affordable; even the working class would venture to these shopping districts for the occasional splurge.

Raffles Place was the bastion of department stores, home to both long-time stalwarts John Little's, Robinson's and Whiteaway's (which had opened in Singapore in 1900), as well as newer rivals such as Gian Singh & Co., set up in 1935 by five brothers who came to Singapore from Punjab.[48] Nearby Change Alley and the Arcade were popular for "a display of goods almost bewildering in its variety and almost all tempting to the tourist".[49]

In the same postwar period, the High Street/North Bridge Road area became *the* place to shop at and would later be remembered as Singapore's version of London's Carnaby Street in the Swinging Sixties.[50]

Still flourishing were the Indian-owned textile stores, which so dominated the area by the 1960s that one oral history account recalls there being "50 to 60 shops all catering to textiles, retail plus wholesale, and about 500 other textile wholesalers at the time in High Street alone, all Indians".[51] While these numbers were most certainly exaggerated in the interviewee's

In the postwar decades, the High Street/North Bridge Road area was a popular shopping district, with a plethora of shops selling clothes, shoes and other goods. (1968)

memory, they remind us of the distinct cultural milieu of High Street – its identity being what we would now call a "shopping destination".[52]

High Street was where students went to S.A. Majeed's every year to buy school uniforms, and shops such as Chotirmall's and Khemchand and Sons stocked imported shirts from Arrow, Manhattan and Van Heusen.[53] The Melwani fashion empire (now known as the Jay Gee Group) ran successful fashion stores on High Street such as Chanrai's, Chanrita and Melwani's Men's Shop.[54] Bata, an international shoe store chain of Czech origin, has been on North Bridge Road since 1931, first at the Capitol Building, then in its own purpose-built store since 1940; in the postwar decades and after, it sold affordable shoes to generations of Singaporeans, especially its white school shoes.[55]

High Street also had department stores and clothing shops to rival those at Raffles Place, some of them in business since the 1930s. Besides the Indian-owned ones such as Chotirmall's and Pamanand Brothers, there were enterprises owned by ethnic Chinese: Aurora, the Singapore branch of a chain from Java; and Peking Co., started by Kuo Fung Ting, who was from Beijing.[56] In 1957, they were joined by a new kid on the block, the very first Metro store, set up by Ong Tjoe Kim, an immigrant from Xiamen who had worked in department store chains in Java. As one Singapore newspaper described it, "the triangle among the three department stores – Aurora, Peking, and Metro – became a big attraction for the shoppers during the late 1950s".[57]

It is worth noting the business foresight that drove this growing buzz at High Street. Kuo later explained that he converted Peking Co. from a curio shop into a department store in the 1950s when he realised that "after the war, the tendency would be for people to be more fashion-conscious. They would want more of the latest fashions in clothes, and other things, synonymous with prosperity."[58]

Similarly, after over 30 years in Singapore, global textile trader J. Kimatrai & Co. deliberately expanded into the local retail trade by opening a "Family Store" on High Street in 1965. Its managing director for Southeast Asia said at the time:

Singapore is a fast-moving city. And the people are sophisticated, keeping up with the latest trends in fashion. We feel that a fashionable store in High Street will go a long way to keep up with the tempo and way of life of the people.[59]

ADVERTISEMENTS AS A PEEK INTO THE PAST

Singapore's shopping culture, as well as the influence of print and other forms of advertising on all aspects of Singapore culture, continued to evolve, but this book draws the line after the 1960s. With the start of television broadcasting in 1963, and other changes to the media environment in subsequent years, the interaction between the consumer, the advertiser and the advertisement (be it print or broadcast) has to be read and interpreted in a different light from the purely print advertisements of the earlier era.

However, whether we are looking at a recent YouTube advertisement or a printed fragment from the distant past, it is important to remember, as media scholar Chris Wharton cautions, that "the people who now view or listen to the advert are a quite different set of people inhabiting different economies and cultures for whom the advertisement was first devised".

For the historian interested in studying the past through advertisements, the challenge is "to understand the culture in which the historical advertisements were both produced and received ... by comparing and contrasting the advert against a range of other artefacts and forms of evidence".[60]

The advertisements reprinted in this volume, as well as the vast quantity available in the National Library's collection, offer a valuable and intriguing window into certain aspects of Singapore's business, social and cultural life

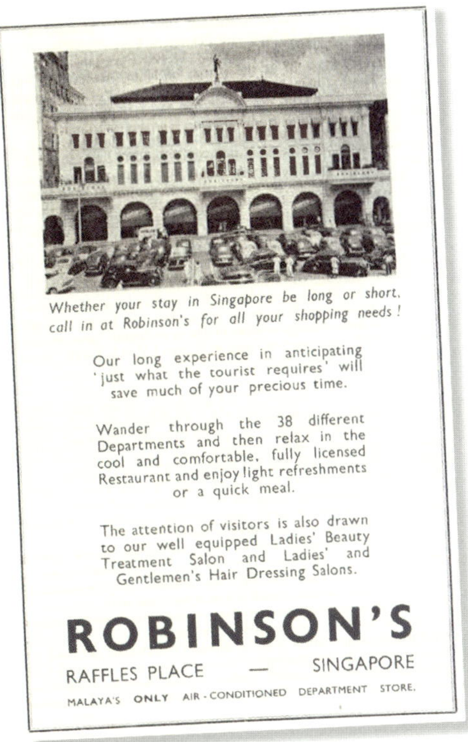

Robinson's was founded in Singapore in 1858 at Raffles Place. Over the years, it expanded to become a full-fledged department store, with an iconic storefront and location that attracted customers from all over Malaya. (1956)

in decades past. They can supplement what we know from other sources, perhaps even inadvertently providing insight into certain class, ethnic and social prejudices of the time.

Ultimately, however, advertisements were produced to sell things, and it may be helpful to hark back to the wise words of distinguished English writer Samuel Johnson, who in 1759 observed, "Promise, large promise, is the soul of an advertisement."[61] Promise, not always actuality – just convincing enough of a tale to get a potential buyer into a shop.

Yu-Mei Balasingamchow

A Rich Advertising Heritage

The first advertisements placed by advertising agents in Singapore appeared around the 1910s. In return for a fee, ad agents helped clients create and place advertisements in newspapers. It was common for ad agencies to "sign off" with the company's name or initials on advertisements they produced – for instance, "Master's" for Masters Limited, "Warins" for Warin Publicity Services and "APB" for Advertising and Publicity Bureau. These would often be inserted unobtrusively into the advertisements, leaving traces for later historians to discover their provenance.

Singapore's thriving advertising business before the Second World War was dominated by a few prominent ad agencies headed by Europeans. There were at least 20 firms specialising in advertising, publicity and marketing in Singapore and Malaya in the prewar era.[62]

The growing economy, and consequently demand for advertising in major Asian cities, fuelled the business of some of these early agencies. The Advertising and Publicity Bureau (APB) was the first regional agency to set up shop in Singapore in 1931. It had been established in Hong Kong in 1922 by Englishwoman Beatrice Thompson to serve the advertising

Siow Choon Leng, one of the early advertising agencies in Singapore, selling its copywriting services. (1919)

An advertisement by ad agency Masters Ltd. celebrating 21 years of business in Malaya. (1949)

An advertisement by – and for – Warin Publicity Services, a leading prewar agency in Singapore. (1939)

Artists at work at Warin Studios located in the old Union Building in Collyer Quay. (1935)

needs of its British and American clients in Asia.[63] By 1940, APB was servicing many household brands and prominent firms, claiming to be the "largest advertising agency in the Far East".[64]

There were also agencies started in Singapore that later became well known, one of which was Masters, founded in 1928 by Australian-born Ernst George Mozar, whose works can often be seen in early local publications.

Among the first homegrown ad agencies in Singapore, one stood out for its vibrant and attractive print advertisements: Warin Publicity Services, founded by Briton William Joseph Warin.[65] Warin first arrived in Malaya in 1915 as a rubber planter.[66] After his plantation business was hit by the Great Depression, Warin reinvented himself as a commercial artist and in 1932 set up his advertising firm, Warin Studios (renamed Warin Publicity Services in 1937).[67] Business flourished and within three years, Warin's clientele had included major corporations and import houses in Singapore and Malaya, and it had associates in London and New York.[68] The agency's success was largely due to the high-quality and creative works produced by its artists,[69] among whom was the Russian-born artist Vladimir Tretchikoff, who later found international fame for his painting, *Chinese Girl*.[70]

Chung Sang Hong*

---

* This is an excerpt from the essay "The Stuff of Dreams: Singapore's Early Print Ads" published in *BiblioAsia*, Jul–Sep 2018, 14(2). Retrieved from BiblioAsia website: http://www.nlb.gov.sg/biblioasia

A 1939 advertisement for Jaguar sports cars. Car ads appeared regularly in magazines published by the Automobile Association of Malaya.

WHEELS OF CHANGE

The word "automobilism", meaning the use of automobiles,[1] entered the English lexicon in the late 19th century with the emergence of motor vehicles as a viable mode of private transportation. Karl Benz's "Patent-Motorwagen", first built in 1885, sparked a vehicular revolution that saw animal power replaced by the internal combustion engine. Thus was born the automobile – literally "self-moving" car. Since then, although the term "automobilism" has fallen into disuse, the world's love affair with automobiles has never waned, with succeeding generations embracing it with as much enthusiasm as did the early adopters.

HORSELESS CARRIAGE

The Katz Brothers ushered in the age of automobilism in Singapore when they imported the first automobiles in August 1896. Before this, the horse and carriage, imported from Britain since the 1820s, was a popular means of passenger transport. Another common mode of transportation in the late 19th century was the *jinrickshaw* (man-drawn rickshaw), originally from Japan and introduced in Singapore in 1880 via Shanghai.[2]

The Katz Brothers were the sole agents for Benz and Co.'s "Motor-Velociped", which was advertised as a "horseless carriage". A favourable review in *The Singapore Free Press and Mercantile Advertiser* newspaper described it as a "neat-looking four-wheeled carriage" that did not require an "expert driver", but commented that its $1,600 price was "somewhat high".[3]

Automobile ads continued to make reference to "horseless carriages" through the years, even into the mid-1950s. This was

(1923)

(1956)

(1951)

Many advertisers referenced the "horseless
carriage" to imply their involvement in the
automobile industry since the beginning.

usually to draw attention to the fact that the product or company had existed since the dawn of the automobile industry and grown along with it. Examples of such advertisements included those for Dunlop Tyres, Shell (formerly the Asiatic Petroleum Company) and Chloride Batteries Limited (see facing page).

The introduction of automobiles was enthusiastically embraced by the who's-who of Singapore and Malaya. B. Frost of the Eastern Extension Telegraph Company and subsequently Charles B. Buckley, publisher and famed author of *An Anecdotal History of Singapore*, were the first to own and drive the Benz in Singapore.[4] Soon, more automobiles were brought into Singapore. The Benz was followed by a De Dion Bouton and then an Albion.[5] All three models shared a reputation for being very noisy and hence did not require any horns to make themselves heard. Buckley dubbed his car "The Coffee Machine" because of the grinding noises it made.[6]

WHO DARES WINS

Singapore's first lady motorist was Mrs G.M. Dare, who drove a Star motor car before switching to a two-seater Adams-Hewitt in 1906.[7] That year, car registration came into force and Mrs Dare enjoyed the distinction of driving Singapore's first registered car, which bore the licence plate number S-1.[8] She nicknamed it "Ichiban" (Japanese for "Number One"), but the locals,

An advertisement put up by either Mrs G.M. Dare or her husband to sell her first car. (1906)

Mrs G.M. Dare and her husband on their Adams-Hewitt bearing the licence plate S-1. (1930/31)

amazed and possibly fearful in equal measure at seeing her at the wheel, called it the "Devil Wind Carriage".[9] Even more amazing was the fact that she clocked more than 69,000 miles (111,000 km) driving the car all over Singapore, Malaya, Java, England and Scotland.[10] Mrs Dare was also credited for teaching driving to the first Malay to obtain a driving licence, a chauffeur by the name of Hassan bin Mohamed.[11]

RISE OF THE AUTOMOBILE

In 1907, the Singapore Automobile Club (SAC) was formed, with Governor John Anderson as its president. Notable members included the Sultan of Johor, Walter John Napier (a lawyer-academic who was the first editor of the *Straits Settlements Law Reports*) and E.G. Broadrick (president of the Singapore Municipality from 1904 to 1910 who later became the British Resident of Selangor).[12] Remarkably, by 1908 – when the world automobile industry was still coming of age[13] – there were already 214 individuals in Singapore licensed to drive "motor-cars, motor-bicycles and steam-rollers".[14]

In June 1907, *The Straits Times* announced that it was devoting a special column to automobilism.[15] The column became known as "Motors & Motoring" in 1910, was renamed "The Motoring World" in 1911, and ran until 1928.[16] Its longevity attested to the interest in and fascination with cars amongst the paper's readers, if not the general population.

The monthly *Motor Car and Athletic Journal* was started in March 1908, but it was short-lived

A 1949 advertisement for the newly launched Morris Six.

and ceased publication after 12 issues.[17] It was only in the 1930s that the Automobile Association of Malaya (AAM) (which SAC became a branch of in 1932) began to venture into publishing, with *Malayan Motorist* (first issue 1933), *Motoring in Malaya* (1935), *Handbook of the Automobile Association of Malaya* (1939) and, much later, *AAM News Bulletin* (1949).[18] Car advertisements were regularly featured in newspapers and the AAM's magazines.

RELIABILITY AND AFFORDABILITY

Up until the 1920s, car advertisements in the United States and Europe tended to highlight the vehicles' technical features, in order to familiarise audiences with the exciting yet intimidating new technology of automobiles.[19] Manufacturers recognised that scepticism about dependability and reliability were major obstacles to widespread public acceptance of motor vehicles for private transportation.[20]

The case was similar in Singapore. Distributors and agents highlighted both the reliability and affordability of their vehicles by proclaiming the technology behind the cars and the low prices. There were also attempts at associating prestige with the advertised cars, but these were to build up brand reputation and reflected the manufacturers' ambition rather than consumers' desire for high-end vehicles.

Ford in Singapore

In 1909, just a year after Henry Ford's historic Model T was introduced in America and took the world by storm, Ford cars entered the

An early attempt at associating prestige with the advertised car to build brand reputation. (1907/08)

For decades, advertisements typically indicated the price of the car to attract buyers in a competitive market. (1930)

Singapore market.[21] Initially brought in by Gadelius & Company, Ford's presence grew in Singapore when the Ford Motor Company of Malaya was established in 1926 to supervise the supply and distribution of its products in Malaya, the Netherlands East Indies, Siam and Borneo.[22] It initially carried out car-assembly work in a garage on Enggor Street, then in 1930 expanded to larger premises on nearby Prince Edward Road. In 1941, the company moved to a newly built factory in Bukit Timah.[23] Throughout this time, as well as in the decade following the end of the Second World War, Ford's advertisements in Singapore rarely departed from the theme of playing up its cars' efficiency and competitive pricing.

(1909)

(1937)

Advertisements for Ford cars over the decades invariably called readers' attention to their affordability.

The Ford Factory building, designed in Art Deco style, opened in 1941. According to this 1949 ad, the factory was producing an impressive seven models of cars and trucks, and capable of churning out 20 chassis and eight passenger car bodies per work day.

Japanese cars and other motor vehicles began to be imported into Singapore in the late 1950s. (1958)

Japanese Marques

Japanese cars began to be sold in Singapore in the late 1950s. By 1970, one in two cars sold in Singapore was a Japanese car.[24] The main reason for their popularity? Value for money. Japanese cars were cheaper than American and European offerings, and were winning races in local and international motor competitions in the late 1960s. The advertisements cleverly highlighted these achievements and, at the same time, used the tried-and-tested formula of good value, efficiency and reliability to attract Singaporean buyers.

Mazelan Anuar

Apart from making reference to their reliability and affordability, ads for Japanese cars often highlighted their achievements at races and rallies. (1969)

Taxi! Taxi!

First introduced in 1910, the taxi-cab service in Singapore was the brainchild of C.F.F. Wearne and Company. Singapore became the second city in Asia after Calcutta, India, to have such a service and it was lauded as being modern and up to date. Two Rover cars were fitted with "taximeters" and were initially used to provide taxi service for private orders before obtaining the licences to ply the streets for public hire. At a charge of 40 cents per mile and with a seating capacity of five passengers, taxi-cab services could work out to be no more expensive than hiring a first-class rickshaw.[25]

In 1919, the Singapore Motor Taxi Cab and Transport Company Limited was incorporated in the Straits Settlements (Singapore, Penang and Melaka) and put up its prospectus in the local newspapers to raise a capital of $350,000. The company proposed starting a taxi service comprising a fleet of 40 Ford Landaulettes as taxi-cabs. The 20-horsepower six-seater Landaulette was distributed by C.F.F. Wearne and Company.[26]

By the end of 1920, the Singapore Taxicab Co. was advertising a "Call a Taxi" service in *The Straits Times*. Black and yellow taxis were stationed at Raffles Place, the General Post Office, Grand Hotel de l'Europe, Adelphi Hotel, Raffles Hotel and the company's garage at 1 Orchard Road, ready to pick up passengers. The fare

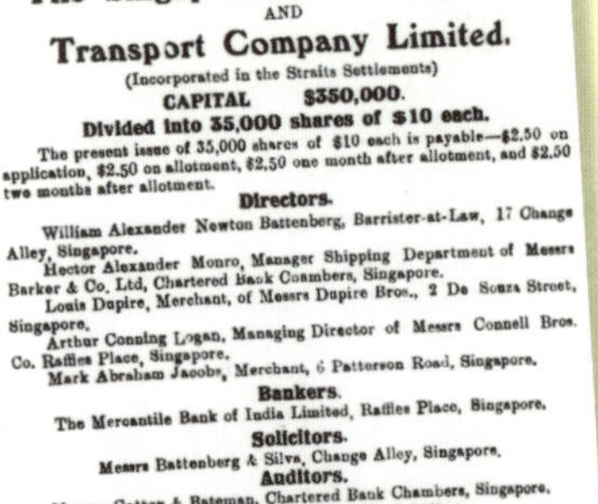

The Singapore Motor Taxi Cab and Transport Company Limited was incorporated in 1919 and put up its prospectus in the local newspapers to raise a capital of $350,000. (1919)

By 1920, customers were able to send a telegram to book a taxi at various locations in Singapore. (1920)

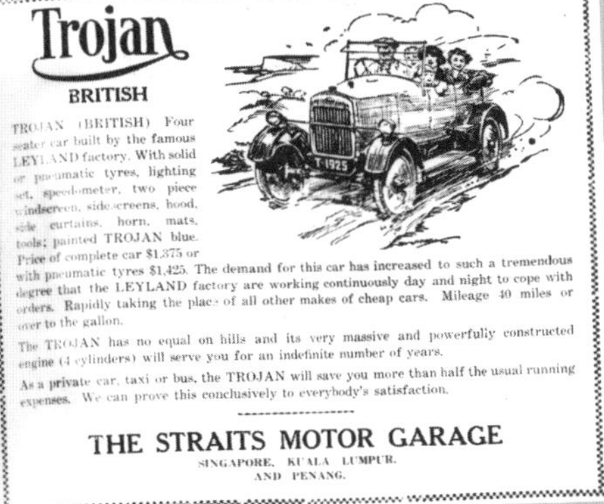

The vehicle-for-hire scheme was advertised as a cheaper alternative to taxis. (1924)

The four-seater Trojan was promoted as a "private car, taxi or bus" that could halve the usual running expenses for a car. (1925)

was 40 cents per mile – the same as when taxi services were introduced a decade earlier.[27]

Abrams' Motor Transport Company started a vehicle-for-hire scheme in the mid-1920s. Customers could hire a car or lorry at $3 per hour, which was touted as being cheaper than a taxi. Among the car models available for hire was the five-seater Gardner.[28]

In 1930, Borneo Motors Limited imported a new taximeter that calculated the fare automatically. Apparently there had been quarrels between drivers and passengers over the correct fare to be paid (taximeters became compulsory only in 1953[29]). The new taximeter had been used in other cities such as Rangoon and Calcutta.[30]

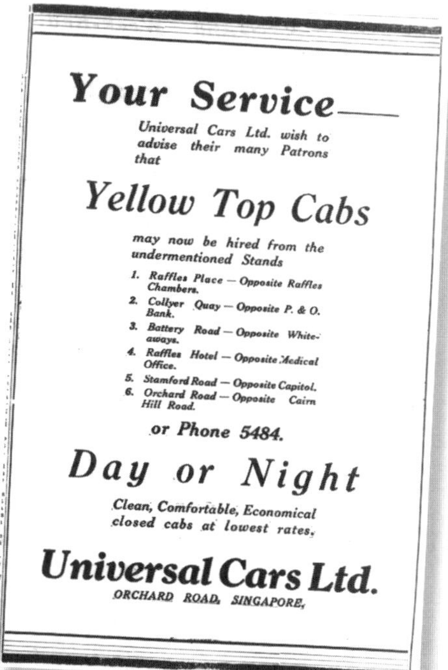

Yellow Top Cabs first appeared in Singapore in 1933 and soon became a familiar sight on the streets. (1933)

Yellow Top Cabs debuted in 1933.[31] Universal Cars Limited started the service and claimed to have the lowest rates for closed cabs.[32] The advertisements it ran for Yellow Top Cabs between 1933 and 1934 boasted of their cleanliness.[33] The cabs were available at taxi stands – at Raffles Place, Collyer Quay, Battery Road, Raffles Hotel, Stamford Road and Orchard Road – as well as by telephone.[34]

After the Second World War, many private cars were used by unlicensed taxi drivers to ply the streets for hire. These "pirate taxis" caused problems for licensed taxi drivers, passengers and the government,[35] though it was also argued that they provided a much-needed public service.[36] In 1970, the National Trades Union Congress started its Comfort taxi service[37] and offered pirate taxi drivers a chance to join its operations.[38] A total ban on pirate taxis came into force in July the following year.[39]

The first automobile in Singapore advertised as a horseless carriage. Its claim of "being quite silent" was most likely an exaggeration. (1896)

Advertisement for an Adams-Hewitt two-seater (with an additional servant's "dicky", or rear seat), which may have been the model driven by Mrs G.M. Dare, Singapore's first lady motorist. (1907)

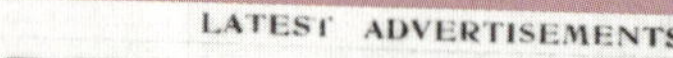

The De Dion Bouton was one of the earliest cars to arrive in Singapore. Affordability and reliability became major themes for car advertisements in the decades to come. (1904)

(1927)

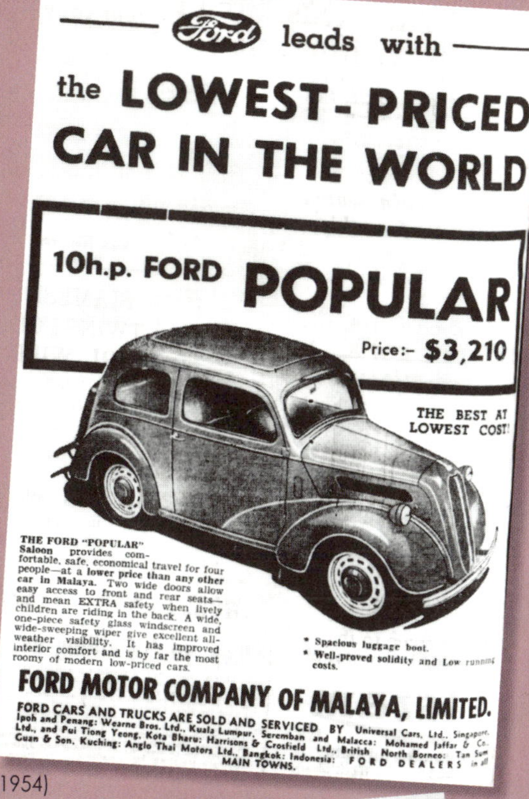

(1954)

(1947)

(1969)

Advertisements for Ford cars over the decades invariably called readers' attention to their affordability.

(1927)

Car advertisements typically indicated
the prices of their offerings to attract
buyers in a competitive market.

(1954)

(1935)

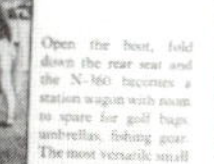

(1967)

(1966)

Japanese marques like Honda, Datsun and Nissan scored successes at local and international races and rallies – and these achievements were regularly trumpeted in their advertisements.

(1967)

This 1928 advertisement for Ferodo brakes implied
that the confidence of lady drivers in crowded
streets was hampered by the strength required to
step on car brakes.

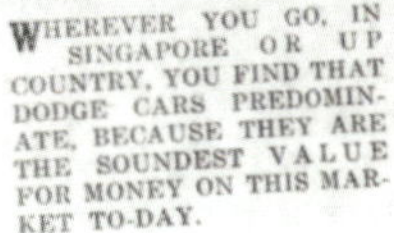

In this 1921 advertisement for Dodge cars, lady
drivers are designated a two-seater model.

The REO Flying Cloud advertised as appealing to
the sensibilities of both men and women. (1929)

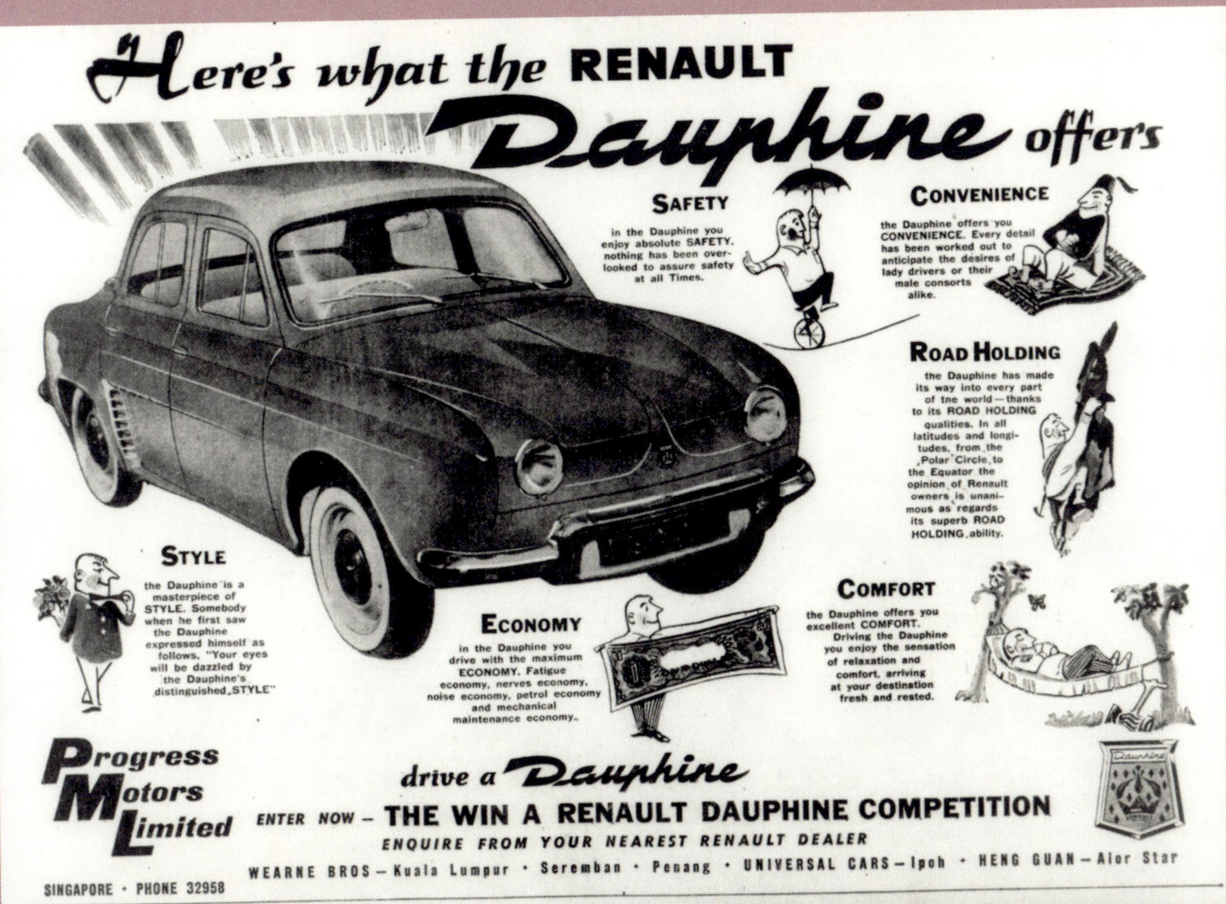

The Renault Dauphine advertised as having every detail worked out to "anticipate the desires of lady drivers or their male consorts". (1959)

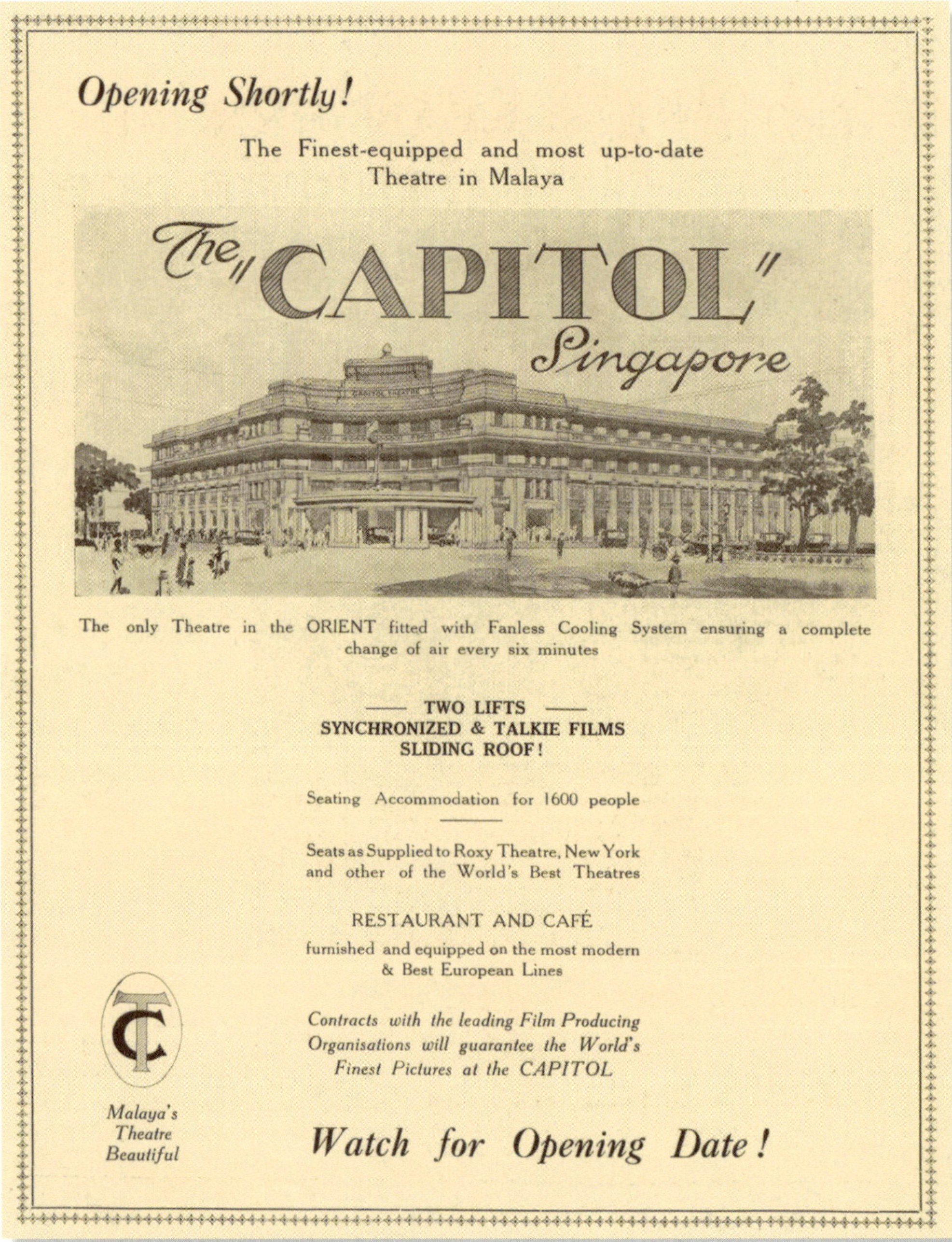

The Capitol promoting its up-to-date facilities
in this pre-opening advertisement. (1929)

THAT'S ENTERTAINMENT

On 19 May 1842, a notice was published in *The Singapore Free Press and Mercantile Advertiser*:

Prospectus for a Theatre

The Dearth of all amusement in Singapore induced several Gentlemen to suggest the establishment of Theatrical Performances by subscription; it has therefore been deemed advisable to circulate this paper, with the view of ascertaining the sentiments of the Gentry and Community in general, as to the desirableness of a scheme of this description.[1]

This view of Singapore's dismal options for "amusement" in the middle of the 19th century is well corroborated by the entertainment-related advertisements in the local English newspapers of the day – or rather, by their conspicuous paucity. However, as the settlement grew and prospered, the situation improved quickly. Observers of the entertainment scene in the late 19th and early 20th centuries described a variety of means for entertaining oneself: flying kites, listening to a storyteller, going to the theatre, dancing, listening to music, riding a bicycle, watching performances in open spaces and on the streets, among other amusements.[2]

In tandem with these developments, advertisements for paid entertainment proliferated, appearing in various publications and printed materials. Public entertainment could be found in venues such as theatres, and later cinemas, as well as amusement parks and travelling circuses.

THEATRE: MULTIPURPOSE ENTERTAINMENT SPACE

The first record of an English-language amateur theatrical performance in Singapore is believed to be an advertisement published on 21 March 1833 in the *Singapore Chronicle*.[3] The show was staged on 25 March at Cross Street, and featured several types of performances, including a tragedy, *The Revenge*; a comedy, *The Mock Doctor*; and songs with music played by a military band.[4] In 1844, a new theatre, Theatre Royal, staged its first performance, *Charles the Second, or the Merry Monarch*, put up by a group of amateur players. This theatre was housed in London Hotel, located on Coleman Street then.[5]

When London Hotel moved in 1845, the theatre ceased to operate. The amateur group that used to stage performances there then refurbished the old Assembly Rooms at the foot of Fort Canning Hill into a theatre, and named it Theatre Royal.[6] Apart from plays, musical concerts were also held there, featuring "vocal and instrumental" performances by European opera singers, pianists, violinists and other musicians, as well as "dancing entertainment" in the form of ballet.[7]

After the old Assembly Rooms were demolished, the newly built Town Hall (1862) served as Singapore's main venue for theatrical performances. In 1909, it was converted into a full-fledged performing house and renamed Victoria Theatre, adjoining Victoria Memorial Hall (1905).[8] Throughout the years, Victoria Theatre hosted a variety of public shows and entertainment, including comedies, concerts, plays, operas, and film screenings,[9] put up by both local and overseas groups. While a sizeable number of the staged performances and films originated from the West, there were also shows from Asia, such as Chinese movies and Indian classical dance performances. Perhaps due to the flexibility of the venue in catering to different forms of entertainment, in 1927 a screening of the Chinese film *Dianying Nümingxing* (《电影女明星》; *Movie Actress*) was followed by a traditional Chinese opera performance by Wang Hanlun (王汉伦), a celebrated actress of the day.

THEATRICAL AMUSEMENTS,
CROSS-STREET, TELUK-AYER.
Patronized by the Gentlemen of Singapore.

IT IS MOST RESPECTFULLY ANNOUNCED
THAT
On Monday, the 25th March, 1833,
WILL BE PERFORMED,
Dr. Young's celebrated and much admired
TRAGEDY OF
THE REVENGE;
THE WHOLE TO CONCLUDE
WITH THE LAUGHABLE FARCE OF
THE MOCK DOCTOR.

In the course of the Evening will be introduced several comic and sentimental Songs, and between the Pieces A recitation from Campbell's " Pleasures of Hope."

Boxes Sp. Dlrs. 2 | Pit, Sp. Dlr. 1

Tickets to be had at Messrs. George Armstrong & Co.'s, at Mr. J. Gemmill's, at Messrs. Merryweather & Co's, and from Mr. H. Edwards, Malacca-Steet.

No money will be received at the Door

The Doors to be opened at 6, in the evening, and the Performance to commence at 7 o'clock precisely.

Advertisement for the first known amateur theatrical performance in Singapore. (1833)

The Town Hall in the 1880s, on the site of present-day Victoria Theatre and Concert Hall.

Victoria Theatre and Victoria Memorial Hall in the 1920s.

昨晚南洋劉貝錦自製影片公司之新客試映記

南洋劉貝錦自製影片公司第一次出品新客一片：期昨晚假座大鑼樓試映一節：曾誌前報：茲悉昨晚各界前往參觀者：極為擁擠：時居入時許：新客卽開映銀幕之上：計是片共九大本：惟當地政府：祗准其演至第六本而止：綜觀是片：取外景：則光線填稱明晰：惟字意則顚撲模糊：手演員之藝術：以初次挺身銀幕之人：而能演此：赤算難得：倘能從此精益求精：則邁進步試來可量：不僅列國內諸明星蓋鵞齊驅已也：餤予望之：

Newspaper report on the preview of the earliest known Malaya-made film, *Xin Ke* (《新客》; *New Immigrant*), which was screened at Victoria Theatre. (1927)

The Star Opera Company and Theatre Royal along North Bridge Road were owned by brothers Cheong Koon Seng and Cheong Koon Hong. (c. 1910)

On the other hand, the new Theatre Royal along North Bridge Road, set up by brothers Cheong Koon Seng and Cheong Koon Hong, was particularly associated with *bangsawan*, a popular form of Malay theatrical performance. It was known as the home of Star Opera Company, a *bangsawan* troupe that shared the same proprietors.[10] After Theatre Royal came under Amalgamated Theatres, Ltd., it was renovated and reopened in 1935 with facilities for film screening.[11] Following that, the theatre advertised more entertainment offerings, including magic shows and Tamil movies.

CINEMA: POPULAR ENTERTAINMENT FOR THE MASSES

Cinematography, the new technology invented by the Lumière brothers, arrived in Singapore shortly after the first public screening in Paris in 1895. Early screenings were made either in the Town Hall theatre, makeshift halls in places like hotels, or temporary structures such as tents.[12] In 1904, the Levy Hermanos brothers screened imported movies in a building at 320 Victoria Street. Named Paris Cinematograph, the venue had proper seats and a projection booth. This was the first cinema hall in Singapore,[13] and it claimed to have the "largest Electric Cinematograph ever seen in Singapore".[14]

As movies gained popularity, more cinemas were opened.[15] In 1929, a commentary on the local cinema scene identified the Alhambra on Beach Road and Pavilion on Orchard Road as the most popular theatres among the Europeans. The growing local market also contributed to the burgeoning industry,[16] with cinemas reaching out to the various communities. Harima Hall on North Bridge Road put up advertisements for the same film in multiple newspapers, across different languages, while Capitol Theatre's postwar handbills for *Trapeze*, a recording of a circus performance, featured advertising copy in English, Chinese and Malay.

Paris Cinematograph, at 320 Victoria Street, was the first cinema hall in Singapore. (1904)

Alhambra Theatre on Beach Road was the first cinema in Singapore to have an air-conditioning system installed. (c. 1938)

Capitol Theatre in the 1930s.

(1950)

Pavilion Theatre (left) and Marlborough Theatre were two prewar cinemas in Singapore.

(1938/39)

With audiences coming from varied backgrounds, and being allowed to stay the whole evening at the cinema after buying a ticket, local operators had to find ways to cater to different preferences. One such innovation was the "double programme", where two different types of shows were planned for the evening. The first programme would usually be a Western action film popular with Asian patrons, while the second mostly comprised the latest releases being shown in leading British and American cinemas, catering to the Europeans.[17]

Besides films, the cinemas also hosted live performances. Capitol Theatre introduced live shows such as revues (featuring songs, dances, skits) in the 1930s, providing the public with more entertainment options. Sometimes live entertainment was combined with film screenings – a 1934 advertisement for a Mickey Mouse matinee at the Capitol promised "Cabaret and Cinema Entertainment" in the same session.

Cinema operators tried to appeal to audiences by highlighting the new technologies used in their films. The advertisements of Alhambra and Marlborough cinemas published in 1931 described their screenings as "all-talking", signalling the end of the silent-film era. Colour filmmaking – a major technological innovation of the 1930s[18] – was the next big selling point. *The Broadway Melody*, screened by Alhambra Cinema in 1930, boasted of having an entire scene shot in Technicolour.[19]

Having modern facilities was another area where the various cinemas tried to outdo the competition. Capitol Theatre advertised itself as "the only Theatre in the Orient fitted with Fanless Cooling System ensuring a complete change of air every six minutes" and installed with "seats supplied to Roxy Theatre, New York and other of the World's Best Theatres" (p. 36).

In 1938, the Alhambra became the first cinema in Singapore to install an air-conditioning system, which it duly trumpeted in its advertisements.[20] The air-conditioning system garnered a lot of public interest, and there were numerous newspaper reports on it, including one that gave a detailed description of how the cooling system worked, and referred to the result as replicating a "mountain-air climate in Singapore".[21]

Since the early 20th century, there had been attempts to produce local movies, particularly in Chinese and Malay. The mid-1930s saw the rise of two big players, Cathay Organisation and Shaw Brothers, which operated cinemas and produced movies in Malaya. Their growth was disrupted by the Japanese Occupation (1942–45), but after the war they became major players in the local Malay film industry from the 1950s to the early '60s, a period considered the golden age of Malay cinema in Singapore.[22] Shaw Brothers' Malay Film Productions and Cathay Organisation's Cathay-Keris produced more than 250 Malay movies between 1947 and 1967.[23] Both companies also made Chinese films, some of which were produced locally.[24]

Production companies and cinemas would sometimes make it a point to highlight that a particular film was produced locally in their advertisements. For example, *Leila Majnun* (1934), credited as the first Malay film produced in Singapore, was advertised as "entirely produced in Singapore". Similarly, Cathay-Keris's 1960 Mandarin production, *Shizi Cheng* (《狮子城》; *Lion City*), was marketed as "the first Malayanised Mandarin movie with local talents and filmed locally" (p. 49), though this honour was, in fact, taken by *Xin Ke* (p. 39), a Chinese silent film that had been produced in Malaya much earlier in 1927.[25]

AMUSEMENT PARKS: ONE-STOP ENTERTAINMENT

In the early 20th century, the growing population and wealth in urban Singapore set the stage for a new type of entertainment venue. Being a major international trading port, Singapore was influenced by the emerging forms of entertainment and consumer culture

The entrance to Happy World in Geylang. (1938–39)

Great World amusement park on Kim Seng Road. (1950s)

An archway bedecked with advertisements inside
Great World, the largest of the amusement parks in
Singapore. (1937)

in the West and would have known of the various commercial events, such as fairs and trade exhibitions, taking place in other parts of the world. These events, together with entertainment complexes like Great World (1912) and New World (1917) opening up in Shanghai,[26] inspired the development of amusement parks in Singapore.

The first amusement park in Singapore is said to have been Happy Valley, which opened in 1922 in Tanjong Pagar.[27] It was short-lived, however, and the three parks that came later – New World (1923), Great World (1931) and Happy World (1935; later renamed Gay World) – are better known today.[28] These amusement parks introduced a new entertainment concept to local audiences, bringing various forms of entertainment together in one place.[29]

The parks offered an array of entertainments, such as opera in various Chinese dialects, Malay theatre, film screenings, cabarets, dance and music halls, magic performances, boxing matches, restaurants and many other attractions and activities.[30] In their advertisements, the parks marketed themselves as worlds of fun, offering their patrons the latest, most modern facilities.

These advertisements for theatres, cinemas and amusement parks reflected a shift in the nature of entertainment consumed in Singapore over a century, from communal to more commercial and individualised, with a range of offerings to cater to increasingly differentiated preferences. With further technological advancements, the concept of entertainment in Singapore evolved even more, moving from public venues into private spaces like the home, through radio and television.[31]

Goh Yu Mei

"Pop-up" Entertainment

Public entertainment in Singapore began in temporary performing venues. The first reported public entertainment in Singapore is said to have been a concert performed in 1831 on the Esplanade (the Padang today).[32] While this may have been due to a lack of permanent venues for some of the early cases, many were housed in temporary set-ups because of their itinerant nature. Advertisements show that some public entertainment continued to take place in temporary venues even after proper performing and screening areas had been established.

One highly visible example of such "pop-up" entertainments were the travelling circuses, hailing from countries such as Germany, Italy and the United States. They advertised in the local papers, boasting of their acrobatic performances and animal shows, as well as the popularity they had enjoyed in other places. More often than not, these circuses had also performed in China, Japan, Australia, Batavia (present-

Temporary entertainment venues, such as the one for the Italian circus shown in this ad, were often set up at the foot of Fort Canning Hill. (1887)

The public could occasionally look forward to novel forms of entertainment, such as hot-air balloon displays and rides, as shown in this 1897 advertisement.

Advertisement for dramatic troupes from India performing at Kampong Melaka on Merchant Road. (1924)

(1900)

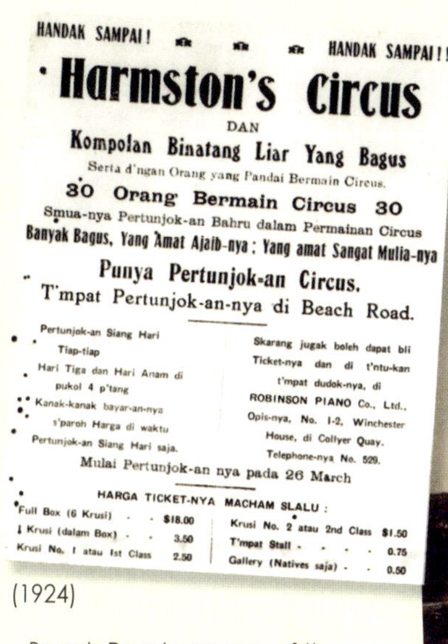

(1924)

Beach Road was one of the popular temporary venues for travelling circuses and cinemas.

Beach Road in the early 1900s.

day Jakarta) and other areas in the region. Although these circuses could be found at various locations – such as Victoria Street, Bukit Timah Road and others – a large proportion of them were set up at the foot of Fort Canning Hill and at Beach Road. To cater to local audience preferences, some circuses provided separate seating for women. These were reserved specially for "native ladies" and the female family members of Chinese businessmen.

Besides circuses, the public could also look forward to other occasional outdoor entertainment. One could catch a puppet show with accompanying music at the foot of Fort Canning Hill in the evenings – the puppets and sets demonstrated fine craftsmanship, and were an eye-opener for the local audience. Or one could hire a travelling cinematograph screener to screen a new film, or a troupe of acrobats to perform their feats. There were also floral expositions, where nurseries would send in their best flowers for display.

Also frequently seen were travelling theatricals, for example, the Ganesananda Dramatic Troupe from Tamil Nadu, India, who came to Singapore in 1924 and staged a show in Kampong Melaka. On a very rare occasion in 1897, one could watch a hot-air balloon demonstration and even take a ride in the balloon to enjoy views of Singapore and neighbouring areas such as Johor and Riau.

Theatre performances by overseas companies as well as local ones were staged at the Town Hall. (1894)

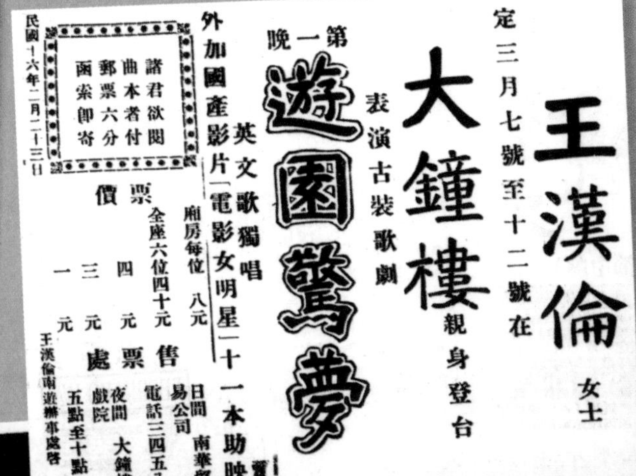

Advertisement for a performance of Chinese opera by movie actress Wang Hanlun at Victoria Theatre. The performance was coupled with a movie screening. (1927)

Uday Shankar, a famous Indian classical dancer, performing at Victoria Theatre. (1935)

An advertisement for *bangsawan* (Malay opera) staged at the Theatre Royal along North Bridge Road. (1908)

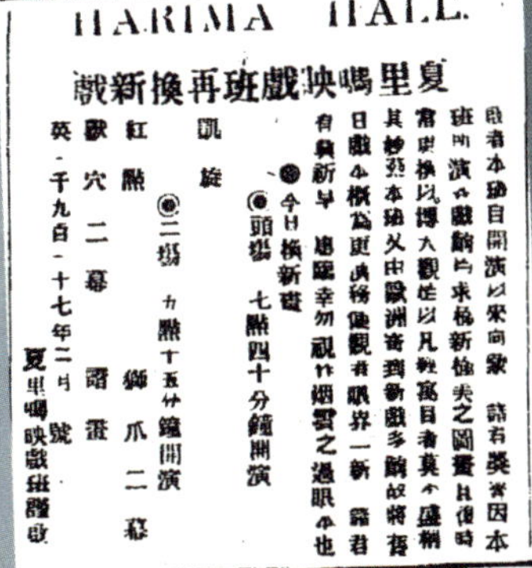

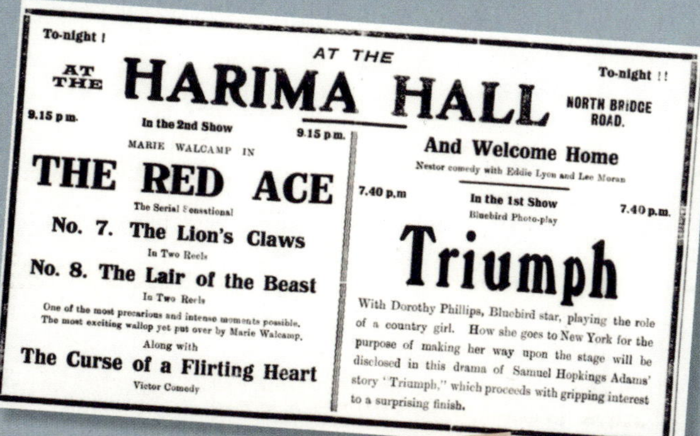

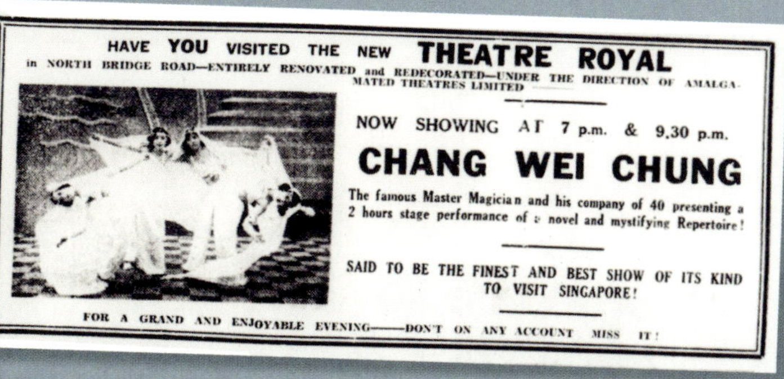

These three advertisements by Harima Hall were published in newspapers of different languages on the same day. (1918)

AT THE CINEMAS

Tamil Talkie At The Theatre Royal

The Tamil talkie now showing at the Theatre Royal, North Bridge Road, entitled "Mohini Rukmangadha," is one of the finest Tamil pictures so far shown here. It is the story of "Ekadasi Vritha Mahamyam" which is well known to Indians.

Some well-known Indian actors and actresses are featured and a number of beautiful songs and dances are rendered.

In addition to live performances, Theatre Royal also screened films after its reopening. (1935)

Advertisement for a magic performance at the newly renovated Theatre Royal on North Bridge Road. (1935)

Leila Majnun was advertised as "entirely produced in Singapore" in several of its newspapers advertisements. (1934)

(1921)

(1925)

The Marlborough screened both Western and Chinese films.

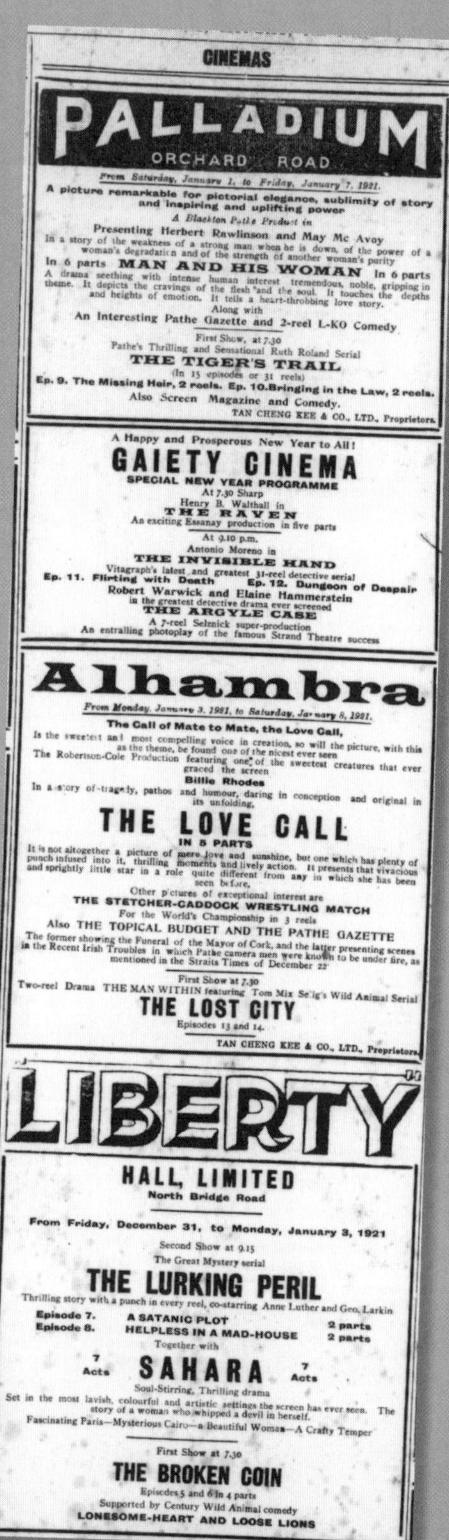

Advertisements by several cinemas. (1921)

A 1960 advertisement marketing *Shizi Cheng* (《狮子城》; *Lion City*) as "the first Malayanised Mandarin movie with local talents and filmed locally". On the contrary, the first locally produced feature film was *Xin Ke* (《新客》; *New Immigrant*), a Chinese silent film, released in 1927 (see ad on page 39).

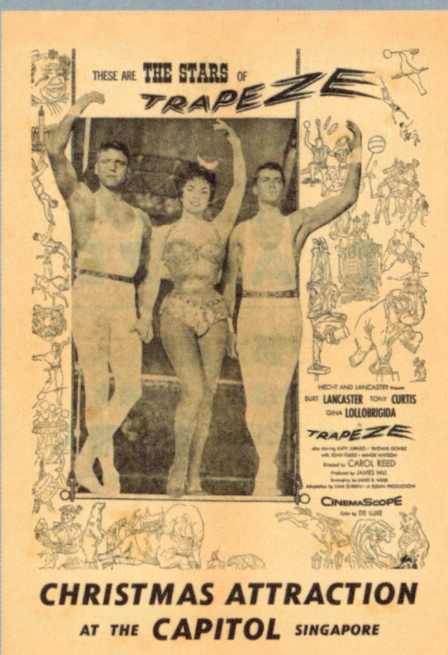

A handbill (front and back pictured) for Capitol's screening of *Trapeze*, with translations in Chinese and Malay (in Jawi script). (c. 1950s)

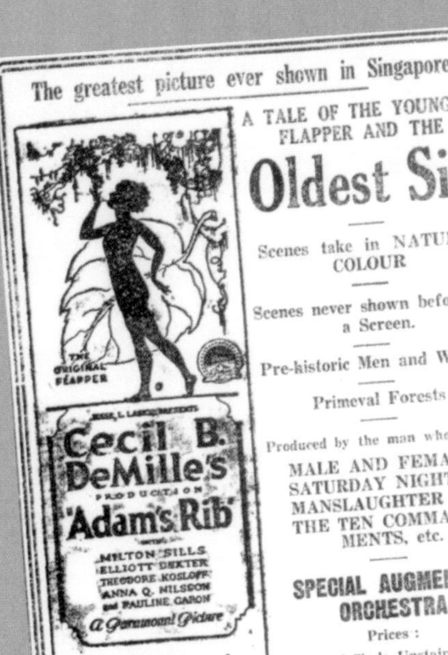

A Mickey Mouse matinee at the Capitol featuring a cabaret and a film screening in the same session. (1934)

Adam's Rib advertised by the Palladium as the "greatest picture ever shown in Singapore" with scenes taken in "natural colour". (1924)

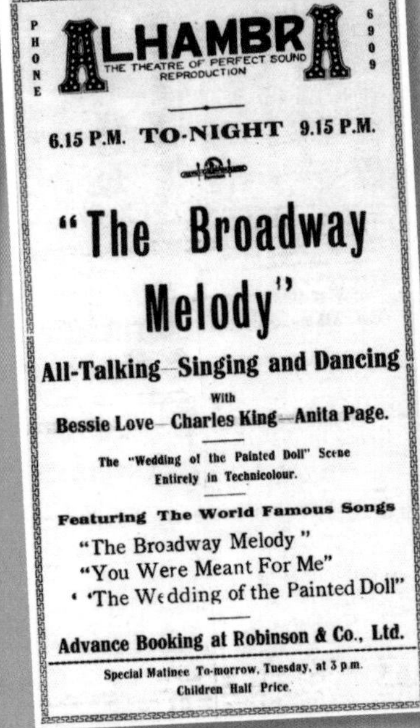

An advertisement by "the air-conditioned Alhambra", featuring lettering mimicking snow-capped mountains. (1938)

The Alhambra's advertisement for a film that was not only "all-talking" but also had a scene in Technicolour. (1930)

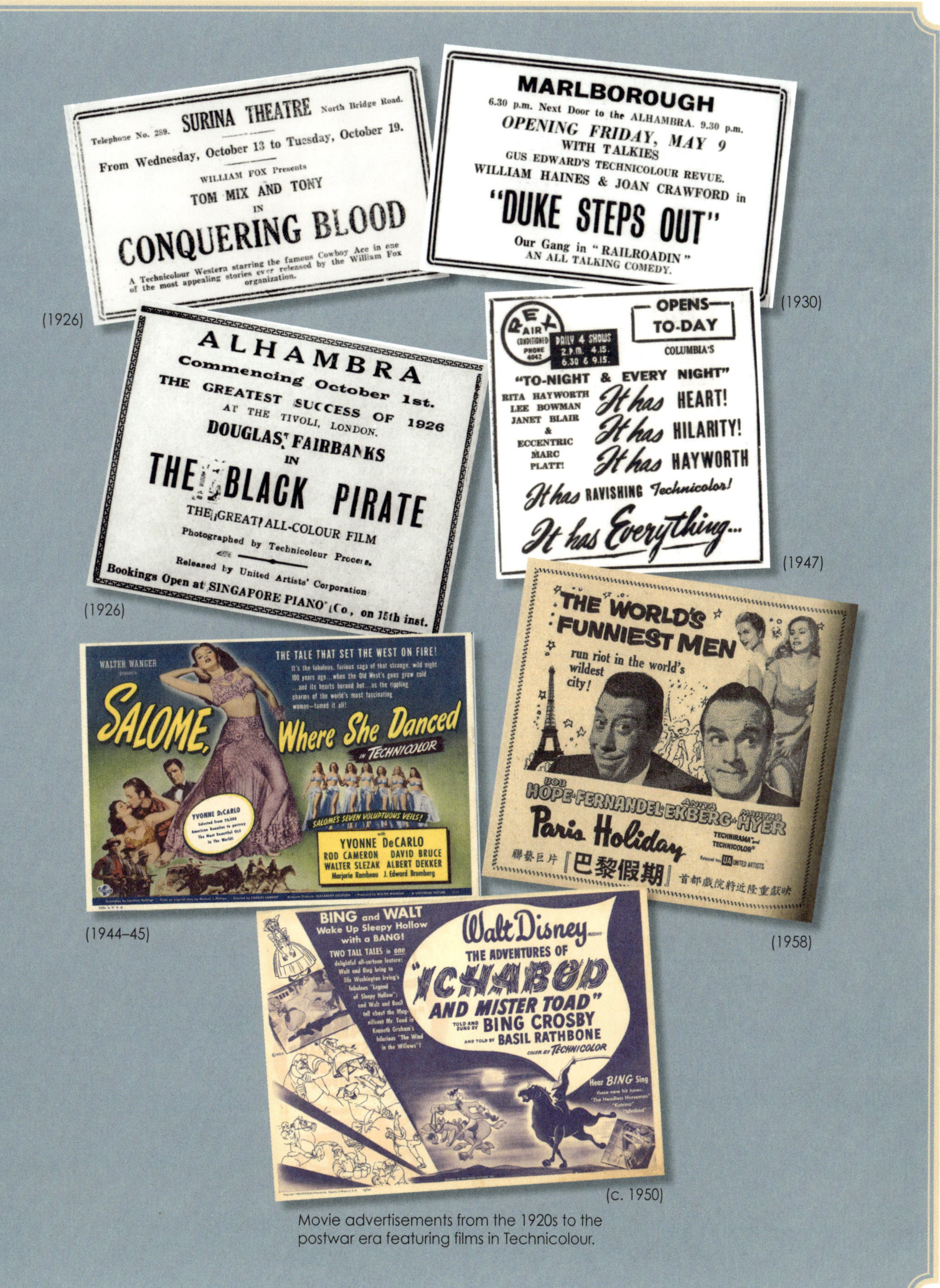

(1926)

(1930)

(1926)

(1947)

(1958)

(1944–45)

(c. 1950)

Movie advertisements from the 1920s to the postwar era featuring films in Technicolour.

A 1930 ad showing images of Happy Valley, including its iconic restaurant in the shape of a ship.

Happy Valley was one of the earliest amusement parks known to have operated in Singapore. (1924)

Besides marketing current attractions, advertisements for amusement parks also provided information on upcoming programmes. (1926)

(1947)

(1959)

Amusement parks – Great World, New World and Happy World – were marketed as modern worlds of entertainment, with all the latest facilities.

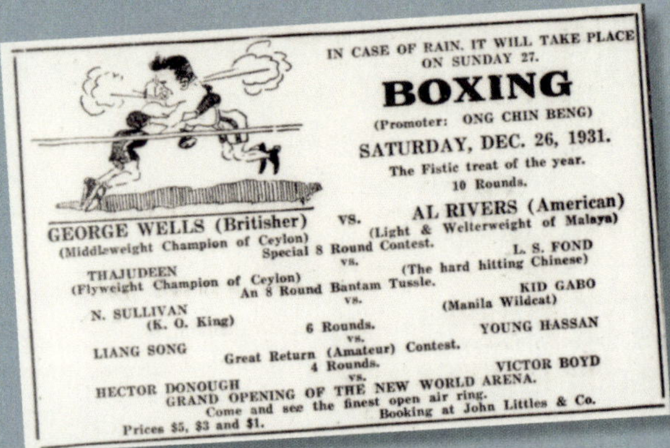

Boxing matches were among the most common spectator sports held in the amusement parks. (1931)

Advertisement for Great World in a 1936 travel guide, appealing to travellers to visit the amusement park when in Singapore.

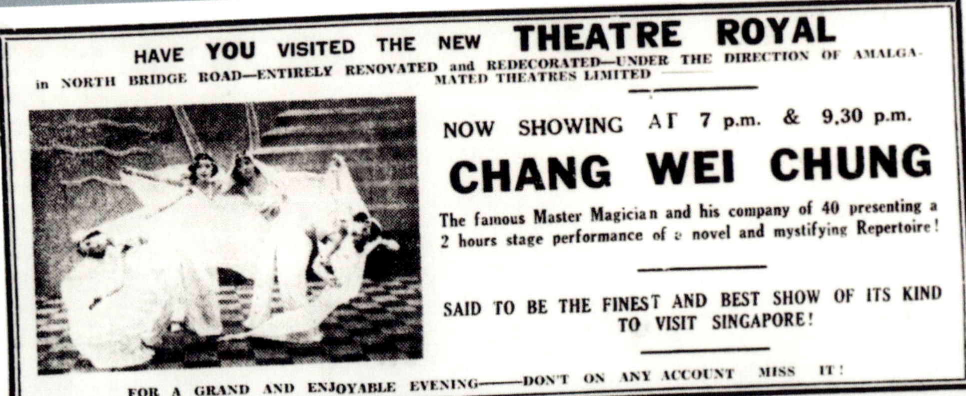

To celebrate the New Year in 1938, Great World had a complete change of programme. The new line-up included a singing competition, a circus from the Philippines, three cinemas, operas, an Indian snake-charmer, and even a small-scale golf course.

A 1970 handbill (front and back pictured) for an acrobatic performance at Gay World.

"A drink of distinction" – luxury alcohol brands appealing to their consumers' desire for status. (1953)

CHANGING TASTES

Food is a key aspect of Singapore's cosmopolitan identity today, with a variety of cuisines and food establishments from all over the world available in the city-state.[1] Global forces have shaped local food culture since colonial times: In the 19th and early 20th centuries, Singapore's position as a thriving port facilitated an inflow of technologies and a multitude of global consumer goods that became embedded in people's lifestyles and identities.[2] Food-related advertisements of the time sought to influence consumers' food preferences and choices. Today, they shed light on the changing practices in food importation, preparation and consumption over the years.

MODERNISING FOOD CONSUMPTION

Trade and technological innovations were two major drivers of change in Singapore's food landscape, bringing global food products to local consumers and spurring the manufacture of new industrial foodstuff.

The opening of the Suez Canal in 1869 resulted in a dramatic increase in international trade. Singapore's position as a major entrepot on the East-West trade route enabled it to receive an extensive range of imported consumer goods, including factory-produced and manufactured foods.[3] These imported foods were products of advances in food technology brought about by the Industrial Revolution.

Indeed, during the late 19th century, food production in the West became increasingly mechanised and scientific, employing new technologies such as canning and continuous process machinery. Mass production and packaging, long-term storage, and long-distance distribution were thus made possible, leading to the production and export of foods such as breakfast cereal and canned fruit.[4]

The arrival of these goods in Singapore was reflected in the increasing number of advertisements. By 1897, Katz Brothers were listing all sorts of manufactured and preserved European foodstuffs for sale, from American canned pears to Cadbury chocolate creams in air-tight tins. Well into the 20th century, advertisements continued to make reference to "scientific methods" and "hygienic conditions" to assure consumers that they were buying the most modern and up-to-date products.

While it imported a significant quantity of foreign food products, Singapore also witnessed a growth in the local production of food and beverages as it steadily developed as an industrial city. Several local industries adapted modern scientific knowledge and technology in their ventures.

One example would be the locally produced aerated waters that were advertised in many publications. Aerated water was a product of 19th-century technological advances. Marketed as a boon in the hot tropics, aerated waters grew from being a scarce commodity to becoming a widely sought-after thirst-quencher.[5]

The local aerated water industry was kick-started in 1883 when Scotsmen John Fraser and David Chalmers Neave established the Singapore and Straits Aerated Water Company – the first facility in Southeast Asia to manufacture carbonated drinks. Later renamed Fraser &

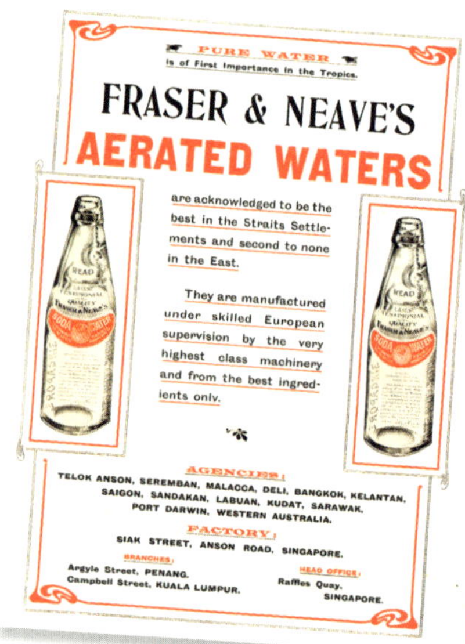

From its early days, Fraser & Neave touted the exceptional quality of its aerated waters, priding itself on its up-to-date production methods. (1907)

Aerated drinks being bottled at the Framroz plant on Allenby Road. (1965)

The main office building of Lee Pineapple Co. Ltd. on Chulia Street. The company was set up in 1931 by businessman and philanthropist Lee Kong Chian. (1935–50)

Pineapple canning was a labour-intensive process. Pineapple cutters removed the eyes and stem of the fruit by hand before cutting them up, while supervisors ensured that the resulting cubes were of the correct size. (1952)

Neave Limited (F&N), the company introduced an array of brands, styles and flavours of soft drinks, which it promoted through eye-catching advertisements.[6]

Other aerated drinks brands included Framroz & Co., founded by Parsi businessman P.M. Framroz in 1904.[7] The brand touted itself as "pioneers of fruit juice beverages", offering consumers "cooling" and "refreshing" drinks made from carefully selected Californian fruits.[8] Phoenix Aerated Water Works, established in 1925 by Navroji R. Mistri,[9] introduced drinks like "grapefruit pop" and "orangepop", and similarly promoted their products as the ideal antidotes to the hot Malayan weather.

Singapore benefited from advances in technologies related to food preservation, storage and distribution. With the discovery of plating in the 1850s and 1860s, canning became possible and revolutionised the food industry.[10] In Singapore, and Malaya generally, pineapple plantation owners made use of the new technology to give their perishable product a longer shelf-life and wider reach. Singapore subsequently emerged as a key centre of the global pineapple canning industry.[11] Among the best-known names was Lee Pineapple Co. Ltd. – founded by businessman Lee Kong Chian in 1931 – whose canned pineapple products were popular locally and overseas.

(1953)

(1949)

Ads for Ayam Brand emphasising the quality and flavour of their products, and featuring mostly items favoured by European consumers such as tinned peas, salmon, olive oil and tomato puree.

Another leading brand of canned goods was Ayam Brand, still a well-known name today. Originally established as A. Clouet & Co. Ltd by Frenchman Alfred Clouet in Malaya in 1892,[12] it became known as Ayam Brand after local traders began referring to it as such – *ayam* is Malay for chicken or rooster, an illustration of which appears on the company's trademark.[13] In its early days, the business focused on supplying British residents with building materials and imported foodstuffs.[14] As can be seen from its advertisements over the years, Ayam Brand later expanded the variety of its offerings, and became best known for its tinned foods such as sardines and green peas.

RISE OF MODERN SUPERMARKETS

Food retail outlets played a significant role in influencing consumers' diet choices. With the emergence of modern supermarkets such as the Singapore Cold Storage and Fitzpatrick's in the 20th century, local food culture was transformed in terms of consumption patterns and the grocery shopping experience.

An iconic name in Singapore, Cold Storage grew from a small retail depot on Orchard Road to the leading player in grocery retailing that it is today.[15] It was founded in 1903 to address the paucity of quality food supplies and the lack of storage facilities capable of keeping imported meat products fresh. The company's founders – Deburgh Persee, chairman of Australia's Queensland Meat Export and Agency Co. Ltd, and H.W.H. Stevens, manager of Victoria River Downs, one of the world's largest cattle stations – introduced cold-storage facilities to preserve and distribute frozen and fresh foods from Australia.[16]

As evident from Cold Storage's advertisements, while the company originally served a European clientele, it subsequently diversified into catering to various communities across the whole of Malaya, distributing a wide range of food products from around the world. From the 1920s and '30s, it also ventured into food production. Its bakeries, creameries, dairy farms and pig farms supplied Singaporeans with products such as bread, milk, ice-cream and pork, and created popular household brand names like Magnolia.[17]

While Cold Storage had begun to evolve from a grocery store to supermarket-style food retailing in the 1930s, it officially took on the term "supermarket" in 1959.[18] It introduced commercial techniques such as self-service and mass merchandising, offering its customers convenience and comfort, and enticing them to buy into this modern form of shopping for food and household necessities.

Decades later, another key player in the food retail landscape was Fitzpatrick's Food Supplies Ltd. Founded in 1948 by W.F. Fitzpatrick and G. Holt, it quickly became one of the leading food retailers in Singapore and Malaya supplying quality foods to various parts of the world.[19] In 1958, it established Singapore's first air-conditioned, self-service supermarket-cum-shopping centre under one roof,[20] and quickly became one of the leading food retailers in Singapore and Malaya that supplied quality foods.[21] Fitzpatrick's advertisements emphasised convenience and affordability in a bid to entice the growing pool of middle-class customers in Singapore.

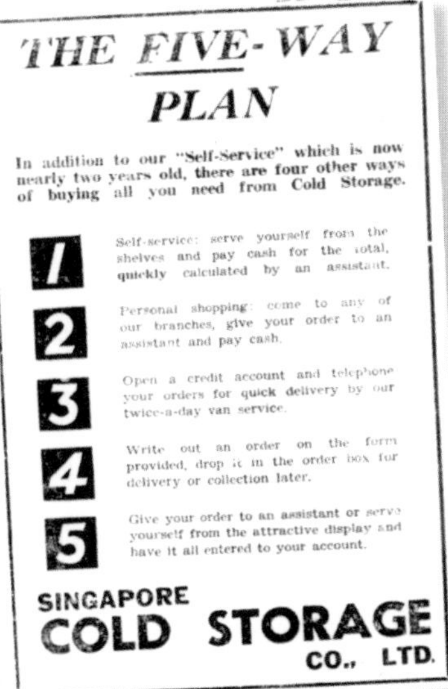

Cold Storage was the pioneer of supermarket-style retail in Malaya, introducing concepts like self-service and mass merchandising. (1949)

Fitzpatrick's Supermarket on Orchard Road, where the Paragon shopping centre now stands. (1962)

DIET AND HEALTH

Health was a key selling point in food advertising across publications in all languages. Many food products claimed to be remedies for the prevailing ailments of the day. Besides malnutrition, there were also diseases like cholera, tuberculosis and malaria, which were exacerbated by overcrowded living conditions and poor sanitation.[22] The Europeans, for their part, believed that their physical and mental wellbeing were adversely affected by prolonged exposure to the tropical climate.[23] Hence, as the relationship between diet and health became better understood, especially from the late 19th century onwards,[24] more food and beverage products started to use good health as a marketing strategy.

For instance, ads for the popular beverage Ovaltine emphasised its health properties, promoting it as a remedy for various ailments such as insomnia and frazzled nerves. Some milk products, such as Swiss Milk and Milkmaid, claimed to have nourishing properties that made them beneficial to inhabitants of the tropics.

(1936)

(1939)

Ovaltine, a popular food beverage, was widely advertised as offering multiple health benefits, from boosting one's energy to curing ailments like insomnia and frazzled nerves.

(1937)

Ads for food products like Rowntree's Cocoa and Bovril meat extract often depicted mothers as the decision-makers in the household, and appealed to them to choose the best products for the sake of their families' health.

(1962)

Milk products from brands like Milkmaid and Bear Brand were advertised as essential for inhabitants of the tropics. The purity and nourishing properties of these products were emphasised.

(1929)

(1929)

Noticeably, most of these advertisements were targeted at women, reflecting their primary role as nurturers and carers. Products like Bovril and Rowntree's Cocoa emphasised their nutritious, tasty and convenient qualities, appealing to mothers to do "what's good for the family".

With many women switching from breast to bottle feeding by the 20th century,[25] tinned milk, baby formula and other baby foods and milk products were increasingly being advertised.

As infant mortality was a concern in early 20th-century Malaya and largely attributed to poor feeding practices,[26] many of these ads promoted supposedly healthy feeding practices. For instance, Horlicks Milkose Baby Food (p. 70) was marketed as a good substitute for breast feeding – a "safe, sure alternative to mother's milk" providing easily digested, balanced and nutritious nourishment.

Liviniyah P.

A Slice of Vice

A group of Chinese men drinking *samsu* at dinner. (1900)

Fresh toddy with hot and spicy snacks was a favourite combination among Indian labourers. Toddy shops often sold snacks like curried crabs, prawns and cuttlefish to cater to their customers' palates. (1951)

Local companies like Malayan Product Manufacturing Co. advertised their products as essential components of, or companions for, the "world famous" Malayan whisky-and-soda drink known as *stengah*. (1940)

In colonial Singapore, locally produced alcoholic beverages such as toddy (palm wine) and *samsu* (rice spirits) were readily available and consumed by the masses, particularly labourers.[27] However, most advertisements in print publications were for imported Western alcoholic beverages such as sherry and Scotch whisky. In these ads, alcohol consumption was often associated with luxury and class, with the drinks described as being of "character" and "distinction".

As imported brands gained wider popularity in Singapore, alcohol advertising took on an indigenous flavour with the hybridisation of drinks and establishment of local breweries. The Europeans often diluted spirits to suit the tropical climate, resulting in beverages with local names like *stengah* (Malay for "half"; a whiskey-and-soda drink), whiskey *ayer* (*air*, pronounced *ayer*, is Malay for "water") and gin *pahit*[28] (Malay for "bitter") that reflected their hybrid identities.[29]

Launched in 1932, the now-famous Tiger Beer was Singapore's first locally brewed beer, manufactured by Malayan Breweries.[30] Tiger Beer ads were ubiquitous in publications of all languages, and typically featured catchy slogans boasting of its exceptional taste and quality as well as local flavour – the beer's name was a symbol of Malaya and it was often marketed as an integral feature of the Malayan way of life.

Interestingly, some alcohol ads also touted the drinks' health-giving properties. According to traditional Chinese

Tiger Beer advertisement promoting the beer as the only fresh beer in Malaya. (1933)

medicine, certain alcoholic beverages are believed to have medicinal properties.[31] For instance, a medicinal wine containing ginseng and antelope horn was advertised as a miracle cure for ailments such as insomnia, and promised to promote overall health and longevity. Similarly, a Tamil advertisement encouraged the consumption of Tiger Beer for good health and energy, while an English advertisement for Hall's Wine targeted Europeans with its promise of being a "tonic restorative" in the enervating tropics.

Southeast Asians have a long history of smoking, with the tobacco plant known in the East for centuries. Machine-made cigarettes, however, were introduced to Singapore by the British-American Tobacco Co. (Straits) Ltd. in 1926.[32] Subsequently, various international tobacco brands began marketing their products to the local populace.

Advertisements for high-end cigarette brands such as Philip Morris and Benson & Hedges often promised consumers a luxurious experience. In their attempt to distinguish themselves from lower-end offerings, these advertisements emphasised their products' superior quality and elaborate packaging. Cigarettes were also marketed as a lifestyle product, a consumable pleasure in one's leisure time as well as in social settings.

Some advertisements specifically targeted women, who were portrayed in these ads as modern, sophisticated and glamorous, thereby associating the cigarette brand with these desirable qualities.

While anti-smoking campaigns are prevalent today, tobacco products were once promoted as "healthy". Far from being understood as injurious to health, cigarettes were actually advertised as a cure for ailments like asthma and sore throats.

Tobacco brands often depicted fashionable women in their ads as a way of endorsing their brands and stimulating appeal. (1963)

Katz Brothers supplied imported packaged goods such as Cadbury chocolate creams, sweets and fruits in "air-tight" tins, "fancy" boxes and bottles, as well as a long list of wines, spirits and liqueurs. (1897)

Chivers and Sons were once the largest individual fruit growers in Great Britain and known as the pioneers of the English fruit canning industry. Their canned goods, including the popular Olde English Marmalade, were advertised as the "purest" available and manufactured under hygienic conditions. (1940)

A 1953 advertisement for Brown & Polson's Raisley baking powder emphasising its scientific manufacturing methods.

Brands like Nescafe and Lassie promised convenience and efficiency with their tasty, ready-to-eat products. (1953)

(1941)

Lee Pineapple Co. Ltd was a pineapple grower, canner and exporter. These advertisements describe how its pineapples were canned hygienically in modern factories, and exported to Western markets in decorative tins.

(1939)

Framroz ads often stated proudly that the company was a pioneer of fruit juice beverages. (1934)

(1933)

(1934)

(1940)

Phoenix Aerated Water Works manufactured fruit drinks with catchy names like "orangepop" and "grape fruit pop", which were touted as refreshing and tasty thirst-quenchers.

Red Lion's Still Orange was a popular F&N beverage in the mid- to late 20th century. The bottles sported F&N's *ang sai* ("red lion" in the Hokkien dialect) logo. The drink was a treat for the young and old, particularly during festive celebrations. (1961)

(1937)

(1958)

Tinned and powdered milk products were increasingly advertised to provide infants with essential nutrients. Products like Horlicks Milkose, Lactogen and SMA were positioned as alternatives to breastmilk.

(1954)

(1968)

(1940)

WEI-YEN MARK TEA

A special tea imported direct from China to suit European taste.

400 Million Chinese | drink Chinese tea
180   " Russians | and they cannot be
60   " Japanese | wrong!

For centuries China has been growing many varieties of teas, some qualities quench the thirst, others are used as medicines. The ART EXCHANGE are importing direct from China a blend combining the two qualities.

Packed in packages of 1 Tael, free from dust or any rejection. Wei-Yen Mark Tea is four times more economical if you follow instructions on each package.

DRINK CHINA TEA, WEI-YEN MARK, from BOE-E.
RELIEVES DIGESTION etc.
A PACKAGE OF ONE TAEL COSTS $1.00.

— — — CUT THIS COUPON — — —

TO THE ART EXCHANGE, 31, Stamford Road, Singapore.

Please forward........packages of ---- WEI-YEN MARK CHINA TEA.

Herewith $.......for ---- packages

Name: ....

Address: ....

You are kindly invited to a trial free of charge at our shop.

Open daily from 9 a.m. to 7 p.m.   Sunday 9 a.m. to 1 p.m.

(1936)

While large quantities of Western consumer goods continued to find their way into Singapore, merchants from other parts of Asia such as China, Japan and India also entered the local food market.

Cold Storage opened its first retail outlet on 24 March 1905 on Orchard Road, selling frozen and fresh food supplies imported from the Queensland Meat Export Agency in Australia. (1905)

Cold Storage procured a variety of food items from all parts of the world to cater to its Western – and Westernised – clientele.

(1954)

(1959)

(1959)

Consumers were encouraged to patronise Fitzpatrick's for a modern, economical and convenient shopping experience.

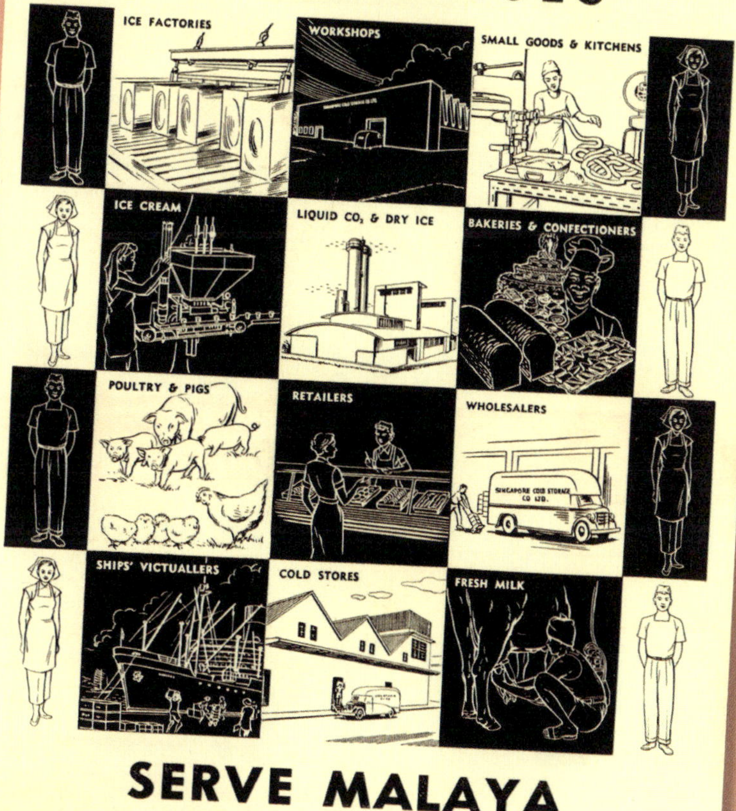

Cold Storage subsequently diversified into food production, establishing creameries, farms and bakeries to cater to Malayans. (1956)

This 1930 advertisement, showing Europeans dancing at a ball, promotes Hall's Wine as "the supreme tonic restorative" against the supposed ill effects of the tropical climate.

"Regal in quality" – a 1936 ad for Black & White scotch whisky.

According to this 1935 ad for a medicinal wine made with ginseng and antelope horn, the product could apparently cure various ailments and promote healthy skin, youth and longevity. It was recommended especially for the elderly.

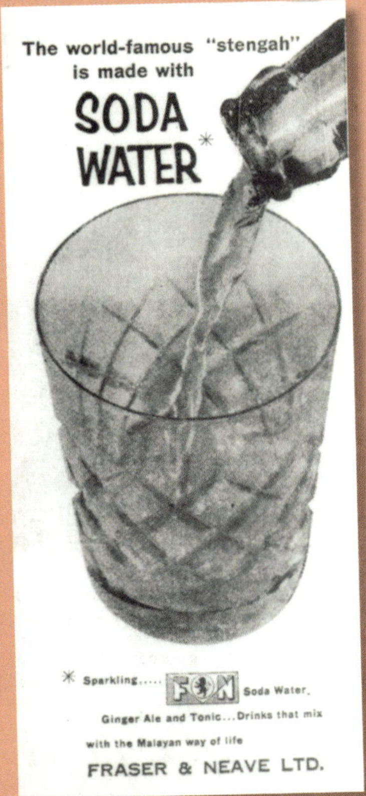

A 1961 ad for F&N soda water marketing it as an indispensable component of the "world-famous" stengah.

(1933)

Tiger Beer advertisements promoting the beer as a symbol of Malayan identity.

(1933)

A 1939 ad in Tamil encouraging the consumption of Tiger Beer for good health.

(1940)

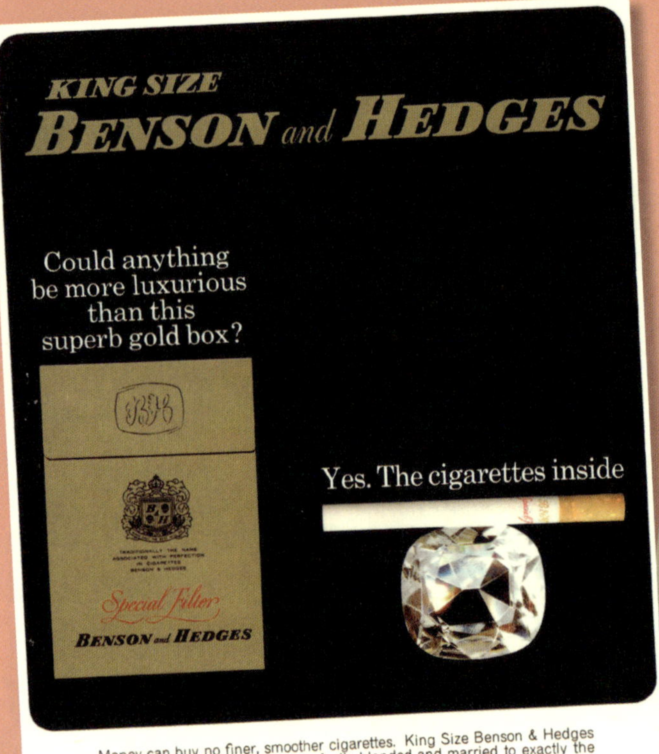

(1967)

(1953)

Advertisements for Western luxury cigarette brands distinguished their products by highlighting aspects such as their fine quality and elaborate packaging.

(1947)

(1928)

Tobacco advertisements promoting smoking as a lifestyle and normalising it as an activity at the workplace and in social gatherings.

(1947)

(1947)

A CURE FOR ASTHMA!!!
GRIMAULT'S

INDIAN CIGARETTES

Asthmatic people who suffer from **Oppression** in breathing, stifling sensations, **Hoarseness**, and **Loss of voice**, Nervous coughs, **Laryngitis**, **Colds**, with **Wheezing**, **Bronchitis**. Insomnia, Catarrhal affections, and **difficulty** in **Expectoration**, are promptly relieved by these Cigarettes.

GRIMAULT & CO., Paris, Sold by all Chemists.

(1894)

Advertisements promoting the health properties of tobacco, which were unfounded. Craven "A" and Martins cigarettes claimed to prevent sore throats, while Grimault's "Indian cigarettes" were touted as a cure for asthma.

(1933)

Bata, hailing from the Czech Republic, was one of the earliest modern shoe sellers in Singapore, opening its first store in 1931 at Capitol Building. It advertised extensively in English, Malay, Tamil and Chinese newspapers. (1958)

A MATTER OF STYLE

Singapore in the 19th century was a thriving cosmopolitan free port that attracted people of diverse ethnicities from all over the world.[1] Travellers such as Isabella Bird, who visited Singapore in 1879, saw a "city ablaze with colour and motley with costume",[2] with Europeans, Malays, Chinese, Indians and other residents and visitors decked out in their own fashion. Initially, the advertisements for apparel in the newspapers did not reflect this rich sartorial mix, being predominantly targeted at the Europeans and affluent Asians, and featuring mostly Western fashion trends and products.

From the 20th century onwards, however, more print advertisements for local and regional traditional wear started to appear. At the same time, Western brands of beauty products increasingly localised their ads – such as by using Asian models – to reach out to the growing local market.

19TH-CENTURY COLONIAL FASHION

Beginning in the 1830s and '40s, popular merchant houses like Little, Cursetjee and Co. and Whampoa and Co. frequently advertised[3] lists of their merchandise such as English and French boots; Parisian bonnets; various types of chemisettes; corsets; gloves; horse-hair petticoats; dresses made of muslin, silk and satin; cashmere shawls; and stockings. These advertisements reflected the Western fashion trends of the period.

The reduction in travel time between Europe and Singapore due to the opening of the Suez Canal in 1869 enabled the demand for European fashion goods to be met more promptly.[4] By the end of the 19th century, advertisements had become more pictorial, with illustrations of Victorian fashion trends, from the popular makes of corsets to the various types of crinolines, gloves, hats, belts and neckties.

These early fashion advertisements reveal that, for the most part, the British continued to dress as they would have done in chilly England. Bird described the European woman in the tropics as an "ungraceful heap of poufs and frills, tottering painfully on high heels, in tight boots, her figure distorted into the shape of a Japanese sake bottle, every movement a struggle or a jerk, the clothing utterly unsuited

In the 19th century, the "hourglass" figure became the new ideal of feminine beauty as well as an indicator of social status. Constricting undergarments such as the corset were used to achieve this.[5] (1898)

The wearing of hats – a marker of social class – reached its zenith at the turn of the 20th century, when no Western gentleman would think of stepping out of his house bare-headed.[6] This 1902 John Little & Co. Ltd. advertisement depicts the various styles of hats available in Singapore: Monte Carlo hats, Singapore sun helmets, single Terai hats, silk hats, Ellwoods helmets and white straw boaters.

to this or any climate, impeding motion, and affecting health, comfort, and beauty alike".[7] Horace Bleackley, a British author, during his visit to Singapore in 1925, recalled seeing well-dressed European women in frocks that followed closely the latest fashions of London and Paris. The men wore European evening dress as their ballroom attire, which in the days before air-conditioning was "the most unsuitable attire for dancing in the tropics that could be imagined".[8]

However, there were also examples of Western fashion adapted to the tropical climate. The European men incorporated the topee, a lightweight helmet made of pith, into their attire. This they wore at all times – even when they went swimming – to prevent sunstroke.[9] From the 1910s to '30s, advertisements show that clothes merchants like John Piggott and Meakers in England were catering to the Europeans living or travelling to tropical climates. Pith helmets, mosquito boots, vests made of absorbent materials, and white and khaki drill suits became popular. Department stores in Singapore such as Robinson & Co. also advertised fabrics such as cotton and linen that gave wearers greater comfort in the local heat and humidity.

MEETING THE NEEDS OF MEN COMING HOME

AT Meakers in Piccadilly a man can buy everything he needs to wear, nothing has been omitted.

The prices are moderate and the merchandise of exceptionally good quality. One floor is devoted to the " New Ready-to-Wear Tailoring " Lounge Suits, another to Overcoats and Weathercoats, a floor for Boots, Shoes and Hats, other sections for Sports Wear, Evening Wear, Gowns, Tropical and Colonial Outfits.

There is an assistant in attendance who has had considerable experience in the Malay States.

A luxurious and modern Barber's Saloon is installed on the Lower Ground Floor. Dressing Rooms and Bath Rooms are also available.

RELIABLE AS OAK

MEAKERS
PICCADILLY
47-48, Piccadilly, London, W.1

Meakers, a men's outfitter in London, advertising their "tropical and colonial outfits". They also had an assistant in attendance with "considerable experience in the Malay States". (1936)

John Piggott, a "tropical outfitter" based in London, advertised in the colony as having "40 years' reputation outfitting colonials". They sold pith helmets, mosquito boots, pyjama suits, white and khaki drill suits, and steel air-tight uniform cases. (1914)

HUSSEN AND FAKIER SAIBS, TAYLORS.

HAVING lately arrived from Madras, humbly beg to inform the Ladies and Gentlemen of the Presidency and the Public in general, that they have opened a Working Shop in Commercial Square. Parties obliging them are here assured that every attention will be paid to all Orders, most neatly and fashionably completed and at moderate terms.

Hailing from Madras, Hussen and Fakier Saibs set up shop in Commercial Square in 1831 and advertised fashionable tailoring services at moderate prices. (1831)

NOTICE.

M. AGUSTINE AVIZAGNET has the honor to inform the Public, that he has arrived from France, and purposes establishing himself at Singapore in the exercise of his profession of MASTER TAILOR.

Having worked for upwards of ten years in Paris, he hopes to give satisfaction to every person who will do him the honor of sending employ.

His address is No. 50 Teluk Ayer Street, at Mr. Westerman's.

A notice from M. Agustine Avizagnet, a Parisian "master tailor" with more than 10 years' experience, announcing his intention to set up shop in Singapore. (1834)

Advertisement by Robinson & Co.'s tailoring department boasting of its European cutters with "life long experience". (1928)

MADE-TO-MEASURE: THE PREFERRED CHOICE

Even as merchant houses and, later, department stores offered a range of ready-made clothing, the preferred choice up to the 1970s was made-to-measure or tailor-made clothing.[10] Beginning in the 19th century, tailors arrived in Singapore from places like Madras and Paris, some advertising themselves as "master tailors" knowledgeable about sartorial requirements in the local climate. Renowned botanist Alfred Russell Wallace, a frequent visitor to Singapore between 1854 and 1862, noted that tailors who worked "well and cheaply" were a common sight in the Chinese bazaar.[11]

The locals wore traditional garments. The Malay men wore a *sarong*[12] or *seluar* (pants) and a *baju* (shirt), while women wore a *baju kurong* (long bouse over a skirt) or a *baju* and *kain* (*sarong*). Indian women from the dominant Tamil community dressed in a six- or nine-yard *saree*,[13] while the men wore a *dhoti*.[14] Chinese traders and merchants favoured a long gown (*p'ao*) as daily wear; working-class men wore versions of the short jacket, waistcoat and padded jacket; and coolies wore loose calf-length slacks.[15] Chinese women dressed in tunics and trousers – a combination known as the *samfoo* – as daily wear and started wearing the *cheongsam* from the 1920s onwards.[16] Advertisements for such garments were, however, rarely found in general. This could have been because locals preferred to buy cloth and bring it to a tailor or dressmaker, rather than buy ready-to-wear garments.

The huge demand for tailor-made clothes was reflected in the profusion of ads for fabric stores and tailoring services. A well-tailored outfit was portrayed as essential for bringing out the wearer's individuality. High Street, a retail paradise in colonial Singapore, was lined with fabric stores such as K.A.J. Chotirmall & Co. and Bajaj Textiles, which sold imported textiles like cretonnes, silk brocades, cottons and linen, and offered tailoring services. Department stores like Aurora and Robinson's also provided tailoring services for men and ladies.[17] By the late 1950s, local designers such as Jenny Chan, who ran

Janilaine on Orchard Road, were making dresses and gowns for the elite of society.[18]

The passing of the Women's Charter in 1961, and women entering the workforce, made local women more independent. As their spending power increased, their dressing style also evolved.[19] Many Western-educated local women abandoned their *samfoo*, *saree* and *sarong kebaya* for Western outfits. Local women would buy fabrics at the upmarket High Street or from colourful fabric shops in Serangoon, Geylang or Chinatown, and then head to their neighbourhood dressmaker, or pay a visit to

a Shanghainese tailor, or call up one of the immaculately dressed Indian tailors who went to customers' homes to take measurements. Women also sewed clothes themselves, using McCall's and Butterick dress patterns or those found in women's magazines like *Her World*.[20] By the 1960s, brands like Singer, Pinnock and Usha were marketing sewing machines to local women and offering sewing lessons.

K.A.J. Chotirmall & Co., a popular fabric store and dressmaker on High Street, advertising their custom wedding dresses. (1936)

Singer sewing machines advertised as "the first essential investment" and "first sign of prosperity". (1960)

MARKETING STRATEGIES

By the dawn of the 20th century, advertising strategies were changing. Fashion and beauty advertisements started moving away from merely listing or illustrating products and their prices. Products became associated with particular lifestyles, desirable qualities, or celebrities. Clothes came to define the wearer's status or personality more than ever before. Stores advertised fashion trends to be worn at the horse races – a favoured form of entertainment among the affluent then – for those who aspired to dress to impress. Perfumes from the Arab world and East Asia were marketed as "exotic" and targeted at "women with taste", while celebrity endorsements and claims of royal patronage were used to sell everything from soap to shoes.

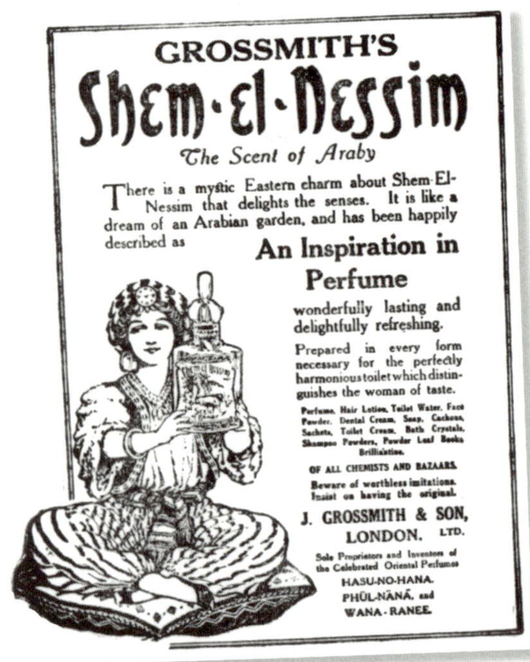

The scent of Arabia in a bottle – this 1921 perfume advertisement promises its wearers mystic Eastern charm with its range of fragrances and toiletry products.

Robinson & Co. marketing "Black Prince" shoes and boots as the footwear of choice of the late King Edward VII. (1921)

Going to horse races allowed one to show off one's smartest clothes. (1922)

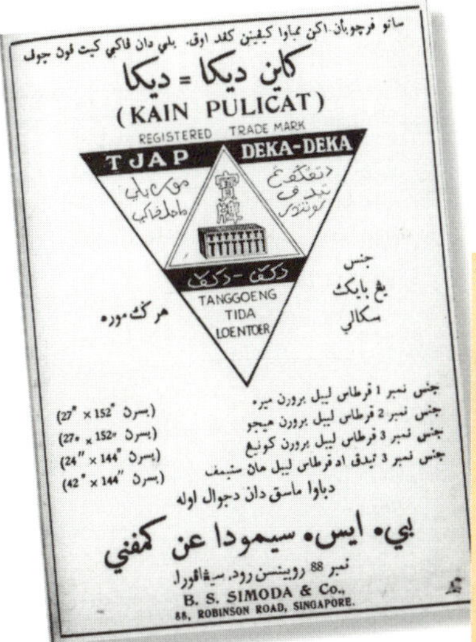

Advertisement in Jawi for *kain pelikat*, or *sarong*, worn mostly by Malay men, promoting a brand imported by B.S. Simoda & Co., a Japanese company. (1933)

Max Factor, an international brand, using a Malay model and advertising in Jawi to reach out to the local Malay market. (1961)

Yardley used popular Malay actresses to advertise their products in the region. (1961)

LOCAL APPEAL

While regional brands and traditional wear such as the *sarong* and *saree* were occasionally advertised from the late 19th century, Western beauty products and fashion trends still constituted the staple advertisements up to the 1960s. To appeal to locals, and tap into rising disposable incomes following the early 20th-century rubber boom, Western brands increasingly advertised in local-language newspapers and engaged Asian models as the face of their ad campaigns.

In the 1950s and '60s, local designer boutiques appeared on the scene. This coincided with the period when Malaya and Singapore were gaining independence. There was a newfound pride in Asian traditional garments. Local designers gave Western fashion an Asian twist by using fabrics such as batik, and glamourised traditional wear by adding modern touches to the *cheongsam* and *sarong kebaya*, and some even refashioning the *saree* into a cocktail dress.

Akshata Patkar

The "Ideal" Beauty

From face soaps and cold creams to make-up and hair tonics, the beauty products advertised in Singapore over the years provide interesting insights into the evolving ideals of beauty held by the various communities.

A large proportion of the beauty products advertised in English from the 19th century to the outbreak of the Second World War was made up of Western brands targeted at the colonial community. Thus, their ads invariably echoed European beauty ideals. In the Victorian era (1837–1901), natural beauty was emphasised and the use of cosmetics frowned upon. The best way for a woman to achieve fashionably pale skin was considered to be soap and hot water.[21] The British soap industry advertised soap as a beauty treatment product that would ensure beautiful, delicate skin and hence increase a woman's attractiveness. Such ads were aplenty in Singapore as well, where the Western soap brands that became well established over the decades made their products more appealing to the local population by advertising in vernacular languages and by getting Asian celebrities to endorse them in the postwar period.

Cold creams and vanishing creams, which had become commercially available by the Edwardian era (1901–10), were also promoted as helping to achieve the fair-skin beauty ideal.[22] At the same time, the desire to look young and fresh-faced was

Crème Simon advertised as a skincare product that could counteract the effects of sun and wind, and preserve the youthfulness of one's skin. (1922)

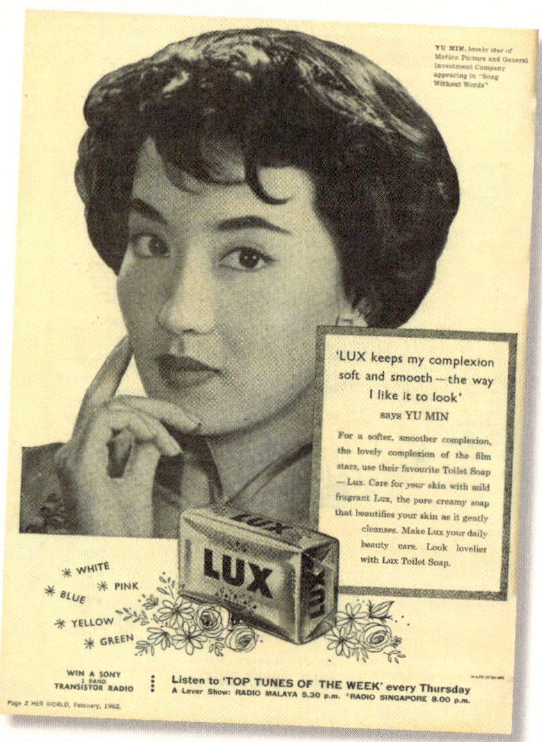

Hong Kong actress Lucilla Yu Min endorsed Lux for giving her a soft and smooth complexion. (1962)

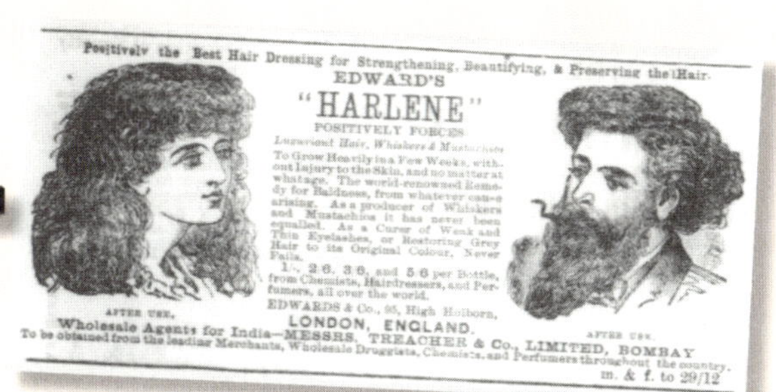

Edward's "Harlene" tonic was marketed to both men and women looking to strengthen, beautify and preserve their hair. (1893)

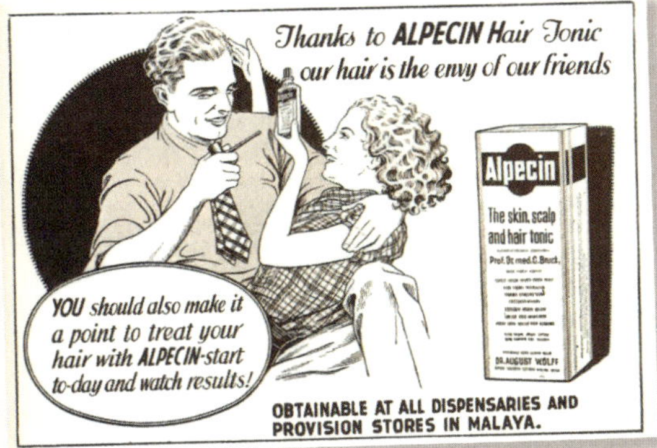

Alpecin was a hair tonic for men and women. (1938)

reflected in the preponderance of ads for beauty creams touting "perpetual youth" and the "banishment of wrinkles".[23]

By the early decades of the 20th century, ads for cosmetics were appearing with great frequency in magazines. One of the most significant developments was the introduction in 1938 of Max Factor's "Pan-Cake", the first water-soluble cake foundation. As it grew in popularity, the range of shades expanded to meet demand,[24] giving women one more way to achieve a "flawless" complexion.

Ads for hair-care products in different languages showed that hair was a prized asset among women and men in all communities. For women, long, luxuriant hair had been a staple feature of the beauty ideal in Eastern and Western cultures for centuries. In the West, this changed when women had to work with factory machinery during the First World War and, for practical reasons, took to cropping their hair. Short hairstyles such as the bob, the shingle and the Eton crop started to mirror a woman's social and economic independence, as well as her love of fashion.[25] During this period, the permanent wave (hence "perm") also became popular. In keeping with these trends, many local Asian women sported short or permed hairstyles in the 1920s and '30s, and hairdressers advertised their perming services with guarantees that the permanent waves would last for months.

However, long hair continued to remain important for many women from the Tamil and Malay communities, as can be inferred from the ads featuring women with thick tresses. Local and regional manufacturers of hair oils and shampoos advertised extensively in vernacular publications, invariably using depictions of attractive, long-haired women to illustrate the efficacy of their products.

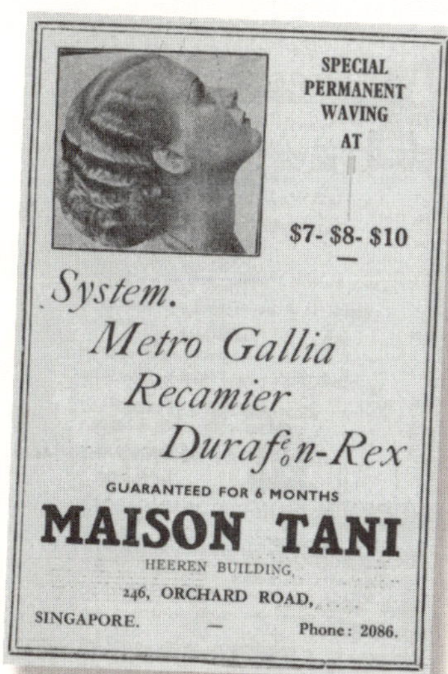

Maison Tani's hair perming services came with a six-month guarantee. (1938)

LIST OF ARTICLES FOR SALE
AT THE COMMISSION ROOMS OF
Little, Cursetjee, and Co.
COMMERCIAL-SQUARE,--SINGAPORE.

LADIES APPAREL.

Berlin wool of colors
Boots and shoes, English and French
Bonnets direct from Paris, silk, satin & nett
——Dunstable and straw
Balzarine Dresses
Caps—blond and Lace
Capes and cuffs
Cardinals, a la mode
Chemisettes of every description
Cambrics—English, French and Scotch
Collars, finely worked
Corsets, without Seam
Corded Petticoats
Dresses—Muslin and Lace (elegantly embroidered) Robed, Tucked, flowered, Tuniced and Mourning
Dress Improvers
Dress Handkerchiefs
Edgings, thread
Figured China silks and satins for dresses
Gloves, French kid and silk—white, black and colored
Handkerchiefs, plain and worked,—Pine, cambric and silk
Horse Hair Petticoats

Jaconet—White and colored
Linen—Fine Irish
Lace—Shawls, scarfs, real and imitation Brussels manufacture
Ladies companions
——Work-boxes, London, Bombay and China manufacture
Mits,—Silk, in great variety
Muslin—Plain, figured and colored
——Dresses' embroidered and plain
——Book and Scotch
Musselin de laine dresses
Pina scarfs, dresses, shawls, collars, handkerchiefs, &c. made at Manila
Parasols—Silk, plain and figured
Robe and morning dresses
Ribbons—Silk, satin, and gauze
Silks and satins—Plain and figured of assorted colors
Silk thread
Shawls and scarfs, pine, crape, satin, Cashmere and Delhi—an elegant assortment
Stockings; silk, cotton, and Lisle thread
Satin—White, blue and pink
Thread edgings
Toilet covers, &c. &c.

Baby Linen &c.

Bonnets in variety
Boots of worsted
Caps of Lace, silk, &c.
Frocks, long and short
Hoods and Bonnets
Socks—Cotton and worsted
Shoes of English manufacture,—&c. &c.

GENTLEMEN'S APPAREL, &C:

Boots, shoes and slippers
Braces—Elastic, silk and cotton
Coats—Ready made dress, surtouts, Codrington's, Pilot, &c.
Corduroy for trowsering
Caps—Military, naval, plain and cloth
Dressing gowns
Duck and drill
Flannel and flannel shirts
Grass cloth for Jackets, &c. unbleached and white
Guernsey Frocks
Hats, black and white; beaver, silk, pith and straw
Huckabuck
Jackets, naval, shooting, &c.
Kid gloves—White, black and colored
Long cloth—Horrocks manufacture
Military & naval epaulettes, buttons, lace, &c
Medical rubber towelling
Neckerchiefs—Silk & satin, black & colored
Shirts—Ready made linen, cotton, Lamb's wool and Merino
Silk, tartans, &c.—an assortment for Waist coating.
Socks—silk, cotton and worsted.
Saxony Mull and Tweel, &c. &c.
Handkerchiefs—grass cloth, cambric and silk

JAPAN & CHINA MANUFACTURES.

Boxes, Tea, Card, Segar, &c.
——Indian inlaid, ivory, &c.
Backgammon-boards.
Cases, segar, trinket, card, &c.
Chess and Backgammon men.
Curtain gauze.
Clocks—Japan manufacture.
Crape Shawls—an assortment.
Dresses.—China silk and satin, plain and flowered.
Fans and punkas.
Grass cloth handkerchiefs.
Japan ware—in great variety.
Ornaments—a great assortment.
Paper cutters—Ivory, Tortoiseshell, &c.
Puzzles, of various kinds.
Silk purses and ornaments.
Silver filagre card cases, &c.
Teapoys, Trays, &c
Tables; work, chess &c.

JEWELLERY.

Bracelets of gold and silver.
Breast Pins, Brooches &c.
Card cases, gold and silver.
Chains—gold silver &c.
Earrings and drops.
Lockets, in variety.
Mourning rings and Brooches.
Needle cases, &c.
Pencil cases, gold and silver.
Rings, for Ladies and Gentlemen.
Seals and Keys.
Watch Hooks
Watches; Ladies and Gentlemen's, of gold and silver.

STATIONERY AND BOOKS.

A fine selection of New Music.
Novels, Histories, Travels &c.
Account books, strongly bound.
Blank books, plain and ruled.
Desks; writing, plain and fancy
Day books.
Drawing Pencils and crayons.
Envelops in cases, or per 100
Foolscap Letter and note paper.
Inks, black, blue and red
Log and cargo books
Ledgers and Journals
Memorandum books
Pens—Steel and Quill
Portfolios and Albums
Travelling cases
Wax—plain and fancy
Wafers—initial, polka, plain, &c.

WINES & SPIRITS

Ales—English and Singapore bottled
Allsopp's and Bass' Beer
Brandy—best Cognac
Champagne—"Geislers"
Claret—first quality
Cordial, cherry and raspberry
Cherry Brandy
Glenlivet whiskey
Gin in cases
Hock—"Johannisberg"
Liqueurs—assorted
Maraschino and ratifia
Old Tom
Port—very superior
Sherry—J. Cockburn's, Campbell's &c.

GILMAN'S STORES.

Beef—spiced and smoked
Bottled fruits and sauces
Bacon—in Tins
Biscuits—Cabin and fancy
Candles—wax and spermicetti
Capers and Olives
Cheeses—constant importations
Dates and Prunes
Fruits (French) in syrup
——brandied.
Ginger (China) preserved in jars
Hams—Yorkshire and Westphalian
Jams and Jellies
Loaf sugar
Maccaroni in tins and boxes
Marmalade in jars
Mustard, in bottles and pots
Malaga raisins
Preserved provisions in tins, regular importations from the first houses
Pickles in great variety
Salad oil, and Sardines
Sausages—Italian and German
Tongues, smoked and salted
Vermicelli

Miscellaneous Articles.

Baskets, China made for Clothes
Buttons, gilt for Coats and Jackets
Camblets (blue) and Cashmere for do.
Cigars, Manila No. 3 and 4
Cigar cases, Manila and china
Colors, oil and water, in tin boxes and cakes
Camphor wood trunks
Crowns, for Naval caps
Dinner and tea services
Dressing cases
Desks, travellers writing
Fowling pieces, single and double barrel, pistols, gunpowder and birding shot.
Gold Lace, 1 and 1½ inch for Naval caps
Hats, Manila and straw
Harness, Saddles, bridles and Girths
Indian Rubber
Lamps, bronzed, gilt and hanging
Oil paintings, a fine selection
Plated and metal curry dishes
Perfumery, from Rowlands and Sons
——Tabor and others
Pencils for drawing
Sketch books
Time pieces, on stands
Travelling Trunks and Portmanteaus
Whips, superior London made

PUBLIC AUCTIONS HELD ON MONDAY AND WEDNESDAY

WHAMPOA AND CO

Have always on Sale an extensive and choice assortment of the following goods, selected specially for their Stores.

WHOLESALE RETAIL & FOR EXPORTATION.

MILLINERY & HOSIERY

Articles for the Work Table
Balzarine dresses
Bonnets of the latest modes, from Paris
Chemisettes of the finest quality,
Childrens Caps and dresses
Dresses—An elegant assortment of Silk, Satin, & Muslin
Dress improvers
Embroidered dresses, Scarfs and Handkerchiefs
Flannel—Plain and printed
French Kid and Silk Gloves of colors
Hose—Cotton and Silk
Handkerchiefs—Silk, Grass cloth, Cambric and Pine.
Horse Hair Petticoats.
Long cloth of Horrocks manufacture.

Berlin Wool of assorted colors
Caps, Cuffs, Collars, of English & Manil manufacture
Lace of English and Brussels manufacture
Muslin and Muslinet Dresses, Curtains, &c.
Mousselin de laine Dresses.
Needles—A choice variety of the best kind.
Pins of London manufacture.
Pine fabrics in great variety.
Parasols of the Latest fashion.
Ribbons—Silk, Satin and Sarsnet.
Stockings and Socks of Silk, Cotton and Worsted.
Satin and silk—plain and figured.
Silk Mits—purses, and silk thread.
Shawls—A great assortment.
Thread and ball cotton.

ARTICLES FOR THE TOILETTE.

A great variety of fancy porcelain.
Brushes—Hair, Hat, Nail tooth and cloth.
Combs—of Ivory & Tortoiseshell in variety.
Dressing cases for Ladies and gentlemen.
Damask Napkins, Towells and covers.
Eau de cologne from Jean Maria Farina—
Hair Pins—English and French.
Hair and Tooth Powder of superior, quality.
Looking Glasses in various mountings.
Razors and Razor Strops.
Soaps—in great variety.
Water—Lavander, Rose, Gold and Honey

A well-known store and shipchandler in Telok Ayer Street in the 1840s, Whampoa & Co. supplied the town with Western goods including millinery, hosiery, toiletries, jewellery and watches, among other goods.[26] (1850)

MILLINERY, &c.
Ex "Drummond Castle."

Pink Ginghams,
Scarlet Llama,
Blue   „
Black Merino,
Scarlet   „
Green Worsted Damask,
Bleached Linen,
Blue Fine Flannel,
Glazed Furniture Chintz,
Boys' Tweed Knickerbocker Suits,
Ladies' White French Kid Gloves,
  „   Colored „   „   „
  „   White   „   „   „ 2 buttons,
  „   „ Berlin   „
  „   Striped Jupon Crinolines,
  „   Mohair Trimmed   „
  „   Harper's Panier „
Gentlemen's Smoking Caps.
JOHN LITTLE & CO.
Singapore, 23rd May, 1872.

Ex: "MENELAUS."

The undersigned have received—
  Gros Pois.
  Petits do.
  Dried Sage.
And
Hambro' Hung Beef in rolls.
JOHN LITTLE & CO.
Singapore, 29th May, 1872.

Between 1845 and 1870, European ladies' fashion saw a major innovation: the crinoline, a stiffened petticoat made of horsehair and linen or cotton that helped create volume beneath a lady's dress. Crinolines became symbols of the higher aristocracy and the new class of emerging bourgeoisie, for whom self-image was critical in the construction of personal identity and a means of social legitimisation.[27] In this 1872 ad for millinery, John Little & Co. advertised various types of crinolines – "Striped Jupon", "Mohair Trimmed" and "Harper's Panier". (1872)

Little, Cursetjee and Co., which opened in 1845 at Commercial Square, carried a range of Western fashion goods for ladies, ranging from English and French boots and shoes to dresses, caps, handkerchiefs, gloves, horse-hair petticoats, shawls and scarves. (1850)

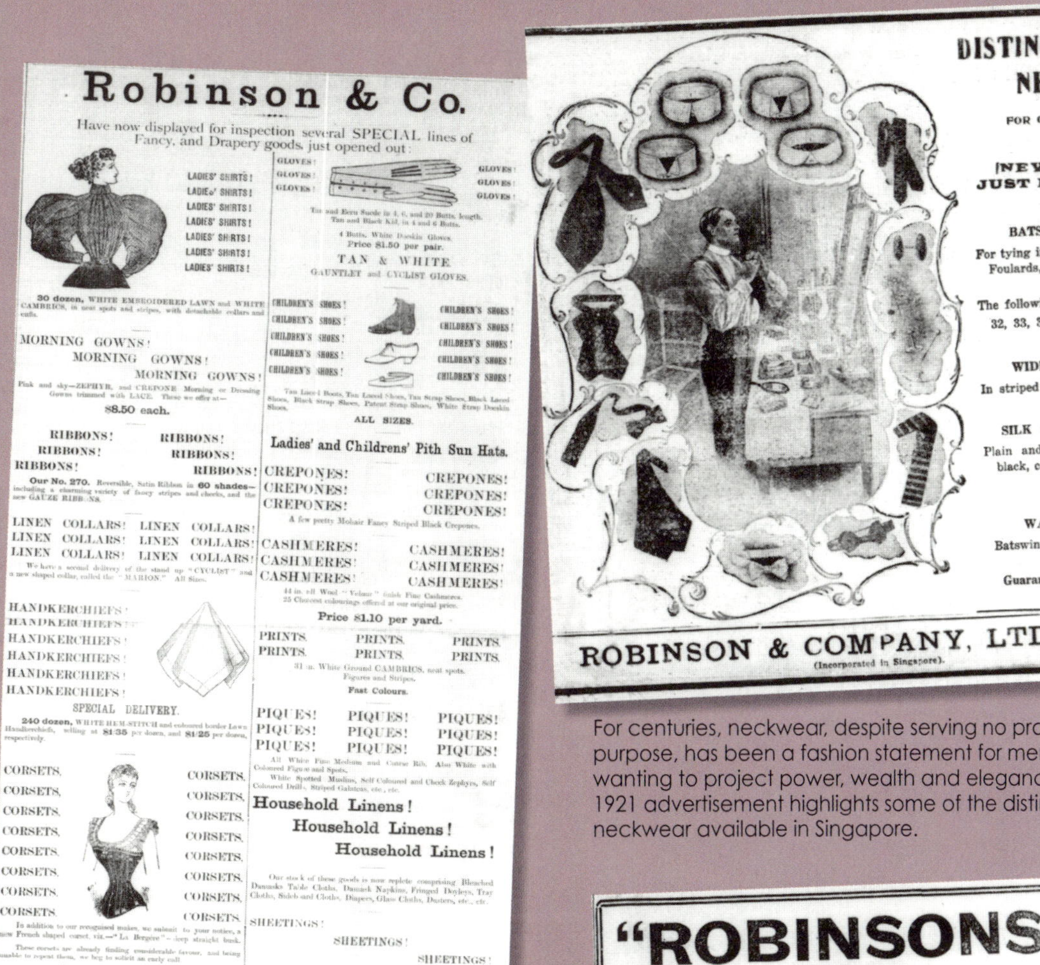

For centuries, neckwear, despite serving no practical purpose, has been a fashion statement for men wanting to project power, wealth and elegance.[29] This 1921 advertisement highlights some of the distinctive neckwear available in Singapore.

In the 19th century, wearing gloves was an indicator of a person's social status among the colonial set. Light-coloured gloves, in particular, came to be particularly esteemed. Towards the end of the century, gloves were no longer as prized as they had been in the early 1800s and were considered optional at social events, but people continued to wear them for most occasions.[28] This 1898 advertisement shows Robinson & Co. selling tan, black and white gloves in different lengths, fabrics and styles. (1898)

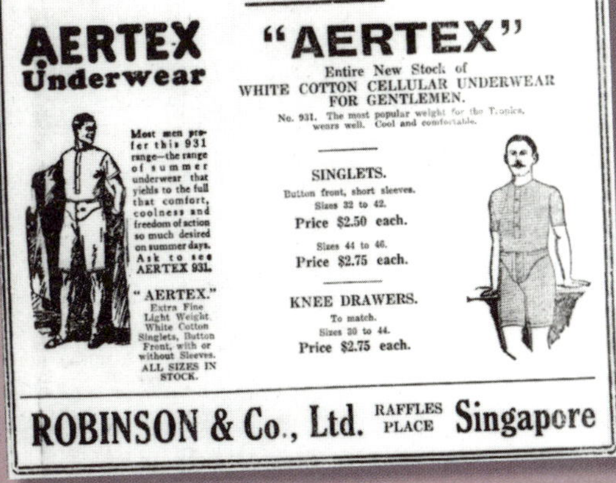

Robinson & Co. Ltd stocked undergarments from Aertex, a British clothing company that manufactured shirts and underwear using their trademark lightweight cotton fabric. By the end of the 19th century, Aertex was the preferred choice of the English middle class. (1927)

(1901)

(1902)

(1901)

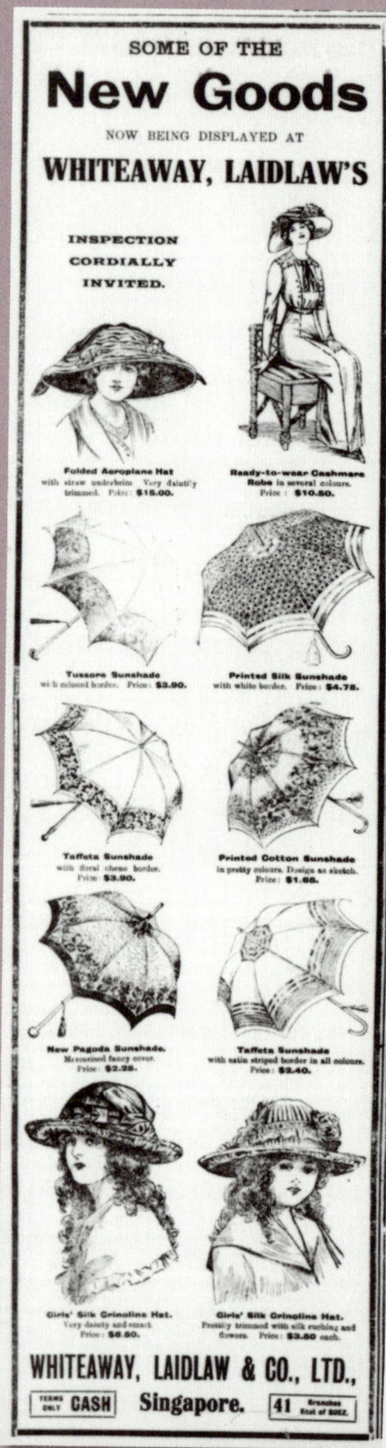

(1913)

Whiteaway, Laidlaw & Co. advertised a range of fashion goods for men, women and children. The prices (expensive for the first decade of the 20th century) indicate that they were targeted at Singapore's more affluent consumers.

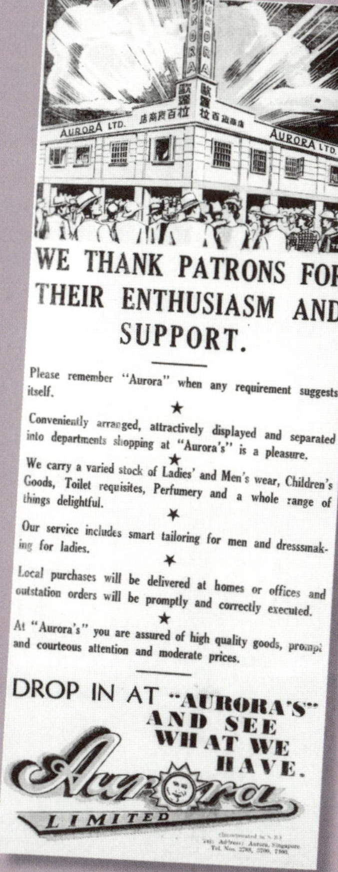

In 1850, Mr. J. Garty, with experience in Madras and "acquainted with the description of dress suitable for a warm climate", offered his services to the gentry of Singapore alongside Miss Garty, who provided millinery and dressmaking services.

When the Aurora department store opened in 1938, its services included smart tailoring for men and dressmaking for ladies. (1938)

Advertisement for a fashion show at Goodwood Park Hotel featuring designs by Janilaine, one of Singapore's most prominent made-to-measure clothing shops in the 1960s. (1962)

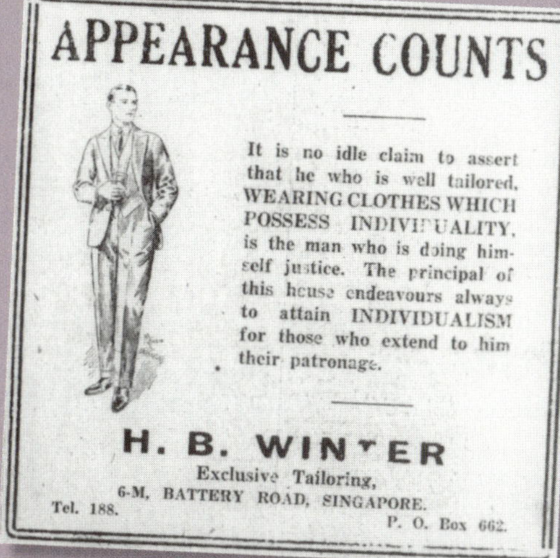

H.B. Winter promoting the ability of its tailored clothes in accentuating the wearer's individuality. (1927)

Bajaj Textiles, a well-established textile merchant, also offered tailoring services with the tagline "suits... worth waiting for". (1949)

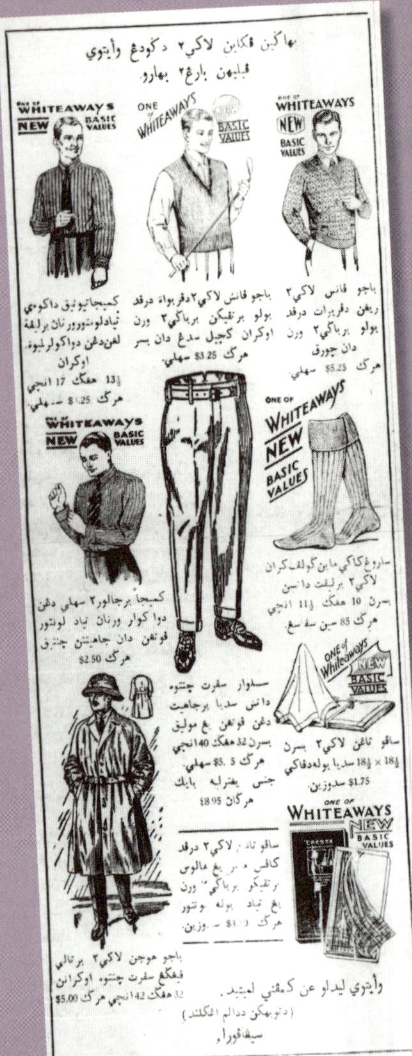

This Whiteaway Laidlaw advertisement in Jawi illustrates the range of men's apparel – from dress shirts to neckties and handkerchiefs – available for purchase. Whiteaway's, which opened in Singapore in 1900, catered primarily to Europeans and wealthy locals. (1933)

Kwong Sang Hong cosmetics, a Hong Kong brand, was a household name in Singapore in the 1930s. (1935)

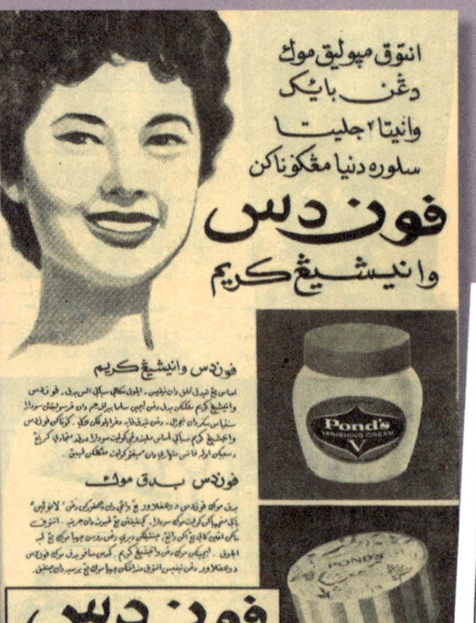

A Pond's advertisement in Jawi providing details on how to beautify the skin. (1961)

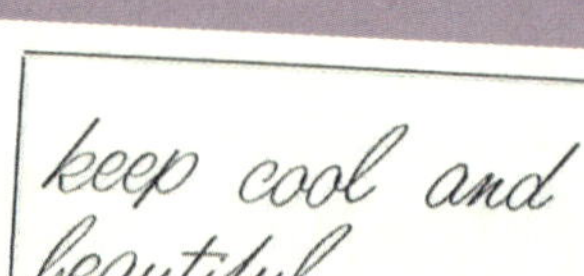

Casual Corner advertised Western-style dresses made from "exotic" Eastern fabrics. (1956)

Antoinette, a fashion boutique located on Orchard Road, sold batik outfits for ladies and men. (1960)

Wristwatches gained popularity among men and women after the Second World War. Brands such as Longines, Rolex and Omega catered to the luxury market, advertising watches as fashion statements and status symbols. (1957)

Balage Porolis de Silva (better known as B.P. de Silva) was a Sinhalese jeweller who set up shop in Singapore in 1872. His royal clientele sealed his reputation as a jeweller of international repute.[30] In 1928 the company was appointed by Omega to be its local distributor of watches. (1936)

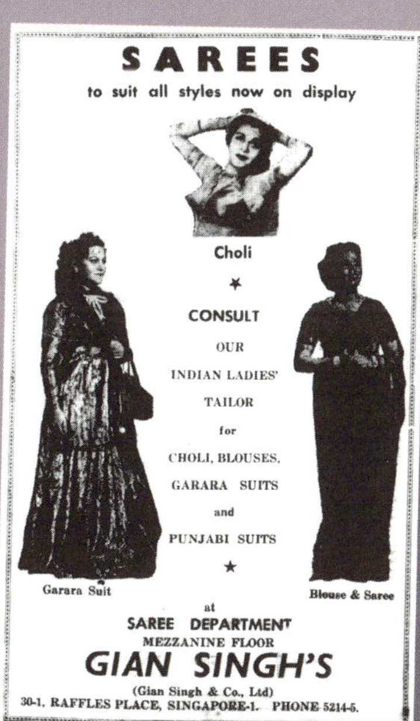

Department store Gian Singh's offered a wide selection of *saree*, blouses, *garara* suits and Punjabi suits. (1952)

This advertisement for Ven-Yusa was one in a long tradition of touting the scientific discoveries behind a product. (1922)

A 1926 ad for Palmolive soap exploiting women's insecurities about losing their youthful bloom ("a wife's greatest asset") with the passing of the years.

Applying Pond's cold cream every morning and night was touted as a regimen that would make a woman more desirable. (1947)

The most significant development in cosmetics in 1938 was the appearance of Max Factor's Pan-Cake, the first water-soluble cake foundation.[31] (1947)

Two minutes of "hormone-enriched" Endocil care every night for three weeks was all it took to make one's skin young again, according to this 1964 ad.

Manufactured in India, Tata's perfumed castor oil for hair and coconut oil shampoo were advertised as essential for healthy tresses. (1963)

A "purifying and beautifying" soap, Cuticura purported to give its users lovely skin and luxuriant hair. (1897)

Anjla Hair Oil, advertised in Tamil, promised to give its users long, gorgeous tresses. (1937)

Figaro was a beauty parlour owned by a European lady specialist. The shop advertised its hair perming services at 10 Straits dollars in a Chinese newspaper in 1933.

Gull Bahar, advertised in Jawi, was a scented oil that would strengthen one's hair – its efficacy supposedly attested by thousands of satisfied users. (1933)

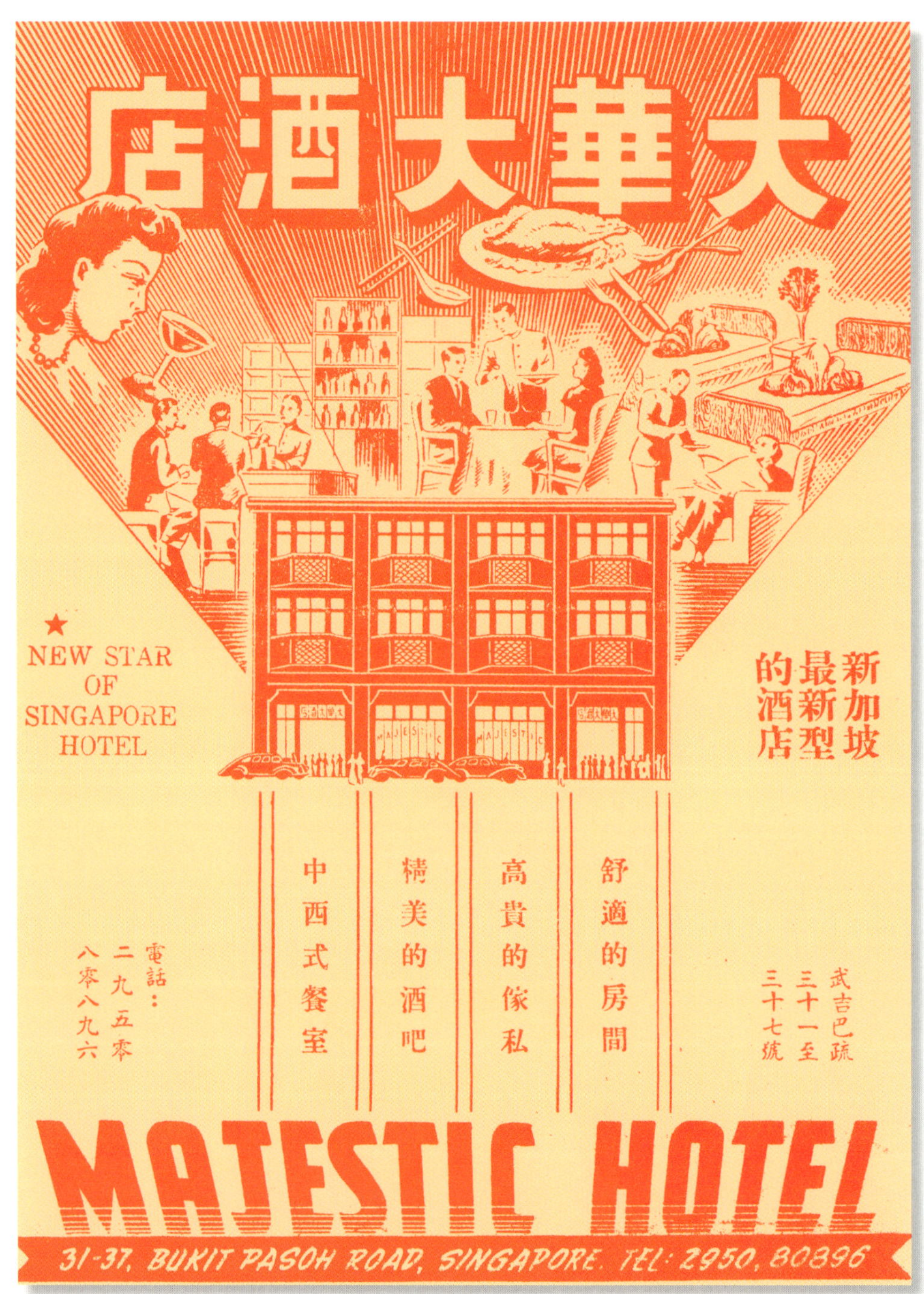

A 1949 advertisement for the newly opened Majestic Hotel on Bukit Pasoh Road in Chinatown highlighting its grand furniture, elegant bar and comfortable rooms.

A WARM WELCOME

The mid-1840s saw the first steamships arriving in Singapore from Europe. These steam liners not only delivered mail and cargo, but also transported passengers. To cater to visitors and an expanding population, hotels and restaurants began sprouting up, first in the town centre and then radiating outwards as transport infrastructure developed. By the 1920s, Singapore's hospitality scene had blossomed and come into its own with a respectable selection of hotels and restaurants, which courted consumers with promises of luxury, comfort, modernity and gastronomical delights.

EARLY PLAYERS

One of the first establishments to offer commercial accommodation in Singapore was a "board and lodging house" by the Singapore River, on High Street,[1] set up in 1831 by boatyard owner Stephen Hallpike. It was a modest establishment "where Families visiting the Settlement will meet with every attention for their comfort" (p. 98).

Eight years later came the first major player in the nascent hotel scene: London Hotel, opened by the enterprising Gaston Dutronquoy, who was also a professional photographer.[2] Besides the requisite "palankeens" (palanquins) or horse carriages for hire, the hotel also provided tiffin (light lunch) on demand, cold and warm baths, billiard tables and grounds for skittles, a British bowling game (p. 98). Despite what its ads would have us believe, the hotel's reputation left much to be desired. Travellers complained about the facilities and the service, as well as the noise from the debauchery that went on till the wee hours in the alley and billiard room.[3]

ADVERTISEMENT.

S. HALLPIKE returns his thanks to the Public for the encouragement he has hitherto met with, and begs to state that he has opened a Board and Lodging House in High Street, where Families visiting the Settlement will meet with every attention for their comfort.

N. B. S. H. continues to execute Ships Blacksmith Work in general, and paints and repairs Carriages of all descriptions on moderate terms.

Carriages lent on hire.

Singapore, 11th May 1831.

Stephen Hallpike's "board and lodging house" was located on a now-expunged section (Hallpike Street) of High Street near the Singapore River. (1831)

ICES! ICES! ICES!

ICES for the sick, ICES for the healthy, and ICES for the hospitable. While the inhabitants of the City of Palaces are bewailing their hard fate that the non-arrival of the American Ships and consequent deprivation of that most delectable accompaniment to a well garnished table, particularly in a tropical climate and in such melting weather as the present, a veritable philanthropist, an old inhabitant of our youthful settlement has stepped forward in the most laudable manner and offers to supply the inhabitants of Singapore with the luxurious delicacy.

MR. DUTRONQUOY, Proprietor of the LONDON HOTEL has the honor of offering to the ladies and gentlemen of Singapore to supply them with a variety of fruit ices for dinner or evening parties, besides a supply of chrystal ice for cooling their different beverages, à l'Italien, at the moderate price of $ 2½ for a party of eight, or for four dollars for a party of sixteen. He warrants that on receiving two or three hours notice to give satisfaction to those who may honor him with their commands.

Singapore April 21st 1851.

☞ Ladies and gentlemen are respectfully requested taken giving an order to state *precisely* the time when the ice is to be placed on the table. The climate makes this precaution indispensable.

In 1851, the enterprising Gaston Dutronquoy of London Hotel sold ices for guests to enjoy in the "melting weather". Ice was then a novelty in Singapore, and gladly welcome in the tropical heat. (1851)

Advertising Sheet

OF THE

SINGAPORE DIRECTORY, 1855.

LONDON HOTEL.

The LONDON HOTEL, kept by G. DUTRONQUOY, is situated on the Esplanade, commanding a splendid view of the harbour of Singapore, and under the immediate patronage of the Peninsular and Oriental Company. PASSENGERS arriving at Singapore who may honor him with their presence will find every comfort and moderate charge, according to the time of their stay.

There is adjoining a separate hotel for Families.

☞ Hot and cold baths at all hours. Four excellent billiard tables, and a good skittle ground.

———ooo———

THE LONDON HOTEL, tenu par G. DUTRONQUOY est situé sur l'ésplanade, commandant une superbe vue du port de Singapore, et se trouve sous le patronage immediate de la Compagnie Peninsular et Orientale.

Les passagers arrivant à Singapore, qui veulent bien lui honorer de leur présence trouveront tout ce qui est comfortable a des prix moderés selon la durée de leur sejour

Il y a à coté un hotel separé pour des familles.

☞ Des bains chauds et froids à toute heure. Quatre billiards excellents, et un très bon jeu de quilles.

———ooo———

El abajo firmado encargado de la funda titulala LONDON HOTEL, que esta situada en la Esplanada, dominando una perspectiva magnifica del puerto de Singapure, y bajo la immediata proteccion de la Compània Peninsular y Oriental ofrece su hermosa Posada a los Passagares que lleguem à Singapore y quieren honrar e su presentia; asegurando con les que hallaran una esmerada assistencia, y gastos muy modicos, segun el tiempo de su detencion.

Contigua a esta funda hay otra separada para familias.

☞ Banos frios y calientes a todas horas. Cuatro escelentes mesas de billar.

G. DUTRONQUOY.

Contrary to the promises made in this London Hotel advertisement, American businessman George Francis Train definitely did not encounter "every comfort" during his stay there in 1855. As he passionately recounted: "[The hotel was] kept in a manner that would disgrace a landlord in the backwood of Kansas, where your food looks uninviting, and is brought to you by Asiatics and Islanders who always seem to me to have their hands upon their half-clad body, when you want a piece of bread, some Malay curry, or a pineapple."[4] (1854)

EASTERN PROMISES

The opening of the Suez Canal in 1869 gave Singapore's hotel sector a much-needed boost. With the duration of the sea passage from England halved to three weeks, more travellers started venturing eastwards. Accommodation options in Singapore saw a concomitant rise, with many more hotels dotting the town centre.

By the turn of the century, wealthy European and American travellers were most likely to call at either the Hotel de l'Europe or Raffles Hotel, both occupying palatial grounds near the Padang. Other principal hotels of the early 20th century included Adelphi Hotel (p. 108), Hotel van Wijk and Hotel de la Paix (p. 108). Serving Westerners almost exclusively, most of these colonial hotels came to be defined by the grandeur of their European architecture. Their advertisements reflected as much: Instead of images of the guestrooms, photographs of the hotels' facades frequently took centre stage, selling the image of colonial power, luxury and comfort.

More often than not, European visitors had a tough time adjusting to Singapore's climate and culture, and most harboured a condescending attitude towards the Asian populace, as was typical of race relations during the colonial era. Responding to the anxieties of the Western traveller in a foreign land, ads for European hotels often sought to reassure their potential clientele that they would find the familiarity of home at their establishments. Frequently touted selling points of the hotels were their European management, chefs, cuisine, language proficiencies, comforts and so on. The colonial hotel was thus presented as a safe space that protected the affluent European traveller from the idiosyncrasies of the local culture.

BEYOND THE GRAND HOTELS

While the grand hotels were the preserve of well-heeled Europeans, there were also options for visitors of humbler means. In 1917, the Young Women's Christian Association hostel on Fort Canning Road was opened, offering a place of respite for female travellers.[5] On Oxley Rise near River Valley Road was The Mansion, advertised as an upscale boarding house. Situated on elevated ground, The Mansion served food that was supposedly comparable to hotels' offerings.

Established in the mid-1850s, the Hotel de l'Europe became the chief competitor to Raffles Hotel in the early 20th century. In this advertisement, readers are confronted with the hotel's gleaming future embodied in an illustrated panorama of the forthcoming building. (1906)

A montage of images in this Raffles Hotel advertisement shows off the imposing building and the luxurious dining hall, together with a long list of aristocrats and high-ranking officials who were among the hotel's distinguished clientele. (1906)

There were also Chinese-run hotels that catered primarily to Chinese visitors. In the 1930s, there were three major players: Great Southern Hotel, Air View Hotel and Empress Hotel.[6] The Great Southern Hotel, particularly, had a clientele consisting mainly of rich and famous Chinese during its heyday in the prewar era.[7]

Besides advertising in the Chinese newspapers, these hotels also ran ads in English-language newspapers. In fact, an English ad for Majestic Hotel on Bukit Pasoh Road boasted of its "European standards" of service, with a bar that was "always stocked with good genuine Scotch" (p. 111) – an overt attempt to dip into the European market.

Small-scale Chinese establishments, such as Thong Yit Lodging House in Tanjong Pagar, also specialised in accommodation for Chinese travellers. In fact, along Tanjong Pagar Road were numerous such lodging houses, many of which also facilitated the purchase of ship tickets to China and provided remittance services.[8]

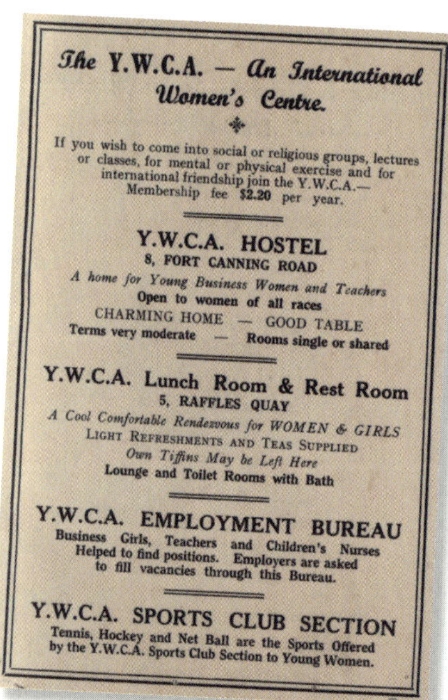

Female travellers could put themselves up at the YWCA hostel on Fort Canning Road, as well as make use of the association's "Lunch Room and Rest Room" at Raffles Quay. (1937)

Built by businessman Eu Tong Sen and opened in 1927,[9] the six-storey Great Southern Hotel was the tallest – and grandest – building in Chinatown then. (1938)

The humble Thong Yit Lodging House occupied a three-storey shophouse in Tanjong Pagar, and offered "concierge" services such as handling the purchase of ship tickets to China and remittances. (1936)

Lion City Hotel opened in Tanjong Katong in 1968. Interestingly, the use of the lion-head motif in the hotel's branding predated the launch of the national symbol in 1986. (1968)

The 7th Storey Hotel opened in 1953 as a five-star luxury hotel. Despite its name, the building had nine floors. Even in 2008, when its demolition was announced, the hotel still maintained its manually operated lift, which had been a quirk of the hotel. (1956)

The 60-room Embassy Hotel on Meyer Road in Katong was opened in 1953 to much fanfare. It was touted as Malaya's biggest hotel in the postwar era. Guests could dance on the roof garden overlooking the sea. (1959)

IN THE AIR

The hotels that survived the Great Depression soon saw the arrival of commercial aviation in the late 1930s. By then, the major names such as Raffles Hotel, Adelphi Hotel and Goodwood Park Hotel (formerly known as Goodwood Hall) were equipped with modern comforts like electricity, electric fans and up-to-date sanitary fittings. Unfortunately, the outbreak of the Second World War put a pause on any potential growth in the industry. After the war, however, there was a surge in tourism due to air travel having become not only faster but also priced less exorbitantly.

The glamour of the historic grand hotels waned had by the 1950s and '60s as new, shiny establishments were built fast and tall to meet the demand of the tourist boom. At least three hotels were unveiled in 1953 alone, including Embassy Hotel, 7th Storey Hotel and South East Asia Hotel.[10] The following year, Cathay Hotel was opened. Air-conditioning was now de rigueur for these establishments – an attractive, modern feature in the tropics that many ads did not fail to mention.

Pastoral Care

The first railway in Singapore was completed in 1903, connecting Tank Road in town to Woodlands, stopping by Bukit Timah. By the 1920s, the engines of urbanisation were revving up and the motorcar had become so prevalent that traffic congestion was a common sight in the city centre. With greater accessibility, more hoteliers began eyeing the affordable, verdant land lying beyond the town centre.

Advertisements for countryside hotels played up the distinction between the urban centre and the rural parts, which had become increasingly apparent due to rapid urbanisation. They commonly invoked the fresh air, sea breeze and accompanying health benefits at these out-of-town locations – in contrast to the congested, dusty and unsanitary town associated with tropical maladies.

Some of these countryside establishments advertised themselves as sanatoriums, while others preferred to be known as "health resorts". A belief common among

The seaside Tanjong Katong Hotel "with all the comforts of a home" was compared with the perceived ills of city living – "dust, noises, and evil odours". Emphasis on the rural-urban dichotomy was common in the ads of country hotels. (1891)

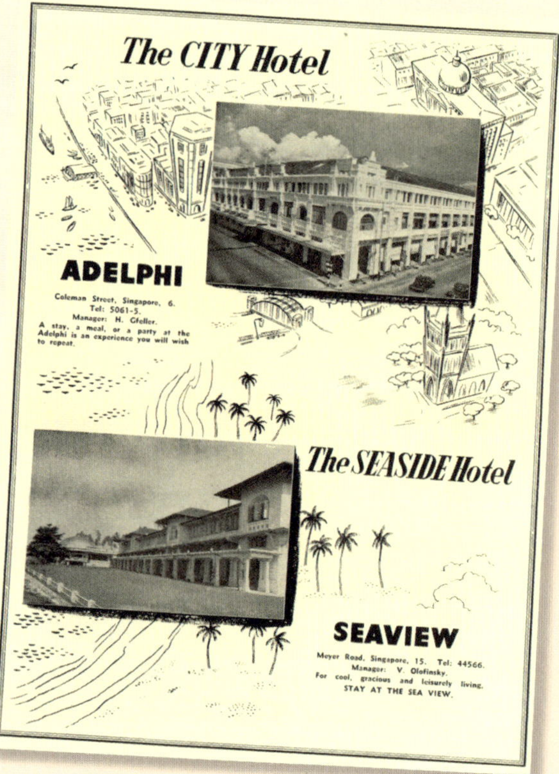

Once under the same management as Adelphi Hotel, Sea View Hotel offered travellers an appealing alternative to being in the city. (1955)

Opened in the early 1900s, Grove Hotel in Tanjong Katong was marketed as a sanatorium where one could enjoy "pure air" at the "coolest spot on the island". (1905)

One could take the tramcar from town to Royal Hotel, `which was touted as the "best sanatorium in Singapore". (1910)

Europeans in the 19th and 20th centuries was "tropical neurasthenia" – fatigue and general ill health that Europeans supposedly suffered as a result of the tropical climate.[11] Hence a major selling point of countryside establishments was the cooler air there.

One of the first seaside hotels in Singapore was Tanjong Katong Hotel, originally built in 1884.[12] However, the most famous of the pastoral destinations was perhaps Sea View Hotel, which was hugely popular in the 1920s and '30s. Marketed as a relaxed, cool alternative to hotels in the city, the Sea View was known for its excellent sea swimming and romantic dinners under the stars.[13]

For the complete getaway experience, during the early 20th century one could also hop onto a boat from Johnston's Pier in Collyer Quay to get to Katong beach.[14] However, the start of the East Coast land reclamation programme in the 1960s spelt the end of Katong's run as Singapore's beloved seaside destination.

Besides Katong, country hotels were also located in areas such as Paya Lebar and Seletar. Visitors could take the electric tram[15] to reach some of these destinations. At times, the tram journey itself was promoted as part of the experience. For instance, the ride to Royal Hotel in Paya Lebar apparently offered "picturesque and interesting views of town and country".

ACQUIRED TASTE

Hotels have always been closely linked with restaurants. European hotels of colonial Singapore were key sites for the conspicuous consumption of food, as social events like balls, charity galas and the celebration of European festivities were regularly hosted in the ballrooms or dining halls.[16] Naturally, hotels' advertisements gave prominence to their food and restaurants.

During the 1920s, a trend swept through the European hotels: the addition of a grill room, where grilled meats were served.[17] Raffles Hotel, referring to the existence of a grill room as a "pressing need", opened its Grill Room (known today as Raffles Grill) in April 1923,[18] while the Europe Hotel unveiled its own within a year.[19] Even Chinese-owned hotels such as Great Southern Hotel, endeavouring to keep up with the Joneses, soon followed suit.

The quality of the food at the Adelphi's grill room was compared to that of "the best London West-End hotels". (1935)

This English ad for the Chinese-owned Southern Hotel (also known as Great Southern Hotel) features the necessary catchphrases and amenities – "up-to-date", "modern sanitary installation", "grill room" – to appeal to consumers aspiring to a modern lifestyle. (1927)

A 1923 ad for the Europe Hotel (one of many names of the Hotel de l'Europe throughout its history) describing the hotel's cuisine as "irreproachable".

A CARD. —

CAFE RESTAURANT DE PARIS,
South Bridge Road, No. 133.
OPENED 1ST JUNE, 1885.
Supplies :—
Breakfast, Tiffin and Dinners, on the short-
est notice, Cold drinks, Ice Cream from 1 P. M.
to 12 P. M. Good accommodation. Terms Mo-
derate—English and Continental Languages
spoken.
MADAME B. SCHWARTZ,
Proprietrix.
Singapore, 9th June, 1885. 9/7

One of the earliest cafe ads was for the Cafe Restaurant de Paris. It served ice-cream – but only between 1pm and 2pm, at the peak of the afternoon. (1885)

THE POLAR CAFE
51, HIGH STREET,
Don't forget Polar Cafe for
ice cream and refreshing drinks
while shopping.

Strategically situated at the old shopping haven of High Street, Polar Cafe tended to target shoppers in its ads. In the 1950s, because of its proximity to the Supreme Court and Parliament House, the cafe also attracted a clientele comprising lawyers, government officials and politicians. (1936)

If hunger begins to assert itself while you are out shopping

Glide along to

CAFÉ DE LUXE

Here you may have anything from a dish of ice cream or the daintiest of dainty little tiffins to the good substantial meal.

Every article of food is served in the most appetising-ly manner possible.

In this clean, bright, cheerful room you may sit and eat the good things set before you with a zest, born of the tempting dishes, and with a satisfaction found only in

CAFÉ DE LUXE
Under European Management
Open till 2.00 A. M.

CAFÉ DE LUXE

25, HIGH STREET.

PHONE - - - - - 6011.

The patrons of cafes in the 1920s and '30s were mostly colonial expatriates – Café de Luxe was no exception. This ad invites tired, hungry shoppers to drop in for ice-cream, "the daintiest of dainty little tiffins" or a full meal. (1936)

CAFE SOCIETY

Ads for cafes began appearing in the 1880s. One of the earliest was for the Cafe Restaurant de Paris on South Bridge Road, which was opened in 1885. It was both a cafe and a restaurant, serving not only cold drinks and ice-cream, but also breakfast, tiffin (light lunch) and dinner. However, there were not many cafes after that, judging from the dearth of cafe ads, until the 1920s, when ice-cream was popularised.

By the '20s there were several cafes along High Street, the premier shopping district of the day. Two of these – Café de Luxe and Polar Cafe – strategically targeted weary shoppers, offering them refuge from the sweltering heat as well as cool treats in the form of ice-cream and iced beverages. Another popular location for cafes was the commercial district of Raffles Place, with its high density of white-collar workers. A landmark in the area, on Battery Road, was G.H. Cafe (p. 116).

After the war, "milk bars" sprouted up to meet the continued demand for all manner of dairy confections such as ice-cream, flavoured milk and milkshakes.[20] They soon became favoured haunts for social gatherings and young couples. Later, as their menus expanded, some of the milk bars became known as snack bars. Serving affordable Western set meals and desserts, the Magnolia Snack Bar at the Capitol Theatre, in particular, held many sweet memories for those who grew up in the 1950s and '60s, being a trendy destination for dates.[21]

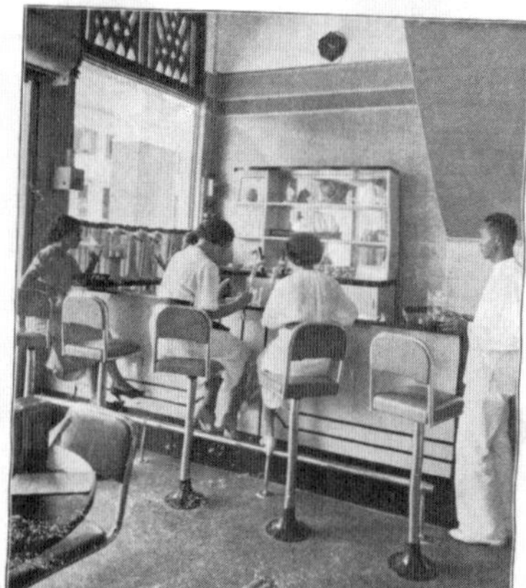

Cold Storage Creameries was a major manufacturer of dairy products. A subsidiary of Cold Storage, it operated several milk bars, and was largely responsible for popularising ice-cream in Singapore. (1939)

With several branches across the island, Magnolia Snack Bars were a favourite of those who grew up in the 1950s and '60s. (1966)

Hopping onto the milk bar bandwagon in 1960 was Tong Lee Milk Bar & Confectionery. It opened on Orchard Road, which would become the hot spot for hospitality and retail in the next decade. (1960)

EATING OUT

While the who's-who of European society continued dining at fancy restaurants and grill rooms in hotels, in the 1930s up to the '50s social events among the well-to-do Chinese – such as association and society gatherings, as well as farewell, birthday and wedding dinners – were commonly held in Chinese restaurants. Some of the most popular venues were Tai Tong Restaurant[22] (大东酒楼), a Cantonese dim sum establishment on Mosque Street with a branch in New World; Nam Tong, located next to Tai Tong on Mosque Street;[23] and another restaurant also called Tai Tong Restaurant in English, but whose Chinese name was 大同酒家, housed within Happy World (p. 114).[24] However, these restaurants were not advertised as much as "Western" restaurants, such as that in the Singapore Airport Hotel at Kallang Airport. One reason could be that they were already attracting a sizeable crowd as a result of their location and reputation and hence had little need for advertisements.

Other Asian restaurants that were sometimes advertised included Jubilee Cafe & Restaurant (p. 115), Islamic Restaurant (p. 114) and Ananda Bhavan, the latter two established in the 1920s and now considered institutions in the local food scene.

Fiona Lim

The restaurant in Singapore Airport Hotel, at Kallang Airport, was famous for its oysters and strawberries – "luxuries that can be enjoyed by everyone at our price". However, this was surely an exaggeration, considering the wide income gap when this ad appeared in 1939.

The original Selegie Road outlet of Ananda Bhavan, established in 1924, is still around today, continuing to serve up its Indian vegetarian cuisine. (1956)

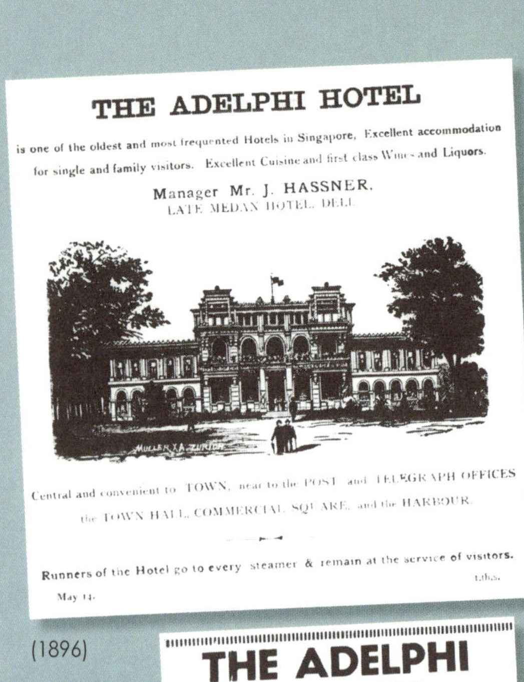

(1896)

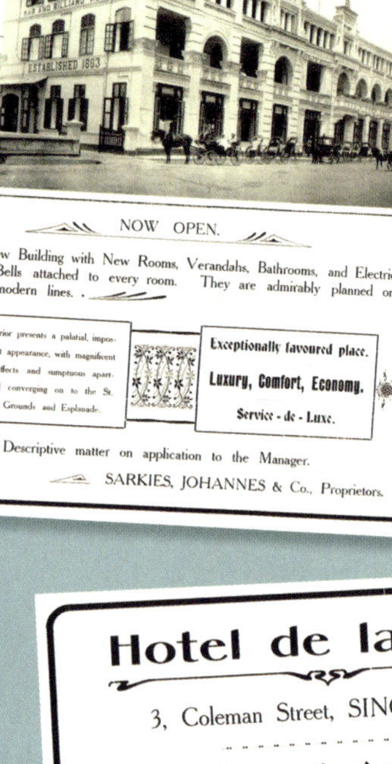

(1906)

(1958)

Opened by 1850,[25] Adelphi Hotel underwent a facelift in the early 1900s and transformed into a 100-room behemoth on Coleman Street. Its stately architecture was frequently showcased in its advertisements. The Adelphi was the longest-running hotel in Singapore when it closed in 1973.

Hotel de la Paix, a more understated establishment compared to the neighbouring Hotel de l'Europe, targeted European families. (1906)

Originally the premises of the Teutonia Club, which served Singapore's German community, the Goodwood building was converted into a hotel after the First World War. (1936)

Perhaps the most famous hotel in Singapore before the Second World War, Raffles Hotel attracted droves of wealthy tourists. The world-class establishment was particularly known for its grand ballroom parties and fine dining. (1938)

From 1950s onwards, many Raffles Hotel advertisements began to feature this quote by writer Somerset Maugham: "[Raffles Hotel] stands for all the fables of the exotic East". Tourists were invited to partake in this orientalist fantasy created by Raffles Hotel. (1959)

(1911)

Boarding houses like The Mansion, Hilltop Guest House and Sunnyside provided decent accommodation to visitors who were staying for extended periods.

(1940)

(1936)

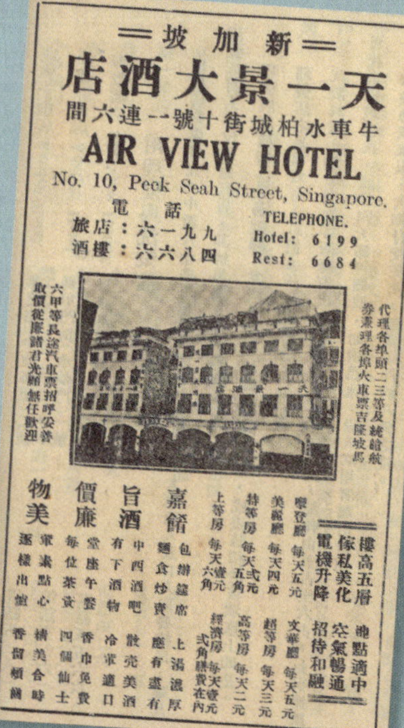

(1936)

(1989)

The daily rates at the Chinese-run Air View Hotel in 1936 ranged from $1.20 to $5. The building that once housed the hotel is still around today at No. 10 Peck Seah Street in Tanjong Pagar.

The Majestic Hotel advertisement:

Do you know?

- That we serve the best Chinese Dishes
- That Chinese Dishes can be served to a party of any size
- That our charges are very reasonable
- That our Service is on European Standard
- That our bed rooms are fitted with baths attached, air-conditioning and rediffusion
- That our Bar is always stocked with good genuine Scotch
- That you have nothing to worry about Food, Drinks and Comfort at the

MAJESTIC HOTEL
RESERVATIONS
PHONE 2950 OR CALL AT
31—37 BUKIT PASOH ROAD

By advertising that its service was of European standard and its bar "always stocked with good genuine Scotch", Majestic Hotel attempted to reach out to European customers, beyond its primarily Chinese clientele. (1949)

Located on Victoria Street, the five-storey Empress Hotel was a landmark in the area. Its rates when it opened in 1934 ranged from $1.50 to $4.50 per night. Contemporary song-and-dance numbers were performed by various artistes at the hotel's restaurant, with a different programme daily. Cabarets were also held on the rooftop. (1934)

While the Europeans hotels pandered to the colonial expatriates, the Great Southern attracted the glamorous Chinese set. (1949)

Kam Leng Hotel on Jalan Besar served Hainanese patrons in particular. In addition to the basic hospitality services, the hotel also facilitated the purchase of ship tickets to Hainan in southern China. The building still stands today and has been converted into a boutique hotel with the same name. (1947)

A ROYAL DIALOGUE.

Holloa! Friend! how are you?

Oh! I feel a bit out of sorts!

Why! What's up?

The idea of having to dine in town on the New Year's Eve.

Why! where else can we go to?

Oh! let us take a run up to the Royal Hotel, Paya Lebar Tram Terminus, where we shall have a excellent Dinner with the best of Wine and Music.

Oh! that's all very nice and inviting but how can we amuse ourselves after Dinner.

By Jove, the New Hall of the Hotel will be opened on that night with a Rollicking Dance to last till 12·30 p.m.

How are we to reach our homes at such a late hour!

Why the able and considerate management of the Tramway Co., has provided a car to leave the Royal Hotel at 1 a.m.

Oh! well if that be the case let us have it out and get some others to join us.

Bye-bye for the present till we meet at the Royal Hotel, Payah Lebar.

A 1908 advertisement pitching Royal Hotel as a convenient refuge from the chaotic town centre during New Year's Eve as it was near the tramcar terminus, even though it was located in then-rural Paya Lebar.

(1949)

(1939)

(1936)

(1939)

Besides the major countryside hotels, there were also smaller coastal outfits such as Seletar Grange, Beach House at Marine Parade, Katong Rest House and Ocean View Sukiyaki House Hotel and Bar. A common feature of seaside hotels was the "bathing *pagar*" (*pagar* is Malay for "fence"), a rudimentary swimming pool formed by erecting an enclosure in the sea.

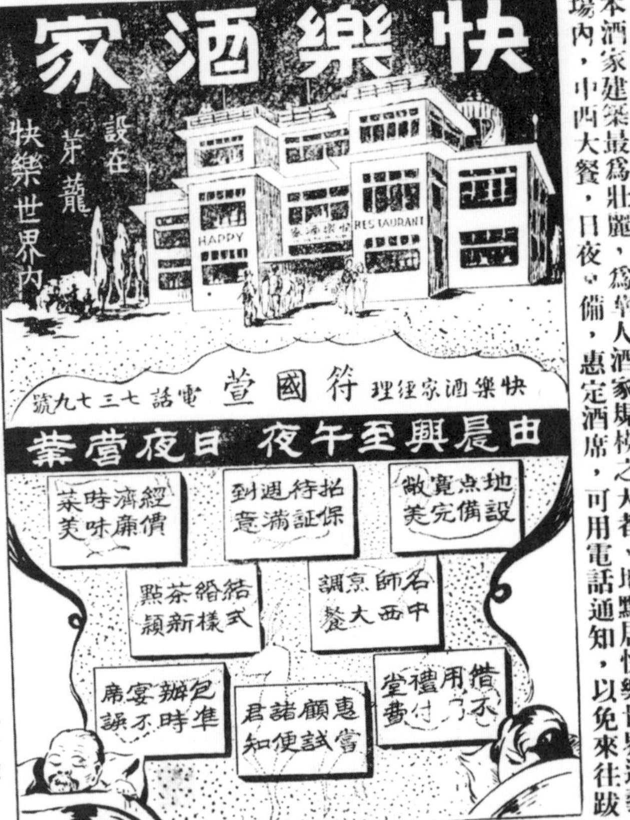

Happy Restaurant in Happy World had a rooftop garden with a sea view. The restaurant served both Western and Chinese cuisine. (1938)

Serving up Cantonese food, Tai Tong Restaurant (大同酒家) in Happy World was a popular venue for large gatherings and weddings. (1950)

Tel: Address 'MATHUSHA'
Phone 85163
For Best Islamic Food
call at

ISLAMIC RESTAURANT

Established 1921
795/797, North Bridge Rd.
— SINGAPORE —

The Founder and owner
M. ABDUL RAHIMAN

●

Supplier of Excellent Food

(Such as Nasi Beriyani and all kinds of Indian curries) for Parties in the Restaurant and also outside catering undertaken at very Moderate charges.

Opened in 1921, Islamic Restaurant is still in operation on North Bridge Road and is known as a premier restaurant for Malay food. (1951)

Jubilee Cafe & Restaurant offered Indian Muslim fare such as *roti maryam* and *roti prata*. According to this ad, a second branch, patronised by "Singapore cosmopolitans", had just opened in Raffles Place. (1967)

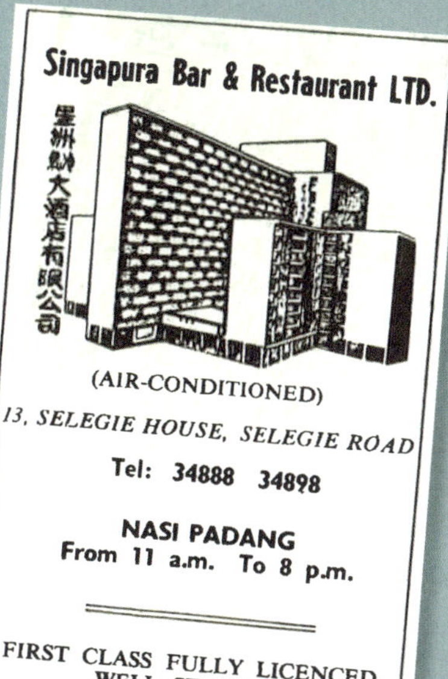

"Specialists in Chinese and European dishes", Singapura Bar & Restaurant served *nasi padang* (rice with Malay dishes) the whole day, according to this ad. It is possible that *nasi padang* here refers more generally to just rice with dishes instead, despite using a Malay term to describe it. (1964)

Still running today, Hung Kang Restaurant serves up authentic Teochew food. Restaurants like this were very popular among the Chinese for social events like birthdays and weddings. (1964)

This 1938 advertisement by Café de Luxe shows off its modern Western interior. The ad also beckons cinema-goers – possibly patrons of the nearby Capitol theatre – to enjoy a meal at the establishment after watching a film.

(1938)

(1939)

Located on Battery Road in the heart of the business district, G.H. Cafe was where many office workers gathered and dined. These two ads speak directly to this customer base – promising them a restful environment where they could take a break from their stressful jobs, and creating the narrative that successful businessmen mingled at the establishment regularly.

Little's Café was part of the John Little & Co. department store in Raffles Place. It was a popular gathering spot for European women in the 1930s.[26]
(1947)

(1959)   Mont d'Or milk bar on Orchard Road served up a diverse selection of local delights such as fish curry, *lontong* and Hokkien mee, in addition to the customary ice-cream.   (1959)

During the colonial era, tiffin was commonly found on restaurant menus. A quintessentially colonial cultural import from British India, tiffin referred to a light lunch typically consisting of curry and rice with other dishes. (1937)

Capitol Milk Bar, housed in the Capitol Building, was a favourite haunt of the young and trendy set. (1958)

A 1952 ad depicting the warm, cosy home atmosphere that Osram lamps promised to create.

THE MODERN MALAYAN HOME

Modern utilities and amenities revolutionised home life across the world in the early 20th century, and Singapore was no exception. What it really boiled down to was the introduction of gas, electricity and running water to households, but in its wake, a vast array of appliances that made use of these innovations soon appeared on the market, radically changing the way people cooked, cleaned and entertained themselves at home.

Singapore's march to modernity from the 19th century onwards was not without its complications. This was primarily due to the vastly differing living situations of the population. Most European expatriates lived in the city centre and its environs, in "modern" homes made of brick, and were generally the first to receive new amenities such as sanitation and electricity. The majority of the Asian population, on the other hand, were either living in the *kampong* (villages) on the outskirts of town and beyond, or else crammed into tenement shophouses, well into the 1960s; the physical construction of their houses did not facilitate the introduction of modern amenities.

A major factor in the modernisation of the home was the introduction of sewerage and running water. Prior to 1910, Singapore's waste disposal system consisted of outhouses and night-soil collection, where residents would pay for collectors to carry off their human waste. Islandwide sanitation was a massive infrastructural project, and it was not until 1987 that the night-soil system was finally phased out.[1]

Running water was another issue that took many decades to resolve. While well-to-do

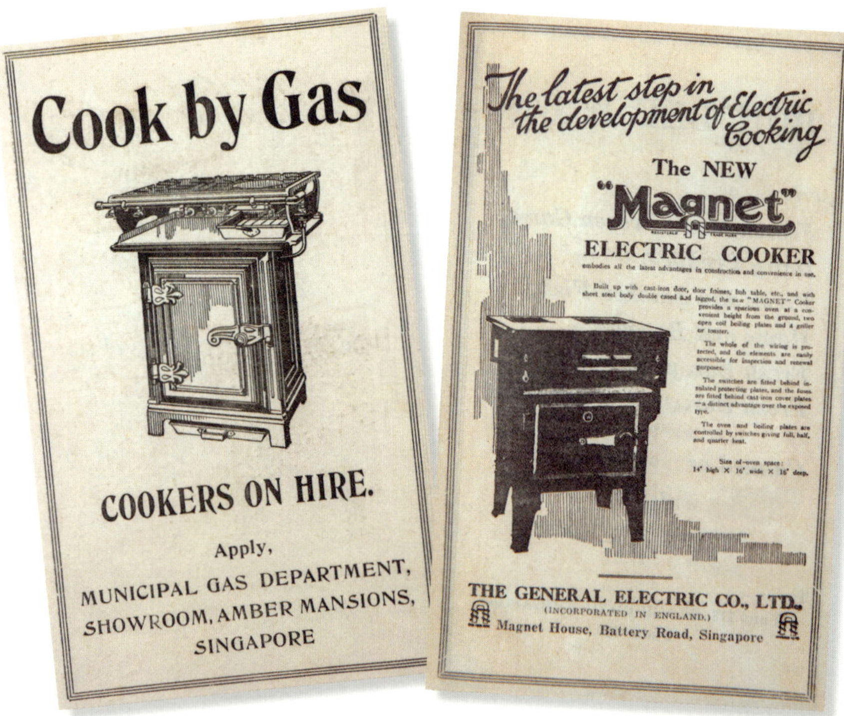

These two ads – for gas and electric cookers – appeared in *The Next Meal Cookery Book* by Mrs W.E. Kinsey, who was known for writing recipes for the colonial population in Malaya. The use of gas and electric cooking and heating in the home developed in parallel with each other, with advertisers competing (sometimes in the same publication) to sell their fuel over the other. (1927)

households in the town centre had access to piped water by the mid-1800s, some villages were still drawing water from communal pumps and wells as late as the 1950s.[2]

Thus home appliances like electric washing machines were targeted at those who had access to running water and electricity. Until the '50s and '60s, when more residents were relocated into public housing that could support a full host of utilities, only a small number of dealerships importing modern home appliances existed.

The Municipal Gas Department promoting gas-powered water heaters as the future of bathing. (1938)

GAS AND ELECTRICITY

Before the advent of gas and electricity in Singapore, municipal and household power – for uses such as street lighting and cooking – came from the burning of oil, coal and wood. In 1862, the Singapore Gas Company opened Kallang Gasworks, the first plant dedicated to manufacturing gas for street lighting.[3] In 1901, gas production was taken over by the Municipal Commissioners and expanded for home use.[4]

Electricity followed swiftly after: In 1906, Raffles Place, North Bridge Road and Boat Quay became the first streets to be lit by electric lighting.[5] Electrical supply was made

A 1940 ad by Hoe Boon Leong showcasing both their bathroom fittings and electrical appliances such as the PYE radio.

available for private use soon after, albeit only to households that could support and afford the installation of wiring systems.

As a result, home gas and electricity became commonly advertised in newspapers, books, and magazines, with the messaging revolving around their economic benefits, reliability, safety and convenience. Advertisers such as the municipal gas and electricity departments took pains to assure customers that the energy saved in the long run would be worth the relatively large start-up cost of installing gas pipes and electrical wiring in their homes.

MODERN CONVENIENCES: HOME GADGETRY AND APPLIANCES

The introduction of electricity in the home created a consumer market for household goods and entertainment, resulting in a flood of new inventions from the United States, Europe and, later, Japan. Besides home staples like electric lights, appliances such as refrigerators, blenders, electric irons, ceiling fans and vacuum cleaners also started to become heavily advertised in the early 20th century.

In general, advertising for household goods in Malaya was undertaken by the local dealerships and department stores that imported them. However, major brands such as the General Electric Company, Morphy-Richards and National also placed advertisements for their own products, as they had the capital to run extensive advertising campaigns to promote their goods in what had become a fairly competitive market for household products.

Initially, only the more affluent had the means to purchase modern household appliances. For example, an electric iron advertised in *The Straits*

Times in 1947 cost $11.50 Straits dollars,[6] which was the equivalent of almost two months of a factory worker's wages at the time.[7] By the 1950s and '60s, however, such appliances had become much more affordable to middle-class households.

Home goods were often marketed as essential to the "modern home". The "ideal household" was a concept that had existed long before home gadgets, but, thanks to early-20th-century advertising, it soon came to mean a home fully equipped with modern conveniences such as a washing machine, gas stove, refrigerator, electric lighting, fans and even air-conditioners. Smaller appliances like electric irons and hair dryers were marketed as practical gifts to buy for friends and relatives that would make their lives a little easier.

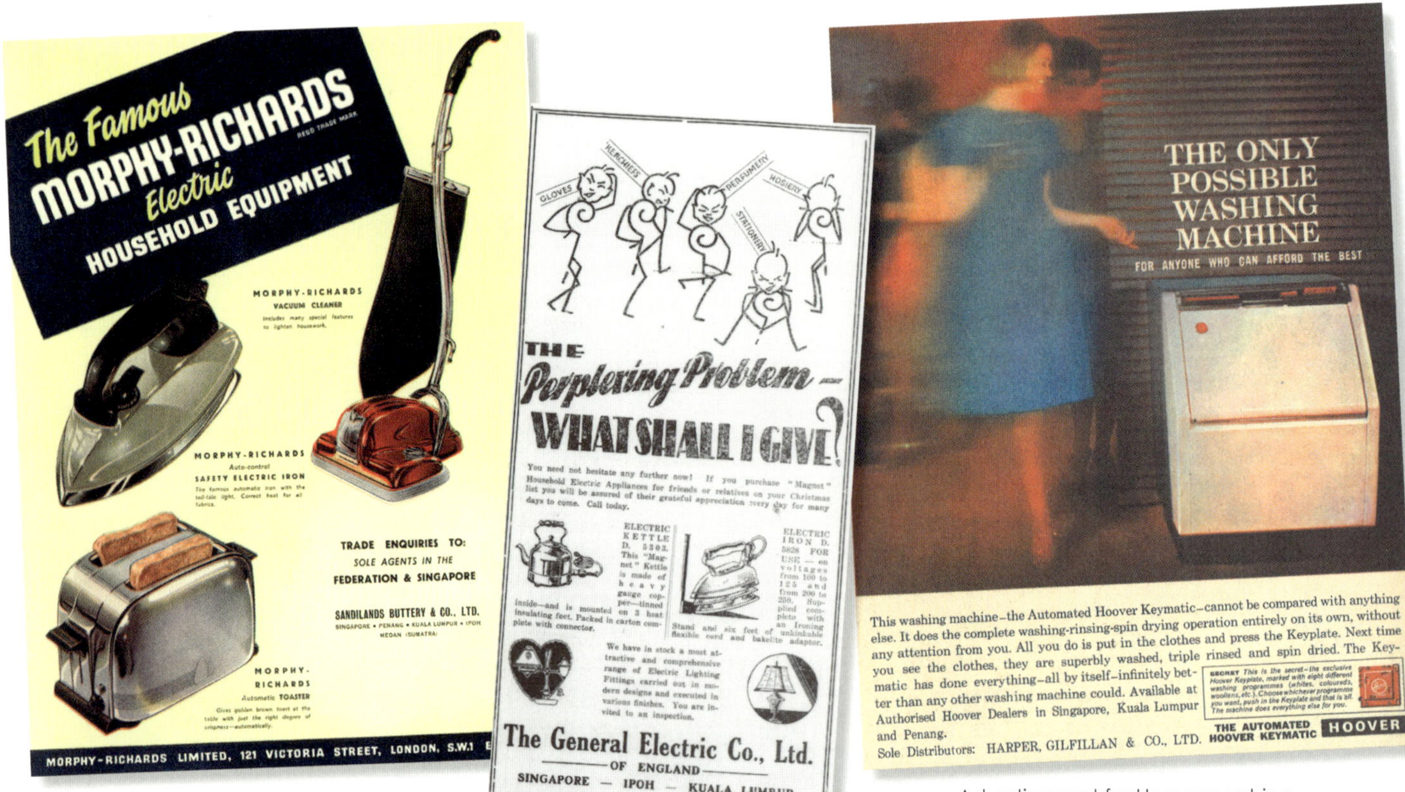

Electric home appliances were still considered luxury items in the 1950s, when much of Singapore was not yet urbanised. (1952)

Appliances like electric kettles and irons were positioned as ideal holiday gifts for loved ones. (1931)

Advertisement for Hoover washing machines boasting maximum convenience with its automatic wash-and-dry cycle "for anyone who can afford the best". (1964)

BEYOND NECESSITY, BEYOND CONVENIENCE: HOME ENTERTAINMENT

One of the most exciting introductions to the early- to mid-20th-century household was home entertainment in the form of radio, television and the gramophone. These innovations grew to become household staples in Singapore, creating an entirely new way for families to spend their time. One could enjoy vinyl recordings of popular and classical music; radio and television shows and dramas; daily news from around the world; as well as sports and racing commentaries and broadcasts – all from the comfort of one's home. Radio and television would eventually grow to dominate media and communication around the world, with advertisers learning quickly to use these new media to sell goods and services.

On the Radio

Radio broadcasting in Singapore began as a niche interest in Singapore in 1924, with the Amateur Wireless Society of Malaysia (AWSM) effectively the preserve of the wealthy wireless enthusiast.[8] This was soon followed by establishment of Radio ZHI by

Grundig marketing its record players as essential components of the stylish modern home. (1961)

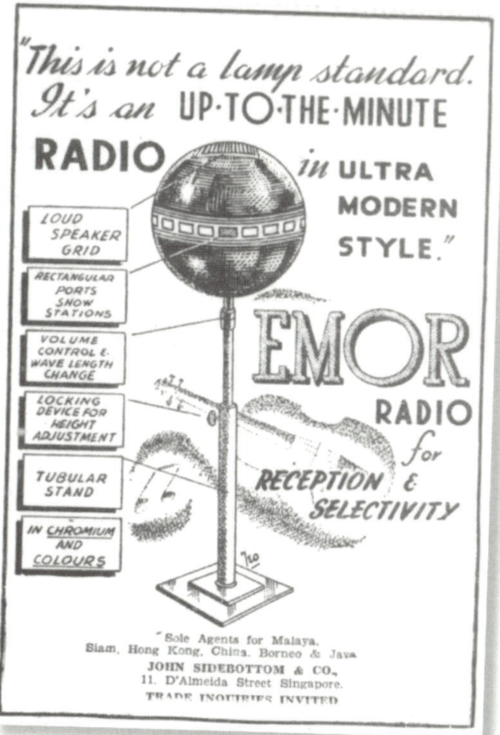

A 1947 ad for an "up-to-the-minute" Emor radio – designed in ultramodern style, and capable of bringing listeners the latest updates from around the world.

Rediffusion presenter Tan Swee Leong capturing American actor Marlon Brando on tape during his visit to the studio at Clemenceau Avenue. (c. 1960s)

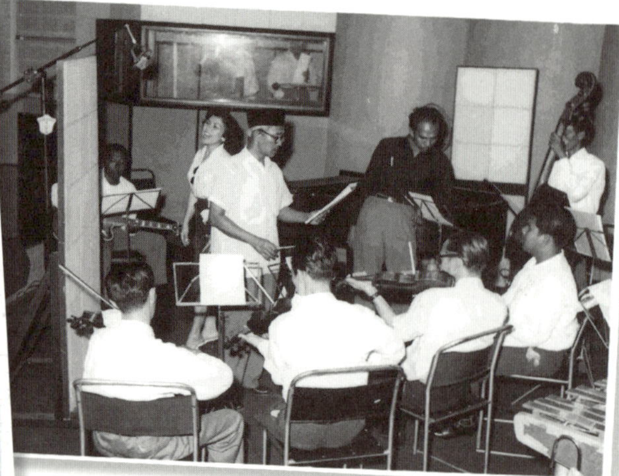

A live musical broadcast from the Rediffusion Auditorium. (1960)

the Radio Service Company of Malaya in 1933, and the British Malayan Broadcasting Corporation in 1935.[9] By the 1930s, radios in Singapore could receive shortwave broadcasts from around the world, such as the Empire Service of the British Broadcasting Corporation (now the BBC World Service).[10]

However, local demand for radios was slow on the uptake: In 1929, the Federated Malay States government received applications for 119 radio licences, in contrast to the 1,000 issued in Hong Kong the same year.[11] This was largely due to public opinion on the reliability of radio reception and the longevity of radio mechanisms in the tropics. It was commonly thought that radio parts would rust and warp in the humid Malayan weather, and that the lack of radio engineers or technicians in the region meant that there might be no real hope of repair.[12] As a result, advertisers

This 1940 General Electric ad emphasises its radios' suitability for the tropics through its depiction of a "Malayan" scene. The illustration was executed by Singapore's Warin Advertising Studios in their signature painterly style.

throughout the early 20th century went out of their way to assure customers that their radio models had been made specially to withstand the tropical climate.

Unsurprisingly, the growth of the industry was driven mainly by the providers of radio services and products, who stoked demand via advertising.[13] The founders of the early broadcasting groups such as AWSM were representatives of companies with vested interest in developing a radio audience, such as General Electric and Marconi's Wireless Telegraph Company.

As demand increased and prices became more affordable, dealers began importing the latest models of radios from various brands. To distinguish themselves from the competition, advertisers would boast of the reliability and reception quality of their products, and assure buyers that they were purchasing the best and latest technology available.

Turn on the Telly

The first television broadcast in Singapore, by Television Singapura, aired in 1963 and ran for five hours. It featured the national anthem, an address by then Minister for Culture S. Rajaratnam, followed by a documentary on Singapore, cartoons, a newsreel, some comedic programmes and a variety show. Singapore households embraced television readily – the first broadcast was watched at home by 2,400 families, as well as by members of the public at Victoria Concert Hall and 52 community viewing centres around the island.[14]

Some of the earliest programmes aired in Singapore were *Huckleberry Hound*, *Adventures of Charlie Chan* and local variety shows like *Rampaian Malaysia*, which featured music from the various local ethnic groups.[15]

Advertisements for television sets not only emphasised their high-quality picture and reception, but also promoted the idea that with their "luxury styling" and "cabinet construction", these new entertainment devices would make attractive furnishings for one's living room.

As television sets grew to become a standard part of living-room furniture, advertisers made it a point to highlight the quality of their cabinet fixtures. (1964)

Georgina Wong

Who Runs the Household?

Throughout the early 20th century, many advertisers of household- and domestic-related goods grew to consider women as their main audience.[16] An overwhelming number of advertisements featured women as the main consumers and users of home technology, with products targeted at men being extremely rare. The prevalence of such depictions – unprecedented before the advent of pictorial advertising[17] – both reflected and influenced public perception of women's role in society:[18] as belonging in the domestic sphere, and responsible for caregiving and household management.

Ads published in Singapore during this time portrayed women – of various ethnicities and economic backgrounds – posing with household goods, either looking glamorous alongside high-end refrigerators, or else engaged in cooking, sewing or doing laundry. A rare household ad targeted at men promoted Singer sewing machines as good gifts for their wives.

By the 1950s and '60s, women in Singapore were entering the work force in fairly large numbers, but they were generally still expected to undertake housekeeping

Lux laundry detergent advertised as being safe for washing more delicate clothing like silks and woollens as it did not damage them. (1933)

This Singer advertisement was the rare ad addressed to a male audience – encouraging them to buy a Singer sewing machine for their wives. The name of this particular model, "Jade Lady", was derived from the Chinese term "玉女", referring to a beautiful woman. (1969)

This 1967 ad portrays a woman as the "best" mother because she chose Shellane's gas cylinders, which made cooking more efficient and thus gave her more time to spend with her children.

A portrait of the "glamorous housewife". Many household advertisements featured women looking put together and fashionable, even whilst in the midst of their chores. (1956)

Women were often depicted in ads going about their housework with a smile on their faces – presumably thankful for the appliances that allowed them to get more work done for less time and money. (1962)

and child-rearing as their primary role. This doubling of duties, among other underlying reasons, relegated many women to shift work and other relatively lower-paying jobs such as factory or secretarial work so that they would have the time to take care of the home after work hours.[19]

With this in mind, the main bulk of household appliance advertising focused on making women's lives as domestic labourers easier. Advertisements stressed how the cost of purchasing their products would be more than justified by the reduced time and effort spent doing housework, rewarding the busy woman with a more carefree, simpler life.

More fundamentally, advertisers tried to mould attitudes to suit household consumerism, for instance, by imbuing housework with a certain idealism and romanticism. Ads sometimes implied that the work performed by a woman around the house was not done out of necessity, but as a labour of love; that the care she put into it was an indicator of her love for her husband and children. Purchasing household appliances that allowed housework to be done better and more efficiently was therefore an investment of care in the family, a symbol of a woman's dedication to her primary role as wife and mother.[20]

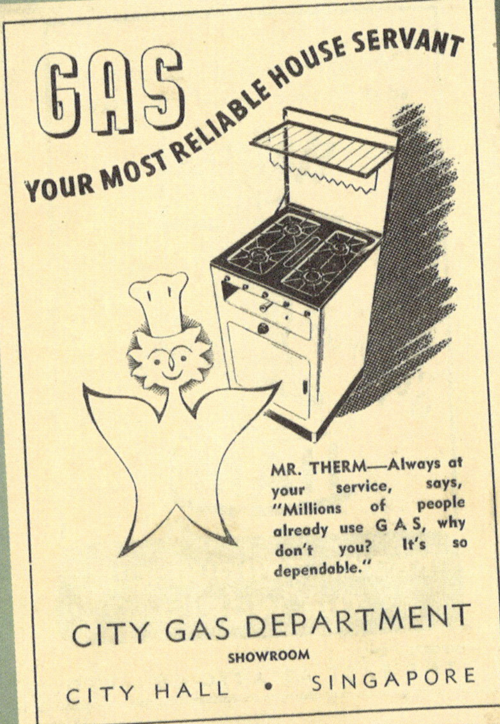

When advertising energy sources, companies often tried to boost their credibility by claiming that their formulas were based on rigorous scientific research – such as in this ad for Mobil Blue Kerosene. This ad also claims that its kerosene burned with more intensity than other brands. (1956)

By the 1920s, some households in Singapore had begun to use gas as a primary fuel source for cooking and for heating water. However, switching to gas required the purchase of new kitchen equipment, so many continued to rely on coal, oil and wood. Advertisements for gas, such as this one by the City Gas Department, were placed in recipe books, among other publications, to specifically target homemakers. (1953)

Shellane gas (now Solane) was a brand of liquid petroleum gas formerly owned by Shell. The company made its name selling home gas to middle-income households and this ad personifies its brand messaging of modernity and economy. (1965)

Many electricity suppliers emphasised the cost-effectiveness of electric lighting in their advertisements. (1907)

Businesses selling electrical products often also offered services to install home electricity. (1926)

This Osram advertisement must have seemed like a futuristic fantasy in the 1940s when it was published. Fluorescent lighting is now a staple in homes and offices around the world. (1941)

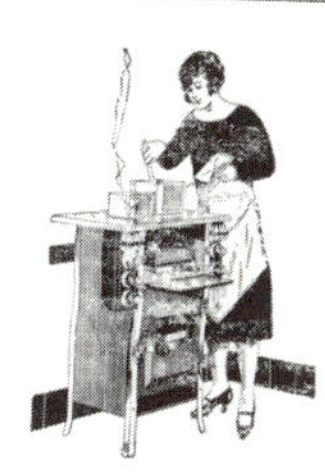

This 1939 ad by the Municipal Electricity Department espouses the benefits of cooking with electricity, including the ability to make every cook a "good cook". Its claims that electric cookers created no dirt may have been a slight exaggeration.

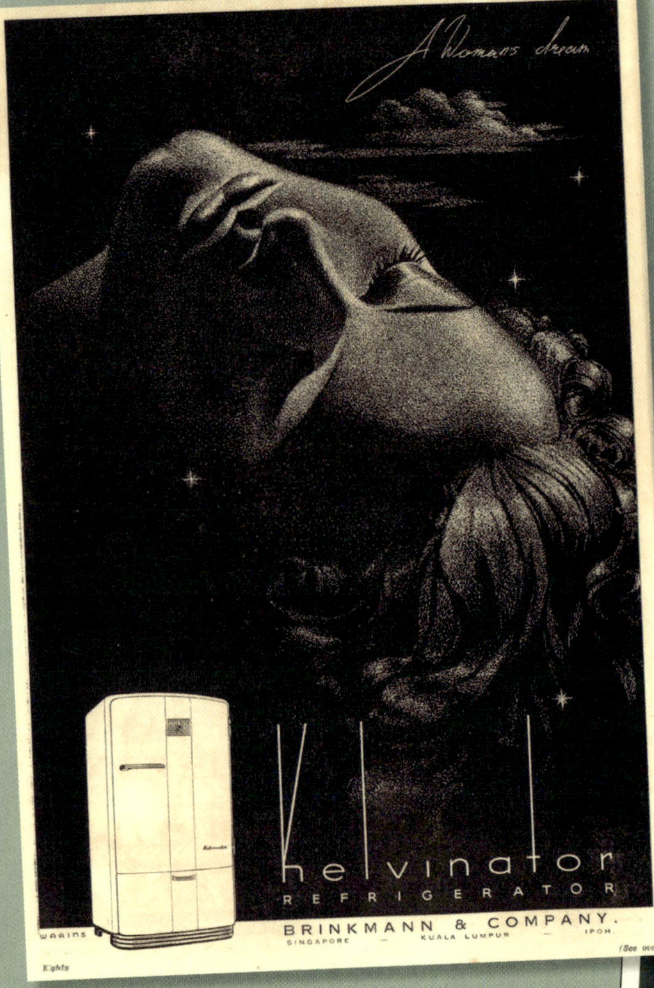

A 1940 Kelvinator ad positioning refrigerators as "a woman's dream", thus suggesting that the perfect kitchen was the sum of a woman's aspirations.

This Singer ad features a handwritten "testimonial" from a child wearing an outfit made by her mother using a Singer sewing machine. Ads often capitalised on women's desire to be "wonderful mother[s]" providing the best for their family. (1967)

What an ideal home requires!

A SILENT KNIGHT REFRIGERATOR Capacity 4½ cubic ft. 3 models available Electric 115v. A.C. D.C. 230v. AC/DC and Kerosiene operated. PRICE $600.00 only.

A "JACKSON" 3 PLATE ELECTRIC COOKER with thermostatic control for oven. For A.C. 230v. PRICE $375.00 only.

"JACKSON" ELECTRIC WASH BOILER which can easily hold 8 lbs of linen. It holds 10 gallons of water and can also supply boiling water for any purpose.

AVAILABLE FROM STOCK: INSPECTION INVITED.

SOLE DISTRIBUTORS: NAM KWANG & CO., 324, NORTH BRIDGE RD., S'PORE, TEL.: 2315

Advertising for various brands of appliances was often undertaken by the dealers and importers, in much the same way department stores do today. (1947)

That describes

AIR CONDITIONING
by CARRIER

You can provide refreshing coolness whenever and wherever you want it.

You can live at home in comfort, work all day in your office without a thought of discomfort and get a restful night's sleep.

Carrier Air Conditioning is simple, inexpensive, easy to instal and reliable.

Investigate its possibilities today by phoning or writing to the local Carrier agents:—

UNITED ENGINEERS LTD.
SINGAPORE.

ONE HUNDRED AND NINETEEN

(1936)

(1936)

In the 1930s, air-conditioners were a luxury for the home and the office. Advertisements reached out to customers who were yearning for a cool, temperate climate, such as homesick European expatriates. Dreaming of a white Christmas in the tropics? Air-conditioning might be the next best thing.

Comfort, above all other considerations, was the central message of most advertisements for air-cooling devices such as fans. (1964)

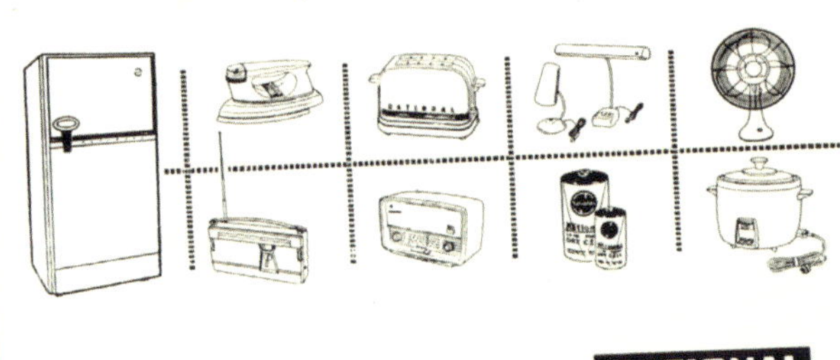

A woman in kimono presenting the "gift of better living" in the form of National home appliances from Japan to two women, dressed respectively in *sarong kebaya* (left) and *cheongsam*, representing local consumers. (1961)

Until the 1950s and '60s, electrical appliances were considered fairly expensive. The prices listed in this 1947 advertisement would have been out of reach for most households.

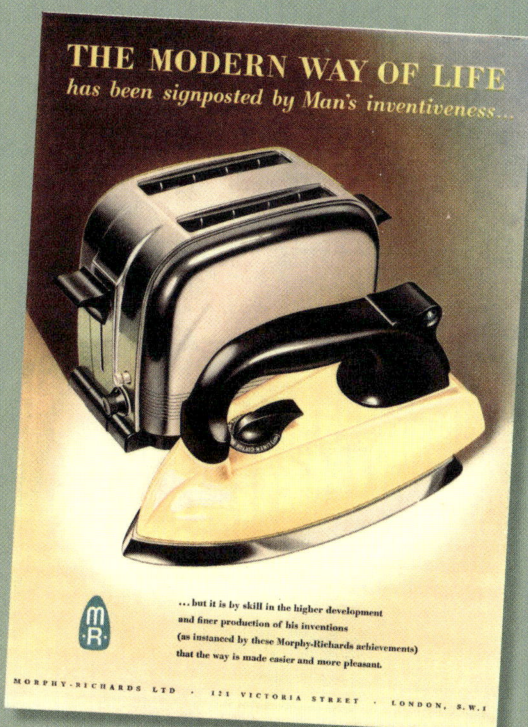

Ads such as this one for Morphy-Richards appliances were mostly found in newspapers and magazines read by the more well-to-do. The "modern" way of life was cast as an aspirational ideal. (1953)

Singer put out many creative and visually interesting ad campaigns, the majority of which depicted their products being used by women. (1961)

A Sunbeam ad positioning its appliances as "electric gifts" for the Chinese New Year season. (1962)

(1939)

Columbia, Pathé and His Master's Voice (also known as HMV) were some of the most popular record companies in the early 20th century.

(1947)

(1947)

An Edison radio advertisement inviting potential customers to compare the sound quality of its phonographs with that of its competitors at the daily demonstrations held at its premises on Orchard Road. (1930)

Tuning in to the radio was a way to receive news almost instantly as compared to waiting for telegrams or newspapers. Radio advertisers touted their products as a way of staying connected to the world from the convenience of one's home. (1939)

As the metal components in radio sets were known to warp and rust in humid conditions, many advertisers boasted models that were specially crafted for the tropics. (1939)

Many household appliance advertisements from dealers featured more than one brand, such as this Radio Electric Company ad for both General Electric and Eddystone radios. (1936)

An ad for HMV radios placed by Moutries (Robinson & Co.'s piano and musical instrument shop), describing radios as "high performance instruments". (1950)

Transistor radios entered the market in the mid-1950s and became highly popular in the '60s and '70s. (1966)

This ad for AEG's Superhet radios taps on the novelty of being connected to worldwide news and content. Users are assured of the capability of AEG radios in picking up overseas broadcast signals. (1956)

A 1966 Mitsubishi ad for a "micro TV".

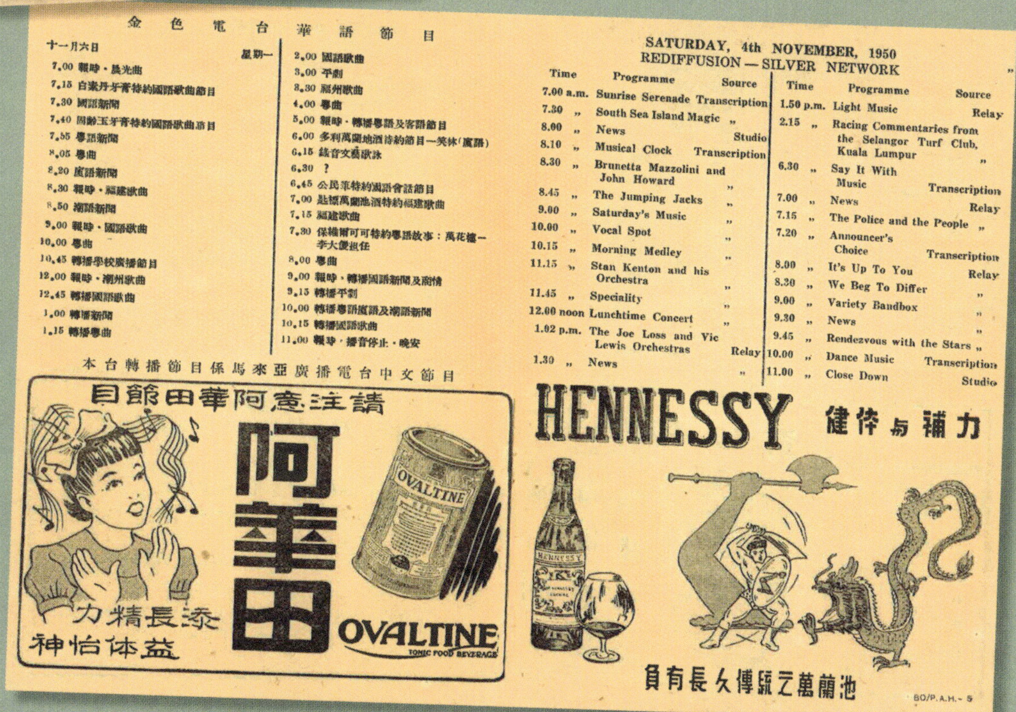

金色電台華語節目

十一月六日	星期一
7.00 報時・晨光曲	2.00 國語歌曲
7.15 白蘭丹牙膏特約國語歌曲節目	3.00 平劇
7.30 國語新聞	3.30 廈州歌曲
7.40 周齡玉牙膏特約國語歌曲節目	4.00 粵曲
7.55 粵語新聞	5.00 報時・轉播粵語及客語節目
8.05 粵曲	6.00 多利萬蘭地酒特約節目—笑林（廈語）
8.20 廈語新聞	6.15 錄音文藝歌詠
8.30 報時・福建歌曲	6.30 ？
8.50 潮語新聞	6.45 公民葉特約國語會話節目
9.00 報時・國語歌曲	7.00 匙標萬蘭地酒特約福建歌曲
10.00 粵曲	7.15 福建歌曲
10.45 轉播學校廣播節目	7.30 保維爾可可特約粵語故事：萬花樓—李大傻說任
12.00 報時・潮州歌曲	8.00 粵曲
12.45 轉播國語歌曲	9.00 報時・轉播國語新聞及商情
1.00 轉播新聞	9.15 轉播平劇
1.15 轉播粵曲	10.00 轉播粵語廈語及潮語新聞
	10.15 轉播國語歌曲
	11.00 報時・播音停止・晚安

本台轉播節目係馬來亞廣播電台中文節目

SATURDAY, 4th NOVEMBER, 1950
REDIFFUSION — SILVER NETWORK

Time	Programme	Source	Time	Programme	Source
7.00 a.m.	Sunrise Serenade	Transcription	1.50 p.m.	Light Music	Relay
7.30 "	South Sea Island Magic	"	2.15 "	Racing Commentaries from the Selangor Turf Club, Kuala Lumpur	"
8.00 "	News	Studio	6.30 "	Say It With Music	Transcription
8.10 "	Musical Clock	Transcription	7.00 "	News	Relay
8.30 "	Brunetta Mazzolini and John Howard	"	7.15 "	The Police and the People	"
8.45 "	The Jumping Jacks	"	7.20 "	Announcer's Choice	Transcription
9.00 "	Saturday's Music	"	8.00 "	It's Up To You	Relay
10.00 "	Vocal Spot	"	8.30 "	We Beg To Differ	"
10.15 "	Morning Medley	"	9.00 "	Variety Bandbox	"
11.15 "	Stan Kenton and his Orchestra	"	9.30 "	News	"
11.45 "	Speciality	"	9.45 "	Rendezvous with the Stars	"
12.00 noon	Lunchtime Concert	"	10.00 "	Dance Music	Transcription
1.02 p.m.	The Joe Loss and Vic Lewis Orchestras	Relay	11.00 "	Close Down	Studio
1.30 "	News	"			

From 1949 onwards, radio stations such as Rediffusion became staples of Singapore entertainment. Rediffusion distributed a free magazine (cover at top left) listing the week's radio programming. Listeners could look forward to broadcasts of live music, racing commentary and world news in English and various Chinese dialects. (1950)

A 1963 advertisement for SevenSeas cod liver oil, one of the many over-the-counter patent medicines that entered the Singapore market from the late 19th century onwards.

TREATING A POPULATION

Medical advertisements proliferated in Singapore in the late 19th and early 20th centuries – for clinics, dispensaries and medical halls, as well as for a plethora of over-the-counter patent medicines, supplements and tonics.

Until such ads came under legal regulation in the 1950s, there was nothing to stop advertisers from promising all sorts of instant cures for myriad ailments. Seen together, these ads mirror not only the prevalent health concerns of the day and the improvements in medical provisions over time, but also advertisers' astuteness in adapting to shifts in public-health policy and consumer demand.

PROVISION OF MEDICAL SERVICES

Government-organised hospital care in the earliest days of the settlement of Singapore was rudimentary. The "General Hospital" – initially no more than a shed, then rebuilt several times over the years[1] – was by 1830 in an advanced state of dilapidation, so much so that "no one would seek admission except in dire need".[2]

In contrast, private medical practices established in the same period – by British doctors as well as apothecaries trained in the Straits Settlements (Singapore, Penang and Melaka) – gained a foothold. They seemed more reliable and, as proclaimed in their advertisements,

SINGAPORE DISPENSARY.

IN consequence of the Establishment of a Government Hospital, the undersigned have (in the mean time) given up the Private Hospital attached to the above Dispensary OWNERS AND MASTERS OF VESSELS, are respectfully informed that they, their Passengers and Crew, can be attended *at any hour of the day, or night,* for which purpose Mr. Little is Resident on the Premises, Commercial-Square.

MEDICAL ADVICE can be afforded at all hours, while the Dispensary is open for the sale of Medicines, and the answering of Prescriptions from 9 A. M. to 5 P. M. daily.

MEDICINE CHESTS are fitted up with the requisite Medicines, and directions for a tropical climate ; while particular Medicines with their directions can be supplied those visiting countries subject to peculiar Endemics.

M. J. MARTIN. } Surgeons.
R. LITTLE. }

Commercial-Square, Singapore.

Founded in 1832, Singapore Dispensary was one of the earliest private medical practices in Singapore. When it was first established, it attended only to Europeans and seamen. (1845)

offered an array of reliable services.[3] By 1846, there were four private medical practitioners in Singapore: Charles Curties, Robert Little, M.J. Martin and J.I. Woodford.[4]

Up to the 1920s, medical services in British Malaya such as dispensaries, clinics and hospitals catered primarily to European officials and troops. Subsequently, the medical services were extended to those directly associated with the colonial authorities, such as indigenous bureaucrats and plantation workers. Finally, there were attempts, albeit to a very modest degree, to provide care outside the urban centre.[5]

Western medicine was simply one option among many for sectors of the community with their own traditions of health and healing.[6] There were still many people who were apprehensive of Western medicine and found the practices unfamiliar and even outlandish.[7] They continued to consult home-based traditional healers like *bomohs*[8] and midwives, as well as avail themselves of the services offered – and heavily advertised – by medical halls specialising in the Chinese, Ayurvedic and Unani[9] traditions, among others.

Chinese medical practices had become extensive by the 1870s. Philanthropists and clan associations played a big role in providing medical care to the Chinese population by establishing outpatient clinics, medical shops and dispensaries.

(1936)

The Yunani Clinic (left) and Unani Medical Hall advertised treatments for piles, cough, fever, diabetes, gastrointestinal diseases, period problems, male sexual issues and skin diseases, among other ailments. The latter establishment also offered boarding for patients from other cities – signalling its popularity and reach beyond Singapore.

(1937)

Specialising in the treatment of eye problems and piles, Tabib H.G. Mustaffa Punjab Medical Hall promised patients that they would be "miraculously cured". (1951)

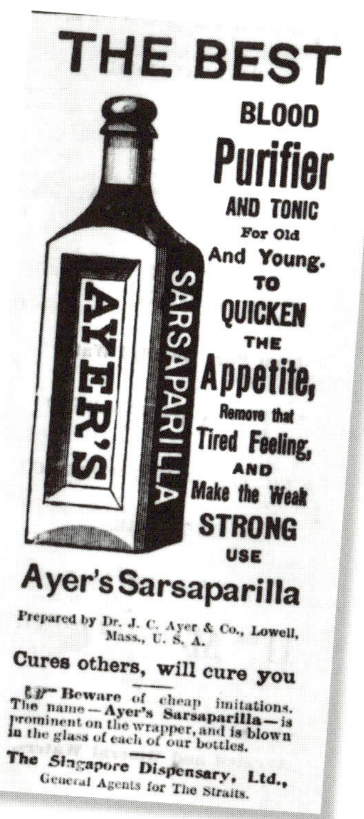

Patent medicines and tonics such as Ayer's Sarsaparilla were available over the counter, offering consumers a convenient alternative to consulting a doctor for minor ailments. (1894)

(1926)

(1930)

Advertisements for patent medicines sometimes alluded to colonial perceptions of the tropical climate as being detrimental to health.

ALL-IN-ONE CURES

Limited access to and scepticism of formal medical services played a part in shifting consumers' attention to the burgeoning market for patent medicine. Chinese, Japanese, British and American pharmaceutical companies entered the local market from the late 19th century, advertising a panoply of over-the-counter drugs and tonics.[10]

Pills and ointments promising users instant remedies and miracle cures were touted as cheaper and quicker alternatives to consulting a doctor, saving users the hassle of queues and consultation fees.[11]

On the other hand, services offered by medical practitioners trained in Western methods were concentrated in the urban areas and thus inaccessible to many living in the outskirts.[12] The lack of personal transport, or public transport in the rural parts, made it difficult, especially for the poor, to seek treatment in hospitals and clinics.[13]

RESPONDING TO THE TIMES

The 1920s witnessed an ambitious effort by the British to improve public health in Malaya.[14] The provision of medical services was becoming a great political imperative as the virulent spread of diseases was adversely affecting both the local workforce and the British authorities to a crippling degree, impeding colonial administration and expansion.[15]

The types of medical advertisements found in English and vernacular newspapers ran hand in hand with the diseases and ailments that were rampant in Singapore and neighbouring states at the time. These included malaria, tuberculosis and smallpox – the latter a scourge since as early as 1819 and prevalent right through to the mid-20th century.[16]

LADIES (AND CHILDREN) FIRST

Local women and children began to be included in the government's healthcare policies in the early 1900s as economic priorities shifted from the production of raw materials to human reproduction for the creation of a sustainable workforce population.[17]

Colonial administrators first focused on the pressing issue of reducing infant mortality. The infant mortality rate in Singapore was significantly higher than in other parts of the

(1951)

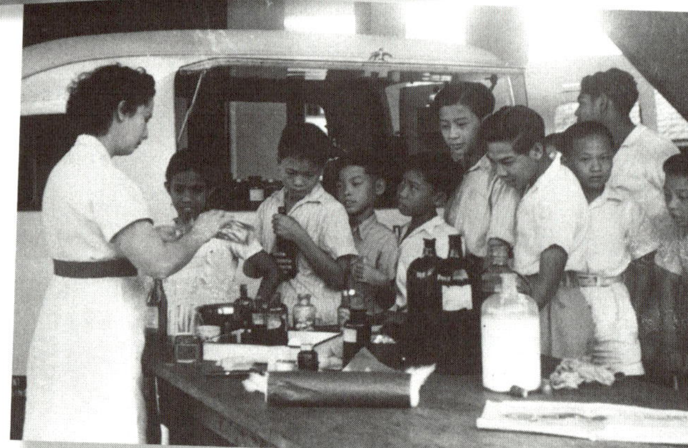

Government mobile dispensaries, which had replaced private ones by the 1930s, travelled to schools and community centres offering a range of services such as vaccinations and medicines.[18]

(1951)

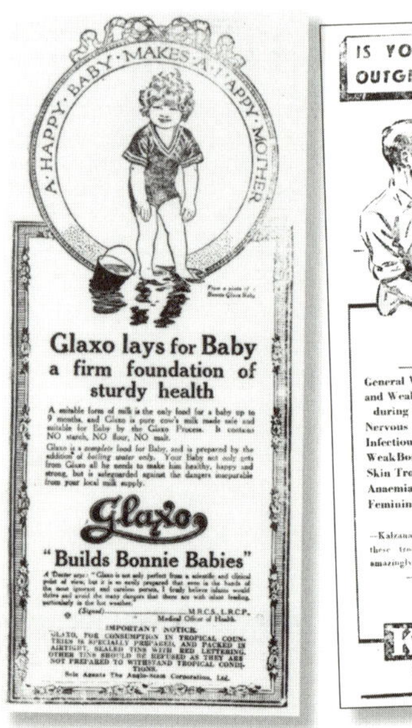

(1921)

(1939)

The messaging for products meant for infants and growing children – such as milk powder and dietary supplements – typically centred on providing the necessary nutrition to support physical and mental development.

(1961)

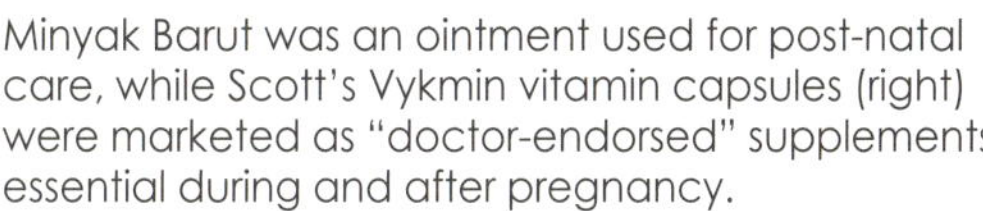

Minyak Barut was an ointment used for post-natal care, while Scott's Vykmin vitamin capsules (right) were marketed as "doctor-endorsed" supplements essential during and after pregnancy.

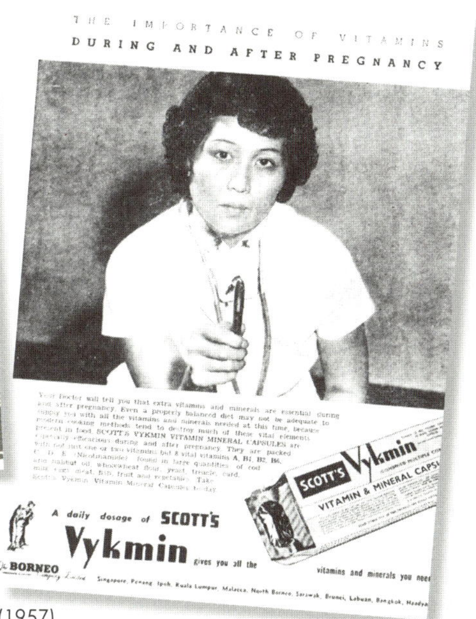

(1957)

Straits Settlements (Singapore, Penang and Melaka), ranging from 300 to 350 per 1,000 births in the period from 1900 to 1911 (though under-registered live births might have inflated these numbers).[19] This was followed by the acknowledgement that infant deaths had remediable conditions.[20] With that, the colonial government launched a flurry of initiatives, from home visits by health inspectors to the setting up of Infant Welfare Centres. And to continue monitoring the health and welfare of the young, School Health Services were started in 1921.

Women's health, mothers' health and children's health were intimately connected – in fact, practically inseparable. This was repeatedly emphasised in both public-health policy and commercial advertisements. In the words of a 1930 advertisement (p. 149) for Sunshine Glaxo milk powder, "The future of the Empire lies in the arms of every nursing mother."

By the 1930s, ads covering pre- and post-natal care had become more common as the economy improved.[21] More women and families could now afford to pay more attention to their well-being during pregnancy and after childbirth, for instance, by investing in vitamin supplements or post-natal creams and ointments.

END TO MISINFORMATION

Medical advertisements started to decline from the early 1960s onwards after the Medicines (Advertisement and Sale) Ordinance was enacted in 1956.[22] The law sought to ensure that advertised medical goods were backed by sound and authoritative research.

Regulations included the prohibition of ads relating to medical skills and services, as well as those relating to sexual functions, kidney diseases and leprosy, among other diseases. This effectively put an end to the heyday of medical ads, whose claims – extravagant as they were – now provide a window into the aspirations and insecurities of Singapore and its people during a bygone era.

Nadirah Norruddin

Intimate Affairs

A survey of newspapers and magazines across the 1930s seems to show a growing number of advertisements focused on combating the spread of venereal diseases during this period, as well as ads for products claiming to promote sexual health. These ads tended to take a pre-emptive and cautionary – rather than a curative or palliative – approach to sexual issues.[23]

PREVENTION, CURE AND EDUCATION

Even though venereal diseases like syphilis and gonorrhea were already prevalent in the Straits Settlements by the early 19th century, the 1920s witnessed a devastating number of cases amongst the local population.[24] Hospital services for venereal disease treatment were not widely available. For men, treatment was typically sought at clinics that had been set up from the late 1800s at locations such as Bencoolen Street, Paya Lebar, North Canal Road and Bukit Timah Road.[25]

For women, under the Contagious Diseases Ordinance of 1870, the female ward of Kandang Kerbau Hospital had been converted into Lock Hospital in 1872 to screen and treat those with venereal diseases.[26] In 1924, St Andrew's Mission Hospital established a clinic for women who were exposed to venereal diseases due to prostitution, which was rife at the time and one of the common modes of transmission.[27]

This 1940 ad points to brothels as the main breeding grounds for the spread of venereal diseases – "a moment of pleasure leads to the trap of 'blood poison'". The advertised Satoben tablets could apparently destroy viruses in the blood after one engaged in casual sex.

Trainee nurses at St Andrew's Mission Hospital. (1930)

Just as in Britain, preventive programmes were instituted in Singapore. Nationwide formal campaigns, public-awareness programmes and the establishment of ablution centres[28] in central districts were some of the measures that had been introduced by the mid-1920s.[29] The Social Hygiene Advisory Board launched campaigns to stem the tide of venereal diseases via film screenings, museum displays, lectures and pamphlets in various languages.[30] These mass education programmes were mirrored in the messaging of venereal disease-related ads for many years to come.[31]

WHETTING APPETITES

Another class of ads related to sexual health were those for supplements aimed at improving sexual function. In ads promoting male virility and female fertility, emphasis was often placed on the enhancement of one's sexual performance so as to increase the chances of conceiving, or simply as a show of sexual prowess.

Sexual health-related ads tended to emphasise the importance of hygiene and safe sex, and typically employed images and symbols of strength, endurance and potency. These ads enjoyed huge advertising exposure for several decades. However, they began to wane following the enactment of the Indecent Advertisements Ordinance of 1941, which suppressed advertisements relating to the treatment of venereal diseases, containing suggestive images, or marketing products with aphrodisiac properties.[32]

Ads for tonics often featured images of muscular and toned bodies and promised to restore a man's lost "vitality". (1946)

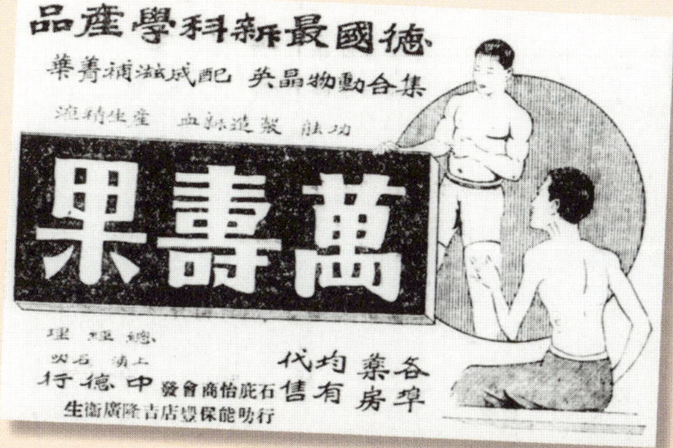

A health tonic ad juxtaposing images of two men – one fit and well built, the other thin and weak – and claiming to stimulate the production of blood and semen due to the presence of animal hormones in its formulation. (1934)

CAMPONG GLAM

DISPENSARY.

ESTABLISHED IN CHURCH-STREET. CAMPONG BENCOOLEN.

Medical Prescriptions will meet with prompt and careful attention at all hours.

THE Undersigned in announcing to the Community, as well as to the Captains of Vessels and others frequenting the Port, that he has just received a fresh supply of drugs and avails himself of this opportunity of returning his grateful thanks to his customers for the liberal patronage they have afforded him—and respectfully solicits a continuation of the same. The Undersigned warrants all his Medicines to be good and genuine, in order to ensure which he receives two supplies regularly during the year, direct from London.

The Undersigned is at all times ready to supply Vessels touching at or frequenting the Port with Medicines securely and neatly packed on the shortest notice—and at as cheap a rate as they can be procured at any of the Presidencies.

Orders will continue to be attended to at the Branch of the above Dispensary, in GEMMILL's Buildings, Commercial-Square, every day (Sundays excepted) from 10 o'clock A M. till 4 P. M.

J. I WOODFORD.

Singapore, 27th May 1845

FOR SALE.—Chamois Skins, Bussorah and Gazeepore Rose Water, Genuine Kayu Putih Oil; Carraway Seeds : Childrens Trusses : Pink Saucers ; Capsules of Balsam of Copaiba, pure, without smell or taste : Essence of Peppermint ; Essence of Ginger : Fluid Magnesia : Pate de Jujubes ; Cheltenham Salts ; Cold Cream ; a few warranted London improved Patent Syringes, &c. &c. &.

J.I. Woodford founded Campong Glam Dispensary after his training as an apothecary in Penang. (1845)

NOTICE.
Mr. CHARLES WILSON
SURGEON &c.

Having resolved to remain at Singapore and exercise his profession, takes this opportunity of informing the Community of Singapore who may be pleased to employ him, that their applications will meet with immediate attention.

Ships' Crews promptly attended and comfortable accommodations provided on shore during their sickness, for moderate remuneration.

Address No. 2, Mr. Gemmill's New Buildings.

N. B.— Prescriptions carefully prepared by Mr. Wilson, with the best Medicines.

Apart from providing medical services, Charles Wilson also offered accommodation for ships' crew who were under treatment. Western medical practitioners often extended a helping hand to Europeans in the administrative, military and mercantile sectors. (1834)

Cheong Chun Tin,
DENTIST,
No. 27, SOUTH BRIDGE ROAD, UPSTAIRS.

Two rooms available for use, the front room for Europeans, and the back one for Natives.

N.B.—Please note present address.

—:o:—

TESTIMONIALS.

Singapore, 9th Dec., 1885.—This is to certify that Mr. Cheong Chun Tin has practised here for about five years as a dentist. His work in the way of fitting artificial teeth plates, &c., is most excellent, and I can highly recommend him to any one needing his services. His charges are fair and moderate.—N. B. DENNYS, Magistrate & Justice of the Peace.

Singapore, 22nd July, 1889.—Just had a wisdom tooth drawn most successfully. The lancing was painlessly done, and the drawing took only two seconds.— ALEX: J. GUNN, 44, Raffles Place.

November, 1890.—I have known Mr. Cheong Chun Tin, Dentist, for about ten years, and can testify to his ability in extracting and stopping teeth.—A. MACKAY.

November, 1890.—Cheong Chun Tin, Dentist, seems to understand his work. Treated an aching tooth very successfully. Is accessible at all hours.—R. W. MUNSON.

Singapore, 2nd Dec., 1890.   6 m.

This 1890 ad for Cheong Chun Tin's dental practice features testimonials from notable patients. And, according to the ad, there was preferential treatment by ethnicity: The clinic's front room was reserved for Europeans, while "natives" were attended to in the back room.

DR. CHEW YIT HONG.

福建漳澄周一方先生醫痲瘋論畧
物味濁血成形早晚發現猶感毒輕軍也今天運南離水火欵重脛癘毒盛固多此症
盖天有可消毒生之災人有可愈澄福之疾一尪一濟一亂一治有奇病必有奇藥今用俗
古云禍因惡遇凶醫也福緣善餘慶逢吉人也今秘法語汝醫痲瘋神藥根頭名曰換骨脫壳仙液早下山濟身懷濟世善惡之因勿
逆天心但余受師命初到不得不畧述敢欺人欺天耶並列專精醫治目錄　福建周一方精理　包治痲瘋破爛
寶斷根痲瘋藥　精醫眼科咽喉　瘰癧珠痘疔毒　楊梅瘡瘋鼻爛　鬼怪癲下消癲　包戒烟三日新　地理廛公眞傳　邪症鬼病
法治　大小沖犯關煞　內外方脈什症　痲瘋脫壳眞藥
大清光緒十九年十二月十六日　　移寓嬪峨大坡苑生宅蝨街懇篤主人告白

Dr Chew Yit Hong advertising his services in treating leprosy and opium addiction – a type of ad commonly found in Chinese-language newspapers. (1894)

The Medical Hall catered to Europeans. This ad lists the European languages spoken by its staff as well as supplies of medicines available to ships, estates and hospitals. (1905)

The Pharmacy on Battery Road, with its team of chemists, druggists and opticians, targeted a European clientele. (1905)

General practitioners and apothecaries contributed to the growing popularity of patent medicines. Not only did they stock an array of medical goods, they also served as distributors.[33]

MEDICAL NOTICE.

Western Dispensary.

NO. 48, HILL STREET,

(opposite the Armenian Church.)

OPEN daily from 7 A. M. to 9 P. M. Sundays from 8 to 11 A. M. and 4 to 7 P. M.

DR. JANSZ in attendance from 8 to 10 A. M. and from 2 to 5 P. M.; residence No. 102, Waterloo Street.

Prescriptions carefully prepared, and Patent Medicines, &c, for sale. Singapore, 19th January, 1891.

(1891)

SINGAPORE DISPENSARY.

(ESTABLISHED 1825.)

(Adjoining Messrs. J. Little & Co.)

WHOLESALE AND RETAIL CHEMISTS AND DRUGGISTS.

DISPENSING.—The careful compounding of Physicians' Prescriptions is well known to be the most important and responsible duty of the Chemist. The greatest care is therefore taken to keep our dispensing counter well supplied with the purest drugs and chemicals fresh from the London market, while every prescription is dispensed and checked under direct supervision.

ÆRATED MINERAL WATERS.—Lemonade, Ginger Ale and Beer, Lemon Squash, Soda, Potash, and Seltzer Waters, &c. Tonic Water, an excellent and agreeable manner of administering Quinine. These waters are carefully prepared from carefully filtered water, thus ensuring purity, while every ingredient used in the manufacture is of the highest quality. Special reductions in the price of our Waters to Hotels and Ships. Price list on application.

A large and well assorted stock of Patent Medicines and Proprietary Goods always in hand. Tooth, Nail, and Hair Brushes, Cosmetiques, Pomades, Perfumes, Fancy Soaps, &c. Every requisite for the toilet and sick room. Agent for Ayer's American Preparations.

GEO. K. REID,—Manager. Singapore, 17th Nov., 1890.   1 y.

(1890)

(1933)

(1930)

(1845)

(1890)

A selection of advertisements for international patent medicines, many of which – like Listerine, Eno "Fruit Salts" and Scott's Emulsion – are still being sold today.

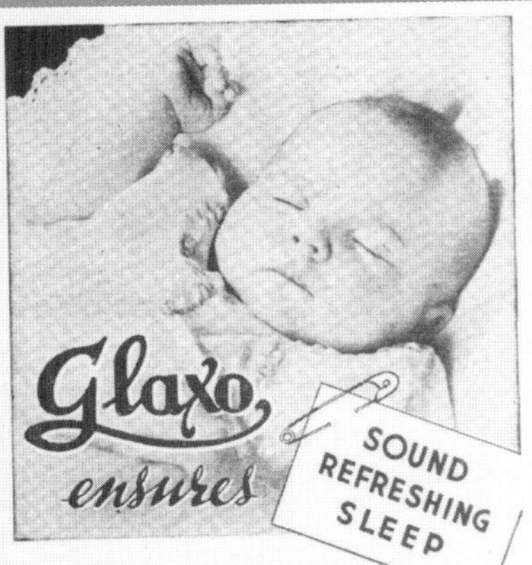

(1940)

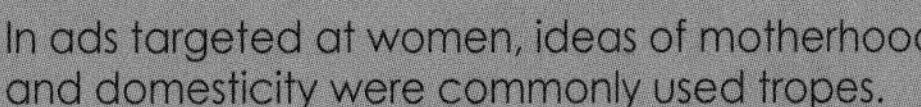

(1930)

In ads targeted at women, ideas of motherhood and domesticity were commonly used tropes.

(1926)

(1961)

(1892)

FRESH
VACCINE LYMPH
FROM
PASTEUR INSTITUTE.
due MONDAY 17th
MEDICAL HALL Ltd.
23 BATTERY ROAD.
SINGAPORE.

(1921)

(1946)

Although smallpox vaccination had been introduced in Singapore by December 1819, it only became widely available in 1870. Medical halls, such as Xin Tong Xing Yaofang (新同兴药房; left), offered vaccinations to locals, while the Pasteur Institute made visits to urban areas to provide tuberculosis and smallpox vaccinations.

Singapore saw a rise in opium syndicates in the mid-19th century as opium and spirit farms grew common.[34] Advertisements for medicines that promised to cure opium addiction were frequently seen. This ad featuring a skull next to an opium pipe coincided with the ban on opium possession by anyone who was not issued a medical practitioner's certificate.[35] Despite this and other similar measures, opium addiction remained widespread in Singapore until the late 1980s. (1935)

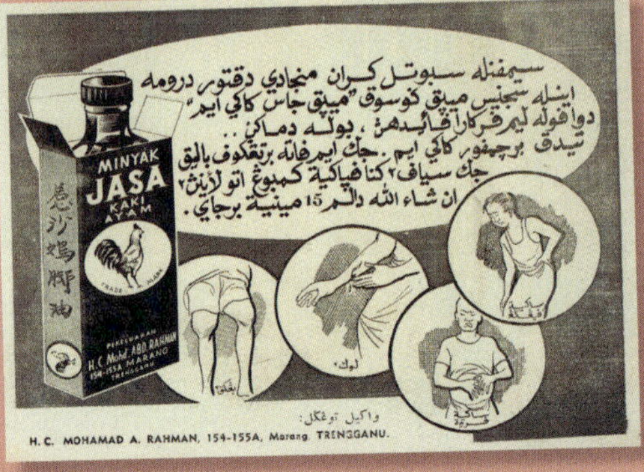

(1961)

All-purpose tonics and ointments were aplenty, all claiming to be instant solutions to various medical ailments.

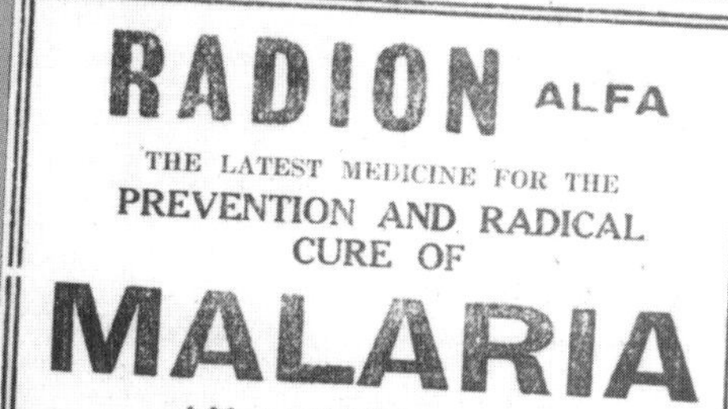

(1927)

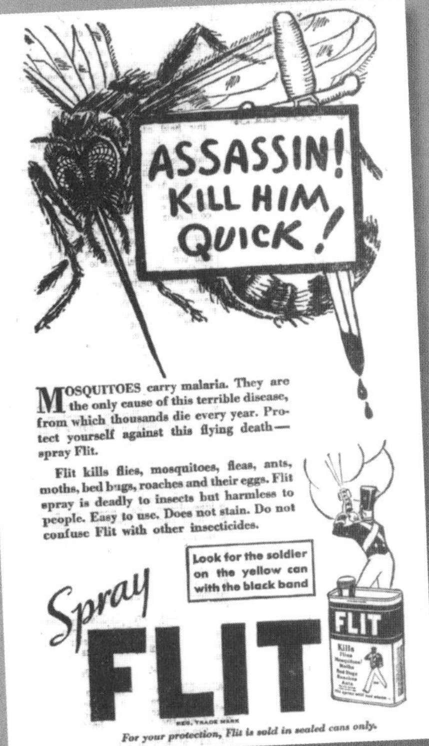

(1932)

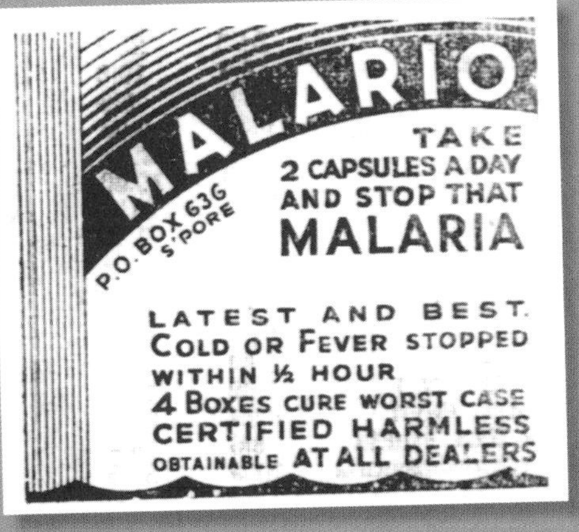

(1937)

(1920)

Malaria is an infectious disease that is best fought with preventive measures. Beginning in the 1920s, the colonial government concentrated on improving drainage infrastructure to prevent the breeding of malaria-carrying mosquitoes,[36] while businesses marketed anti-malarial pills and sprays for added personal protection.

Resolve Now pills were taken for strength and male potency. This 1951 advertisement features the tagline, "Youthful, vigorous men are universally admired".

You Grow Younger As You Grow Older advertisement:

Testrones tablets, targeted at older men, promised to do wonders for hair loss, ageing skin and failing eyesight. (1947)

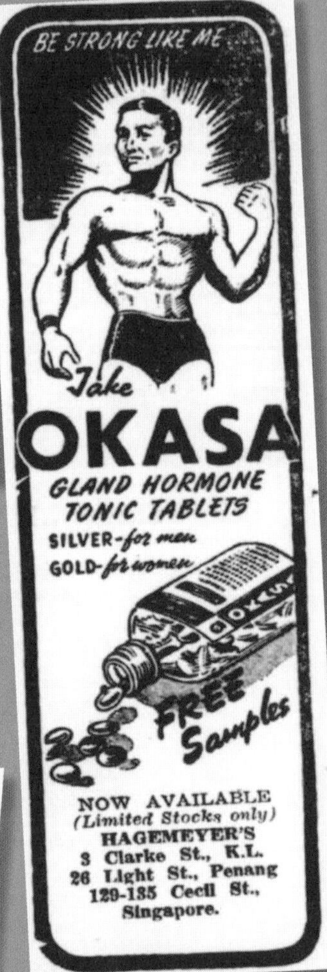

The promise of strength and virility were frequently used to appeal to readers, such as in this ad for Okasa "gland hormone tonic tablets". (1954)

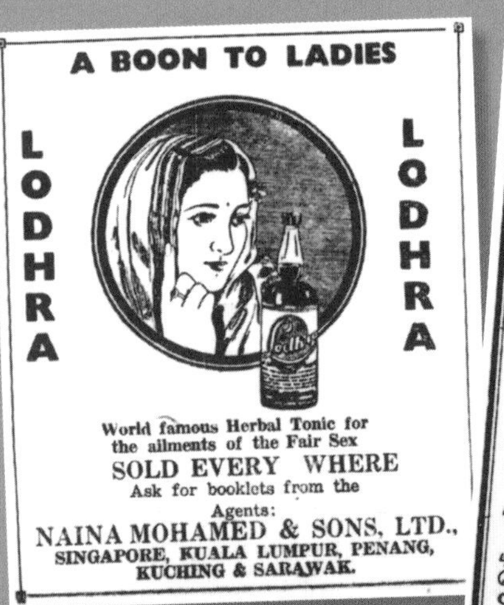

Lodhra, with its Ayurvedic properties, was a well-known herbal tonic that claimed to relieve urinary tract problems and other female ailments. (1954)

Ovarone Pills were targeted at women, promising to help revitalise blood flow, enhance beauty, raise energy levels, and strengthen the wombs of "weak women" – referring to those who had difficulty conceiving. Similar to what we see in today's beauty industry, this ad perpetuates the ideal that an attractive Indian woman is one with fair and smooth skin. (1954)

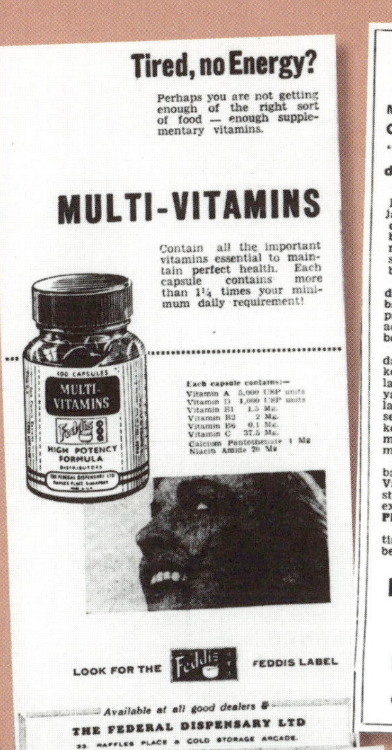

(1960)

(1963)

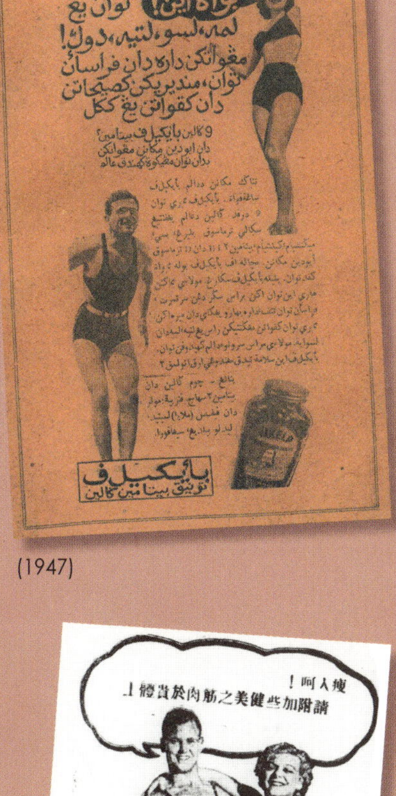

(1947)

By the 1950s, energy boosters and medication with "detoxing" properties had become common, with many highlighting the importance of consuming supplements to revitalise after a hard day's work. Being physically healthy was also associated with sexual prowess and overall attractiveness.

(1924)

Advertised as the "key to marriage", these pills were marketed as a guarantee of a couple's sexual satisfaction. (1962)

Vikelp was a supplement that claimed to help men and women gain weight, emphasising the undesirability of "scrawny bodies". Weight was seen as a measure of one's status and attractiveness. (1937)

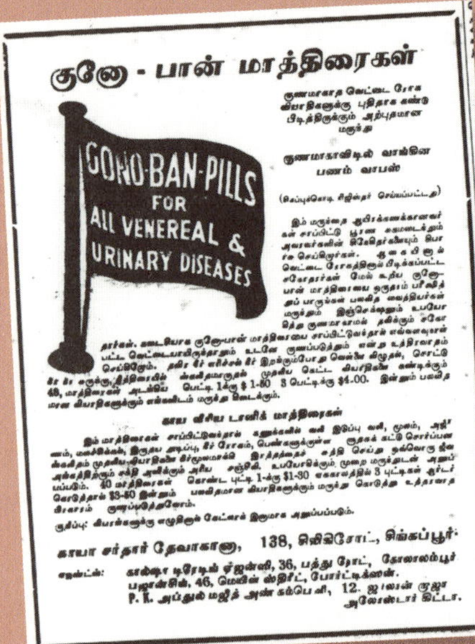

Advertisements for venereal disease medicines often implied that the diseases would gradually spell the end of one's life unless one took the medications. (1939)

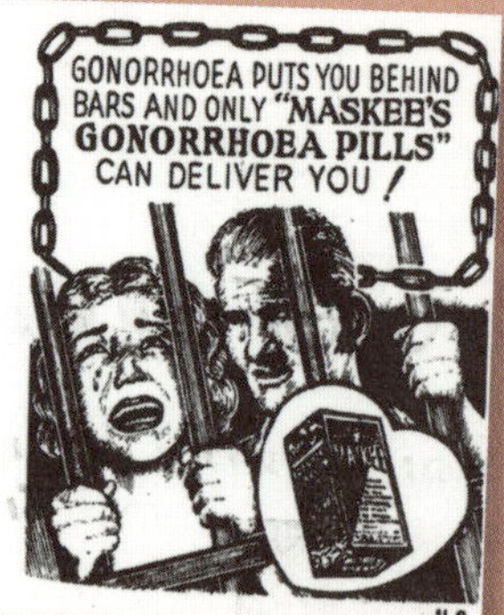

This 1939 ad for Maskee Gonorrhoea Pills warns readers that sleeping with multiple partners could lead to immediate death – a hyperbolic claim, but an attempt at informing readers on how venereal diseases spread.

This 1931 ad for Hai Bo Yao (海波药) carries a foreboding illustration of a skull to convey the fatal consequences of syphilis if left untreated. It also informs readers of the three stages of the disease's progression.

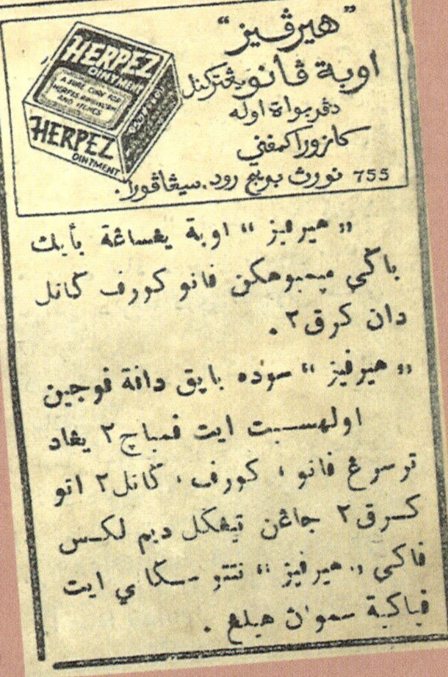

Herpez ointment advertised as a "sure cure for herpes, ringworm and itches". (1948)

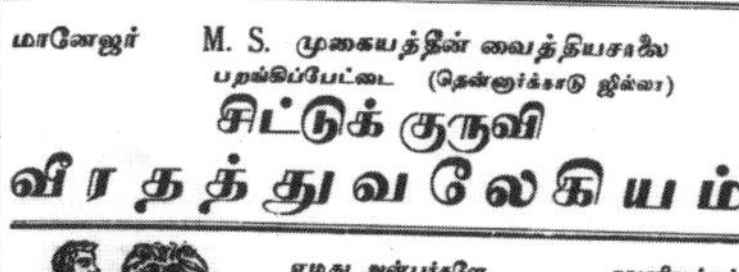

(1937)

Mythological and larger-than-life associations were branding strategies that some companies used to advertise their tonics for "men's health". These two Tamil ads use the imagery of a man subduing a lion to suggest that one could obtain physical strength and virility from consuming the supplements.

An ad for a German medicinal product depicting how a couple managed to have a baby after consuming its pills derived from animal hormones. Ingredients of animal origin were believed to improve virility and fertility in men and women. (1935)

(1939)

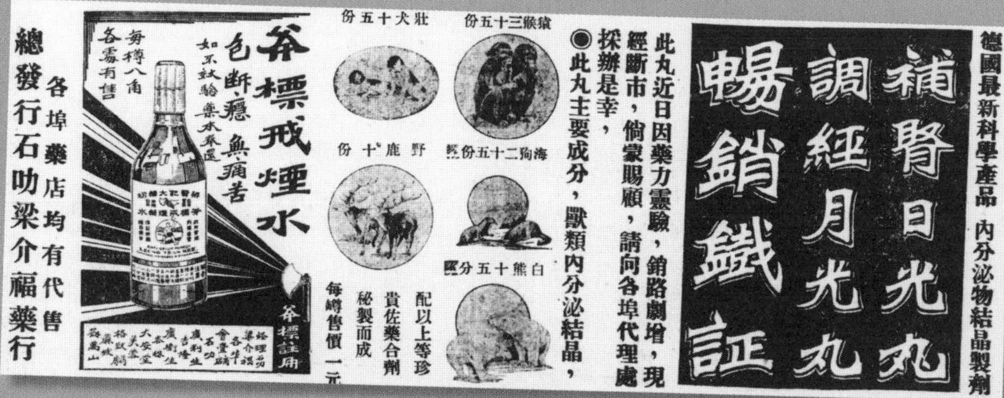

This 1934 ad for Axe Brand medicated water (which was also marketed as an opium addiction cure) states that it contained several animal-derived ingredients and "essences".

A 1958 advertisement showing Malayan Airways' destinations in Southeast Asia. The airline's first commercial flight took off from Singapore in 1947, landing at Kuala Lumpur before going on to Ipoh and Penang.

BON VOYAGE

Travelling for leisure was once the preserve of an exclusive elite class. Few people, apart from the very wealthy, could afford the time and expense needed to travel abroad. In 17th- and 18th-century Europe, the so-called "Grand Tour" was undertaken by young aristocrats, who travelled to France and Italy, among other parts of the continent, in search of art and culture as part of their education. This was the seed of modern tourism, but it nevertheless remained a privilege of the upper classes.

It was not until the middle of the 19th century, with the technological advances of the Industrial Revolution, particularly the advent of steamships and railways, that travelling for leisure became a practical reality for many for the first time in history.

BIRTH OF WORLD TRAVEL

The 1860s ushered in a new era for world travel. Most notably, the opening of the Suez Canal on 17 November 1869 cut the duration of ship passage between Europe and Asia dramatically. A steamship from England now took about three weeks to reach Singapore instead of over six weeks previously.[1]

Coupled with other developments at the time – such as the first railway linking the east and west coasts of North America, and monthly ship services between San Francisco and Yokohama – traversing oceans and continents for leisure became a viable proposition. The unimaginable feat envisioned in Jules Verne's 1873 bestselling novel, *Around the World in 80 Days*, was suddenly achievable – indeed, in

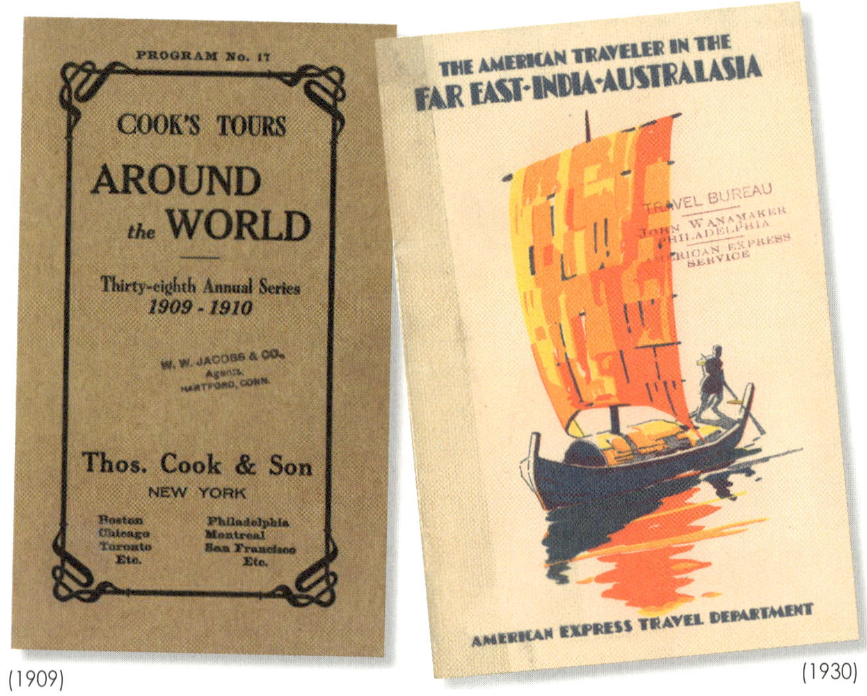

(1909) (1930)

Travel brochures published by Thomas Cook & Son and American Express. Detailed itineraries were provided within.

1892, American journalist Elizabeth Cochrane (better known by her pen name Nellie Bly) beat the novel's protagonists Phileas Fogg and Passepartout by completing the journey in 72 days.[2]

A year before Verne's novel was published, Englishman Thomas Cook, the pioneer of international organised travel, led a group of tourists on an epic world tour, setting off from Liverpool in September 1872.[3] The 222-day journey took the party to the United States, Japan, China, the Straits Settlements, Ceylon, India and Egypt, from where most of Cook's tourists returned to Europe via the Suez Canal. The party spent two days in Singapore, enjoying the botanical gardens and fascinated by the mix of races in the colonial port city.[4]

Thanks to its strategic location, Singapore found itself on the itineraries of world tours and was a major port of call and coaling station from the late 19th century until the outbreak of the Second World War. This travel trend was reflected in the numerous advertisements published in Singapore during the period, promoting itineraries to far-flung destinations as well as round-the-world cruises.

Numerous shipping lines vied for a share of the new business. The major players included the British Peninsular and Oriental Steam Navigation Company (P&O), Koninklijke Paketvaart-Maatschappij (KPM; Royal Packet Navigation Company), Hamburg-America Line, Nippon Yusen Kaisha (Japan Mail Shipping Line) and the Danish East Asiatic Line, to name a few.

Evident from their advertisements, travelling in comfort and luxury was a key selling point. They beckoned potential customers with alluring vignettes of life on board the steam liners – the

Map of sailing route from Europe to East Asia, from a Dutch-language travel brochure by the Norddeutscher Lloyd (North German Lloyd) shipping company, which offered their first East Asia cruise service in 1886. (1920s–30s)

glamorous decor of the first-class cabins, dining saloon and bathing pool; excellent cuisine; fine company among well-heeled fellow travellers; and the thrill of visiting exotic destinations.

The demand for tourism also fostered the growth of complementary industries such as travel agencies, hospitality and retail. Thomas Cook & Son set up its Singapore office in 1922 and American Express did likewise three years later. Advertisements for tour packages typically promoted a full suite of services, guaranteeing a carefree holiday – travellers could look forward to staying in the most luxurious hotels of the day and having all their travel arrangements taken care of.

Travelling was not solely the privilege of affluent Europeans and Americans; advertisements by travel agencies also appeared in Chinese-language publications, which meant that leisure travel was readily accessible to anyone who had the means. In 1926 Thomas Cook & Son publicised a deluxe tour package to Europe exclusively for Chinese patrons (strictly limited to 12), with an extensive itinerary spanning three months.[5]

EARLY TOURISM IN MALAYA

Ship passengers from Europe and India en route to China and Japan, or vice versa, had to pass through Singapore. Typically, travellers saw Singapore as a convenient stopover rather than a destination in its own right. Attempts were made to promote tourism to British Malaya, as evident in advertisements that appeared in travel guides published in the early 20th century.

The British set up the Malay States Information Agency in London in 1910 "to advertise the productions and attractions of the States of the Malay Peninsula under British protection"[6] and to provide information to those who were interested in pursuing business opportunities or leisure travel in this part of the world.[7] Although the agency represented the Federated Malay States, information on the Straits Settlements (Singapore, Melaka and Penang) was also provided. Advertisements by the agency portrayed Singapore and Malaya as a tropical haven rich in natural resources, beauty and opportunities. A 1936 ad described Malaya as "a land basking in perpetual summer", "an ever-changing landscape of constant beauty" and "offer[ing] varied and exceptional chances for business development of every kind" (p. 166, top left).

By 1918, the Federated Malay States Railways (FMSR) linked Singapore to most of the cities and towns of peninsular Malaya, all the way up to the border with Siam (present-day Thailand), where it joined the Siamese State Railways.[8] Originally built to serve the tin-mining industry, the FMSR promoted leisure travel in Malaya and came to be advertised as a tourist attraction in itself. Advertisements and travel publications invited tourists to "Come to Malaya and travel by train" – the title of a 1938 guidebook.

The comfort and romance of travelling on the FMSR were major selling points. Advertisements featured elegant buffet cars, sleeping saloons and, not least, air-conditioning, so that passengers could "enjoy a hill station climate whilst making [their] journey" (p. 166, top right), as one advertisement promised. Rail bookings might also include transport by road to actual hill resorts such as Penang Hill, Fraser's Hill and Cameron Highlands – favoured getaway destinations among the colonial set.

An advertisement of the Federated Malay States Railway on the front cover of the travel guide, *Come to Malaya and Travel by Train*. (1938)

Advertisement promoting travel to British Malaya by the Malayan Information Agency in London. (1936)

KLM (Royal Dutch Airlines) advertisement for its Singapore–London flights, which took five-and-a-half days, a major improvement over the three-week passage by ship. (1937)

A 1956 ad by Qantas-BOAC (British Overseas Airways Corporation; forerunner of British Airways) for holidays to Europe. Travellers could make stopovers at their preferred locations en route to their destinations

ADVENT OF AIR TRAVEL

The age of air travel dawned in Singapore in 1930, when the first commercial flight – operated by the Royal Dutch Indies Airways, or KNILM (a subsidiary of KLM) – landed at the Royal Air Force Seletar Air Base from Batavia (present-day Jakarta).[9] The Seletar Air Base catered to commercial flights before a civil airport was built seven years later.

Commercial aviation grew rapidly as the transportation of mail and passengers by air gained popularity all over the world. Air travel cut travelling time between Europe and Singapore from three weeks by steamship to five-and-a-half days.[10] Because flying could only take place during daylight hours then, such a flight would have been made with several stopovers in between. This dramatic reduction in travelling time – albeit still a far cry from the 12-hour direct flights from London to Singapore today – revolutionised world travel.

Singapore soon became a regional air transport hub. Various international airlines established flights to Singapore, beginning with KLM's Batavia-Singapore-Amsterdam service in 1933. The following year, one could fly from England to Singapore by Imperial Airways and onward to Australia on a connecting flight by Qantas.

With the rising importance of air travel, Singapore's first civil aerodrome, Kallang Airport, was built and officially opened in June 1937. Still, flying remained a luxury limited to the well-to-do, as it cost twice as much as travelling by steamship. Only from the 1950s onwards, as attested by the proliferation of airline advertisements, did planes replace steamers as the mainstream mode of travel. By the 1960s, ship passage to Asia had become increasingly costly and could no longer compete with flying.[11]

Chung Sang Hong

Holiday Destinations of Yesteryear

While the modern tourism industry has allowed people to fly to holiday destinations of their choice anywhere around the globe, advertisements from the late 19th and early 20th centuries suggest that the vacation culture then was very much shaped by local and regional circumstances. Within the Indian subcontinent and Southeast Asia, "hill stations" offered colonial residents respite from the tropical heat. With the establishment of shipping lines and railways worldwide, it was also possible to venture to more distant lands, as long as one had the time and money to spare.

ASCENT TO THE HILLS

An enduring colonial legacy, hill stations were originally developed by the Europeans and Americans beginning in the early 19th century.[14] They served colonial civil servants on local leave and other European residents, who could enjoy a short getaway at these upland resorts, hiking and golfing in the crisp mountain air. From Shimla (Simla) in India to Baguio in the Philippines, many of these hill stations have survived the times and now stand as reminders of a bygone genteel era.

Advertisements for hill stations typically emphasised the cooler climate of these destinations compared to the lowlands. The colonials believed that the tropical climate was detrimental to health and might even shorten one's lifespan. The hill stations offered

Opened in 1938, Smoke House Inn in Cameron Highlands recreated "Old England" in its Tudor-style architecture, landscaping and cuisine, complete with a crazy-paved garden and roast beef on its menu. (1938)

a temporary refuge from the supposed ill effects of tropical heat as well as when epidemics struck the country.[15] The commonly advertised hill resorts included Fraser's Hill, Penang Hill and Cameron Highlands in Malaya, Brastagi (Berastagi) in northern Sumatra and Newera Eliya (Nuwara Eliya) in Ceylon (Sri Lanka).

Hill resorts were often designed to create an environment reminiscent of Europe. This was reflected in the architecture, the social institutions – hotels, clubs and churches – and the temperate flora transplanted there to create the illusion of home for homesick colonials.[16] A 1938 advertisement for the Smoke House Inn in Cameron Highlands (facing page) attempted to charm potential patrons with an illustration of its mock Tudor-style building, evoking the air of an old English cottage.

FURTHER AFIELD

For those on home leave or planning a longer vacation, more exciting options were available. These destinations were either on major shipping routes or under Western colonial influence.[17] Frequently advertised holiday destinations included Australia and South Africa, which were part of the British Empire for much of the 1920s and '30s.

Colonial Hong Kong, marketed as the "Riviera of the Orient", was relatively more accessible to travellers from Singapore, with regular ship services plying between the two cities. The luxurious steam liners of Nippon Yusen Kaisha promoted tourism to Japan, which had several treaty ports with Western presence since 1854. And as transpacific shipping traffic increased, advertisements for touring the United States appeared frequently, enticing those returning home to Europe to take the alternative route and have an American holiday along the way.

Advertisement by the steamship company Burns Philp promoting its regular service from Singapore to Australia, using the country's temperate climate, scenery and koala bears as selling points. (1936)

COOK'S
ESCORTED
TOUR DE LUXE
THROUGH EUROPE
for
CHINESE LADIES
AND GENTLEMEN
is scheduled to leave Singapore
JUNE 4th 1926.
Printed handbook giving full
particulars on application.

THOS COOK & SON, LTD.,
6, Battery Road SINGAPORE.
Cook's New Head Office at Berkeley
Street, Piccadilly, London, will be
opened in April.

A 1926 Thomas Cook & Son advertisement for a tour to Europe specially organised for "Chinese ladies and gentlemen".

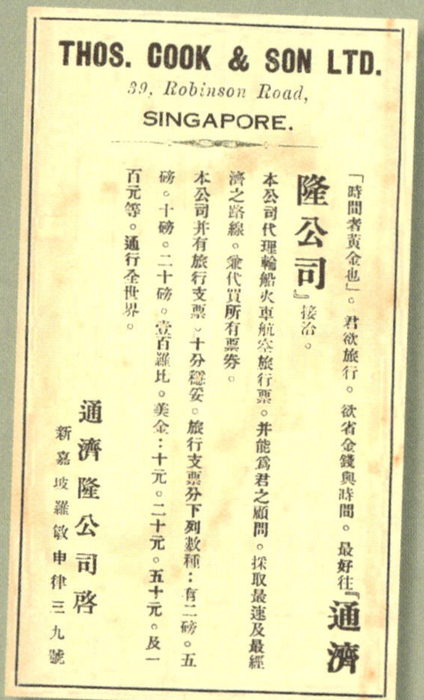

A Thomas Cook & Son advertisement in Chinese, offering its services in organising land, sea and air transport, as well as marketing its traveller's cheques. (1936)

Advertisement by the Hawaii Tourist Bureau promoting the idea of travelling home (presumably to Europe) via Hawaii. This entailed sailing the Pacific, with a stopover in the "land of leis", arriving on the United States west coast, traversing the continent by rail, and finally crossing the Atlantic to Europe. (1926)

SOUTH AFRICA
A TRAVEL LAND OF UNIQUE CHARM

SOUTH AFRICA OFFERS MANY ATTRACTIONS FOR TOURISTS—MATCHLESS VICTORIA FALLS, KRUGER NATIONAL PARK (THE WORLD'S GREATEST NATURAL ZOO), PICTURESQUE NATIVE LIFE, THE DIAMOND MINES OF KIMBERLEY, AND JOHANNESBURG—THE HUB OF SOUTHERN AFRICA AND CENTRE OF THE WORLD'S BIGGEST GOLD MINING INDUSTRY.

GORGEOUS MOUNTAIN SCENERY—BEAUTIFUL SEASIDE RESORTS—CHARMING HOSPITALITY—AND ABOVE ALL—A REALLY DELIGHTFUL CLIMATE.

MODERN AIRLINE, RAILWAY AND MOTOR CAR TRANSPORTATION MAKE ALL HIGH POINTS OF TOURIST INTEREST EASILY ACCESSIBLE.

GOING TO EUROPE? WHY NOT TRAVEL VIA THE CAPE OF GOOD HOPE AND TOUR SOUTH AFRICA EN ROUTE? YOU WILL NOT REGRET IT.

Booklets and information obtainable from :—
TRADE COMMISSIONER OF THE UNION OF SOUTH AFRICA, OLD K.P.M. BUILDING, SLUISBRUGPLEIN 1, BATAVIA-CENTRUM, JAVA.
or
MANAGER, PUBLICITY AND TRAVEL DEPARTMENT P. O. BOX 1111, JOHANNESBURG, SOUTH AFRICA.
or
SIME, DARBY & CO., MALACCA.
or
LEADING TRAVEL AGENCIES THROUGHOUT THE WORLD.

One Hundred and Thirty Seven

South Africa, once part of the British Empire, was accessible by several steamship lines. This advertisement encouraged travellers to make a detour to the country on their way to Europe. (1938)

(1930)

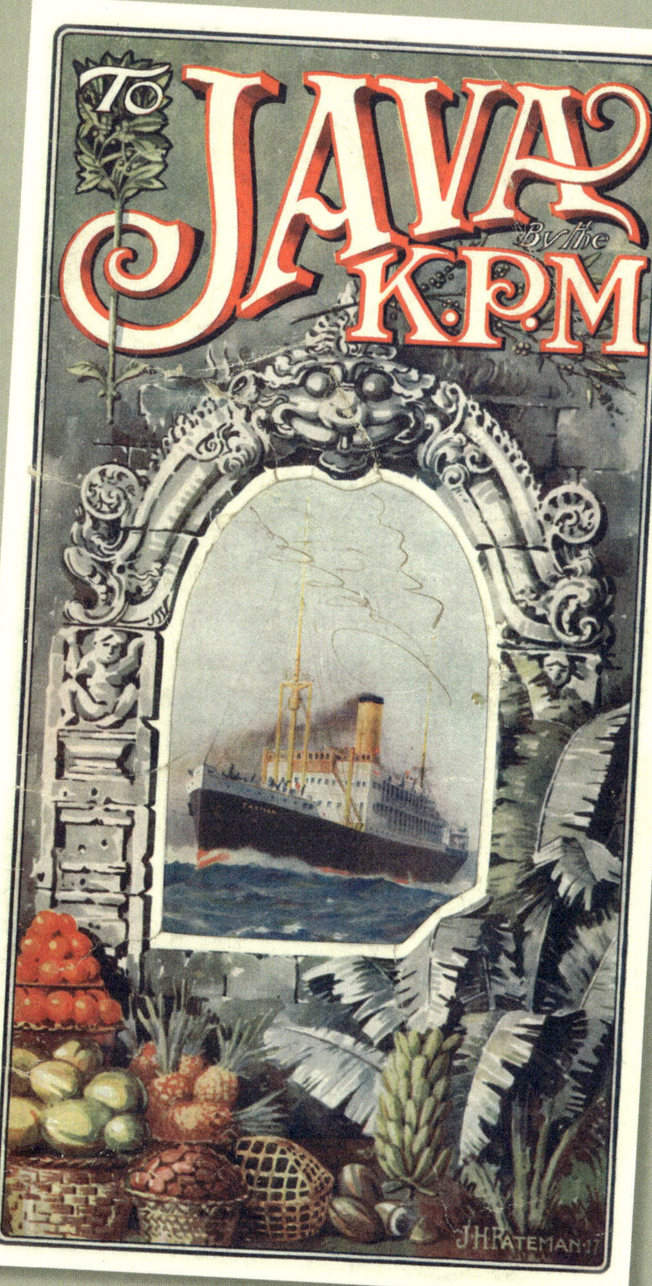

(1910s–20s)

Colourful prewar brochures published by KPM (Royal Packet Navigation Company) promoting tours to Java and Bali. Founded in 1888, KPM was a Dutch shipping company that first provided steamship services in the Indonesian Archipelago. By the Second World War, its shipping lines had extended to over 400 ports in Asia, Africa and Australasia, and the company dominated shipping in the Dutch East Indies.

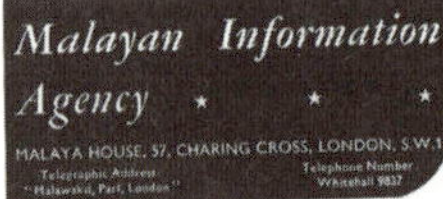

A 1936 advertisement promoting travel to British Malaya by the Malayan Information Agency in London, which aimed to promote business opportunities and tourism to the colonies.

A Federated Malay States Railways (FMSR) advertisement highlighting the air-conditioned buffet cars and sleeping saloons in which travellers could "enjoy a hill station climate whilst making your journey". (1939)

An air-conditioned buffet car of an FMSR train. The Railways introduced air-conditioned coaches in 1937. (1939)

(1933)

Advertisements by the Federated Malay States Railways and the Siamese State Railways. The development of the two railways greatly facilitated tourism to British Malaya and Siam (Thailand). By 1918, the two railways were linked, providing easy connections between the two countries.

(1933)

(1935)

Advertisement for the Grand Hotel in Brastagi (Berastagi), a hill station in Sumatra, Indonesia, situated 1,500 metres above sea level. The Dutch developed this hill resort in the 1900s. Patrons could enjoy outdoor sports, evening entertainment and views of volcanoes. (1940)

(1940)

(1940)

Invigorating mountain air, cool temperatures, outdoor sports and an English atmosphere – these were some of the major draws highlighted by advertisements for hotels in Cameron Highlands.

A 1938 cruise liner advertisement by the Peninsular & Oriental Steam Navigation Company (P&O) and British India Steam Navigation Company (B.I.), which were amalgamated in 1914. In the 1930s, their steamship services covered Europe, the Middle East, India, East Asia, Australia, New Zealand and Africa.

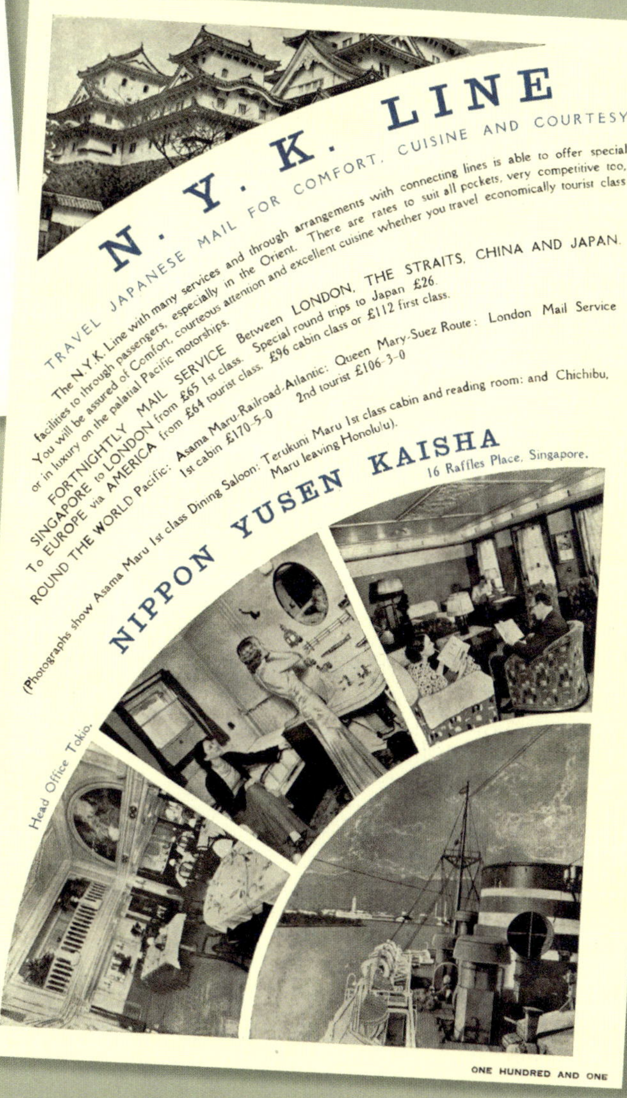

N.Y.K. Line (Nippon Yusen Kaisha, or Japan Mail Shipping Line) advertisement featuring its luxury cruise liner facilities. (1936)

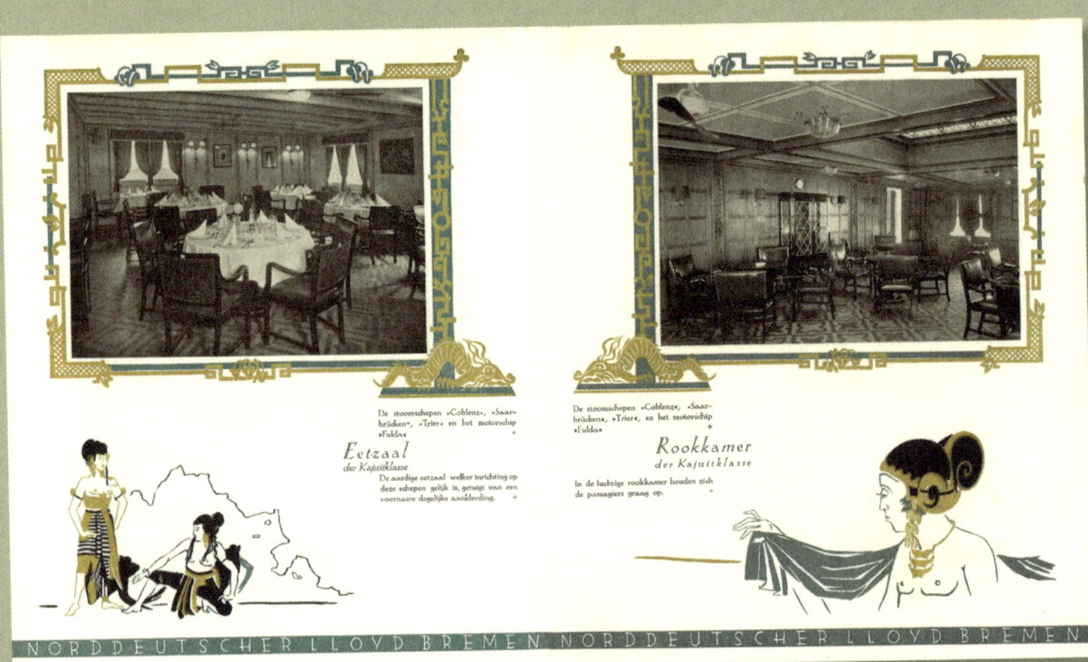

The sumptuous interiors of the cruise liners of the
Norddeutscher Lloyd (North German Lloyd) shipping
company feature prominently in this brochure. The
company started cruise liner services to East Asia in 1886.
(1920s–30s)

(1937)

(1939)

These 1930s
advertisements of
the Royal Dutch Mails
and the Danish East
Asiatic Line evoke the
modernity and glamour
often associated with
luxury cruise liners.

Qantas Empire Airways started flying between Australia and Singapore in 1935, beginning with the first passenger flight from Brisbane. Operating in parallel with the British Overseas Airways Corporation (BOAC), Qantas linked Singapore with Australia and Britain and other countries in between. (1952)

A 1960 Malayan Airways advertisement showing some of the airline's destinations in the region. Following the formation of Malaysia in 1963, the airline changed its name to Malaysian Airways. After Singapore became independent, it was again renamed, as Malaysia-Singapore Airlines (MSA). In 1971, MSA split into two separate national carriers, which became Singapore Airlines and Malaysia Airlines.

(1966)

(1957)

(1969)

By the 1960s, airplanes had replaced steamships
as the default mode of international travel. Airline
advertisements became a common sight in magazines.

Introduction

1. The observations in this essay are based on the author's research in the National Library Board's (NLB) holdings of English newspapers of the period, as well as research findings from non-English newspapers most ably provided by NLB librarians Goh Yu Mei, Liviniyah P., Mazelan Anuar, Nadirah Norruddin and Sundari Balasubramaniam.

2. Gibson-Hill, C.A. (1953). The Singapore Chronicle (1824–37). *Journal of the Malayan Branch of the Royal Asiatic Society*, 26(2), p. 176. Retrieved from JSTOR via NLB's eResources website: http://www.eresources.nlb.gov.sg. See also Mazelan Anuar. (2016, January 26). The first newspaper. *BiblioAsia*, 11(4). Retrieved from NLB website: http://www.nlb.gov.sg/biblioasia/

3. See: George, C. (Ed.). (1995). *150 years of newspapers: The Straits Times July 15, 1845–1995*. Singapore: Singapore Press Holdings, p. 8. (Call no.: RSING 079.5957 ONE); Marina Samad. (1972, January). Early Malay journalism: Jawi Peranakan and the first Malay newspapers. *Leader, Malaysian Journalism Review*, p. 18. (Call no.: RSEA 079.5957 MAR); Chen, M.H. (1967). *The early Chinese newspapers of Singapore, 1881–1912*. Singapore: University of Malaya Press, p. 24. (Call no.: RSING 079.5702 CHE). For Tamil newspapers, Latha d/o Sinasamy notes that it "is difficult to ascertain when the first local Tamil newspaper in Singapore appeared due to the lack of recorded evidence". In English-language records, *Singai Varthagamani* was mentioned in 1876, *Thangai Nesan* was said to have been circulating since 1878, and there was a third publication, *Gnana Sooriyan*; all had ceased publication by 1887. See Latha d/o Sinasamy. (1999/2000). *Tamil Malar: Voice of the Tamil community (1964–1980)* [BA Honours Thesis]. Singapore: National University of Singapore, pp. 1–2. (Call no.: RSING 079.5957 SIN). The oldest Tamil-language newspaper in the National Library Board collection is *Singai Nesan*, which was published from 1887 to 1890; see also Rai, R. (2014). *Indians in Singapore, 1819–1945: Diaspora in the colonial port city*. New Delhi: Oxford University Press, p. 140. (Call no.: RSING 909.049141105957 RAI). For more on Malay-language newspapers, see Ainon Haji Kuntom. (1974). *Malay newspapers, 1876–1973: A historical survey of the literature* [academic exercise]. Pusat Pengajian Ilmu Kemanusiaan, Universiti Sains Malaysia. (Call no.: RSING q079.5951 AIN)

4. Williams, K. (2010). *Read all about it!: A history of the British newspaper*. Abingdon, UK; New York: Routledge, pp. 12, 30, 39. (Call no.: R 072.09 WIL). Of course, many modes of the news circulation have existed likely since the beginnings of human civilisation, such as word of mouth, official announcements (carved into stone, or inscribed onto posters and signs) and handwritten news sheets. However, many of these did not appear at a regular frequency, or if they did, were targeted at the elites of society (e.g. handwritten news sheets in China in 200 BCE), not the public (who were usually illiterate). See Williams, 2010, pp. 12, 26; and Wharton, C. (2015). *Advertising: Critical approaches*. Abingdon, UK; New York: Routledge, p. 25. (Call no.: 659.1 WA-[BIZ])

5. Williams, 2010, p. 50.

6. Quoted in Wharton, 2015, p. 14.

7. Wharton, 2015, p. 38; Clarke, B. (2004). *From Grub Street to Fleet Street: An illustrated history of English newspapers to 1899*. Aldershot, UK; Burlington, VT: Ashgate, p. 142. (Call no.: R 072 CLA)

8. Williams, 2010, p. 76.

9. Clarke, 2004, p. 162.

10. Sandra Hudd notes that "it is likely that printing [in Singapore] had begun in late 1822". See Hudd, S. (2017). London Missionary Society in Singapore. *Singapore Infopedia*. Retrieved from Singapore Infopedia website: http://eresources.nlb.gov.sg/infopedia/

11. Ibid.

12. Gibson-Hill, 1953, pp. 178–179; Mazelan Anuar, 26 Jan 2016. The earliest copy of the *Singapore Chronicle* in the National Library's holdings is from 3 January 1833. Carl Gibson-Hill noted in 1952 that there are no extant copies of the first copy of the *Chronicle* and that the earliest issues he had seen were from 1827; Gibson-Hill, 1953, pp. 176, 178.

13. Gibson-Hill, 1953, pp. 178, 187, 192–193, 196.

14. Chen, 1967, p. 40; The Straits Times story. (n.d.). In W. Fernandez (Ed.), *Living history: 170 years of the Straits Times* [ebook], [p. 30 of PDF]. Retrieved from The Straits Times website: http://graphics.straitstimes.com/STI/STIMEDIA/ebooks/Living-History.pdf

15. Tan, L.G. (2014). Charting multilingualism in Singapore: From the nineteenth century to the present [Final-year project]. Singapore: Nanyang Technological University, p. 24. Retrieved from Nanyang Technological University website: http://www.soh.ntu.edu.sg/Programmes/linguistics/Undergraduate%20Programme/Documents/Good%20Sample%20FYP%20Reports/AY2014/Tan%20Lijia%20Gloria.pdf

16. Marina Samad, Jan 1972, p. 18. Ian Proudfoot has written that modern Malay prose, in the form of "plain expository narrative" (such as that found in newspapers) would have been a novel form of writing and also reading at the time because "[it] was not a style to be enjoyed by reading aloud, as the contemporary popular verse (*syair*) and prose (*hikayat*) forms were; it made no appeal to the ear. It was best suited to individual reading". Proudfoot, I. (1994) *The print threshold in Malaysia* [Working Paper 88]. The Centre of Southeast Asian Studies, Monash University, pp. 11–12. (Call no.: RSEA 070.509595 PRO)

17. Sinasamy, 1999/2000, pp. 1–2; Chen, 1967, pp. 12–14.

18. Chen, 1967, p. 40.

19. Tan, 2014, p. 24.

20. Chia, J.Y.J., & Nor-Afidah Adb Rahman. (2007). Old racecourse (Farrer Park). *Singapore Infopedia*. Retrieved from Singapore Infopedia website: http://www.eresources.nlb.gov.sg/infopedia

21. "Through the agricultural and industrial revolutions [of the mid-17th to 19th centuries] England had been transformed from an economy and culture based on peasant farming and self-sufficient communities into an 'industrialised market society and world capitalist power dominating international trade and colonial expansion'. … Products once produced locally, on a small scale for local consumption, were now produced in industrial quantities and sold on national [and international] markets." This was the global economic context in which colonial Singapore's consumption patterns emerged. Wharton, 2015, pp. 51, 52.

22. "A kitchen servant that more than pays its own salary" – the tagline in an advertisement for Leonard refrigerators placed by Sime Darby & Co. Ltd.: *The Singapore and Malayan Ladies Directory with Shopping Guide 1937–38*. (1938). Singapore: Printers, p. 105. Retrieved from PublicationSG.

23. National Library Board. (2014). King George VI Dock opens. *HistorySG*. Retrieved from HistorySG website: http://eresources.nlb.gov.sg/history/. For more on Singapore's Modernist architecture, see Davison, J. (2014). Swan & Maclaren: Pioneers of Modernist architecture. *BiblioAsia, 13*(2). Retrieved from BiblioAsia website: http://www.nlb.gov.sg/biblioasia/2017/07/06/swan-maclaren-pioneers-of-modernist-architecture/

24. Cited in Turnbull, C.M. (2009). *A history of Singapore, 1819–2005*. Singapore: NUS Press, p. 165. (Call no.: RSING 959.57 TUR-[HIS])

25. Kuo, E.C.Y. (1980). The sociolinguistic situation in Singapore: Unity in diversity. In E.A. Afendras & E.C.Y. Kuo (Eds.), *Language and society in Singapore*. Singapore: Singapore University Press, p. 53. (Call no.: RSING 409.5957 LAN). Interestingly, Tan Lijia Gloria observes that the definition of being literate changed between the 1952 and 1970 censuses: In 1952 it was defined as "the ability to read and write a simple letter", while in 1970 it was defined as the "ability to read with understanding a newspaper in any of the four official languages or any other language"; see Tan, 2014, pp. 30, 33.

26. Uhde, J., & Ng Uhde, Y. (2010). *Latent images: Film in Singapore*. Singapore: NUS Press, p. 203. (Call no.: RSING 791.43095957 UHD); Chung, M.K. (2006). *Vintage Singapore*. Singapore: Editions Didier Millet; National Museum of Singapore, pp. 12, 132–133. (Call no.: RSING 959.57 VIN)

27. Wharton, 2015, p. 182.

28. Bachtiar, I. New, improved and for sale. In C. George (Ed.), 1995, p. 115.

29. For more on advertising and conspicuous consumption, see Wharton, 2015, p. 182.

30. The earliest mention of Singapore as a "shopping paradise" in the National Library Board's digital newspaper archive was on 4 March 1937: Singapore shopping paradise. (1937, March 4). *The Straits Times*, p. 13. Retrieved from NewspaperSG.

31. See, for instance, Goh, C.B. (2003). *Serving Singapore: A hundred years of Cold Storage, 1903–2003*. Singapore: Cold Storage, p. 54. (Call no.: RSING 381.148095957 GOH)

32. Chia, J.Y.J., & Tay, S. (2016). John Little. *Singapore Infopedia*. Retrieved from Singapore Infopedia website: http://eresources.nlb.gov.sg/infopedia/; National Library Board. (2014). Robinson's department store is established. *HistorySG*. Retrieved from HistorySG website: http://eresources.nlb.gov.sg/history/

33. Rimmer, P.J., & Dick, H.W. (2009). *The city in Southeast Asia: Patterns, processes and policy*. Singapore: NUS Press, p. 162, Figure 6.2. (Call no.: RSING 307.76.0959 RIM)

34. [Page 2 Advertisements Column 3]. (1845, September 2). *The Straits Times*, p. 2; [Page 4 Advertisements Column 1]. (1858, October 28). *The Singapore Free Press and Mercantile Advertiser*, p. 4. Retrieved from NewspaperSG.

35. High Street was the first to be macadamed or paved with stones, earning it the title of the oldest street in Singapore. Cornelius, V. (2002). High Street. *Singapore Infopedia*. Retrieved from Singapore Infopedia website: http://eresources.nlb.gov.sg/infopedia/

36. For more on the Sindhi traders' role as "'global middlemen' between the Far East and India", see Rai, 2014, pp. 107–108; and Bhattacharya, J. (2011). *Beyond the myth: Indian business communities in Singapore*. Singapore: Institute of Southeast Asian Studies, pp. 48–50. (Call no.: RSING 338.708991405957 BHA)

37. Rai, 2014, pp. 110, 118.

38. Lim, H.S. (Interviewer). (1981, July 8). *Oral history interview with Rajabali Jumabhoy* [Accession no. 000074/37/8]. Retrieved from National Archives of Singapore website: http://www.nas.gov.sg/archivesonline/. Cited in Bhattacharya, 2011, p. 38.

39. National Heritage Board. (2012). *Kampong Glam: A heritage trail*. Singapore: National Heritage Board, pp. 23, 33. (Call no.: RSING 599.2 KAM)

40. Faris Joraimi. (2017, January 29). Wardah. *s/pores, 15*. Retrieved from s/pores website: http://s-pores.com/2017/01/wardah-by-faris-joraimi; Proudfoot, 1994, p. 28.

41. Kuo, H.-Y. (2104). *Networks beyond empires: Chinese business and nationalism in the Hong Kong-Singapore corridor, 1914–1941*. Leiden & Boston: Brill, p. 232. (Call no.: RSING 338.8895109041 KUO)

42. The earliest English-language newspaper advertisement by Wing On & Co. appeared on 1 October 1912: [Page 2 Advertisements Column 1]. (1912, October 1). *The Straits Times*, p. 2. Retrieved from NewspaperSG. The Singapore branch of Sincere Co. opened in 1917: Chan, W.K.K. (1996). Personal styles, cultural values and management: The Sincere and Wing On companies in Shanghai and Hong Kong, 1900–1941. *Business History Review, 70*(2), p. 148. Retrieved from JSTOR via NLB's eResources website: http://www.eresources.nlb.gov.sg

43. Rai, 2014, p. 119.

44. Bhattacharya, 2011, pp. 56–57; Bhattacharya, J. (2016). Less-remembered spaces and interactions in a changing Singapore: Indian business communities in the post-independence period. In G. Pillai & K. Kesavapany (Eds.), *50 years of Indian community in Singapore*. Singapore; Hackensack, NJ; London: World Scientific, p. 92. (Call no.: RSING 305.89141105957 FIF)

45. Nor-Afidah Abd Rahman. (2004). Echigoya. *Singapore Infopedia*. Retrieved from Singapore Infopedia website: http://eresources.nlb.gov.sg/infopedia/

46. Hiroshi, S., & Hitoshi, H. (1999). *Japan and Singapore in the world economy: Japan's economic advance into Singapore 1870–1965*. Abingdon, UK; New York: Routledge, p. 168. (Call no.: RSING 337.5205957 SHI)

47. A third area, Stamford Road and Orchard Road, had shops that catered more to tourists, selling imported crafts and curios from all over Asia. See G.A. Chatfield. (1962). *Shops and shopping in Singapore*. Singapore: Eastern Universities Press, p. 9. (Call no.: RCLOS 959.51 CHA)

48. Whiteaway Laidlaw's was established in 1900: Makepeace, W., Brooke, G.E., & Braddell, R.S.J. (Eds.). (1991). *One hundred years of Singapore* (Vol. 1). Singapore: Oxford University Press, p. 234. (Call no.: RSING 959.57 ONE-[HIS]). See also: Sidhu, R.S. (2017). *Singapore's early Sikh pioneers: Origins, settlement, contributions and institutions*. Singapore: Central Sikh Gurdwara Board, pp. 130–131. (Call no.: RSING 305.8914205957 SID)

49. Chatfield, 1962, p. 7.

50. James, J. (2001, April 26). High life on High Street. *The Straits Times*, p. 8. Retrieved from NewspaperSG.

51. Chew, D. (Interviewer). (1985, May 8). *Oral history interview with Girishchandra Kothari* [Accession no. 000549/23/14]. Retrieved from National Archives of Singapore website: http://www.nas.gov.sg/archivesonline/. Cited in Bhattacharya, 2016, p. 85.

52. The phrase "shopping destination" did not appear in Singapore's English-language press until a luxury brand advertisement in 1979: [Page 7 Advertisements Column 1]. (1979, July 23). *The Straits Times*, p. 7. Retrieved from NewspaperSG.

53. Kaur, M. (1981, September 11). Memory lane. *The Straits Times*, p. 13; Ran, S. (1985, April 23). High Street – on the road to new life. *The Straits Times*, p. 1. Retrieved from NewspaperSG.

54. Jay Gee Group. (n.d). *Milestones*. Retrieved from Jay Gee Group website: http://jaygee.com.sg/corporate-milestones/. Men's shop opens in S'pore today. (1971, April 2). *The Straits Times*, p. 16. Retrieved from NewspaperSG.

55. Big new Singapore store. (1938, July 24). *The Straits Times*, p. 1. Bata's new premises. (1940, June 26). *Malaya Tribune*, p. 4. Retrieved from NewspaperSG.

56. Where to shop in Singapore: No. III, High Street. (1939, May 3). *The Singapore Free Press and Mercantile Advertiser*, p. 12. Singapore new department store opens. (1938, October 14). *Malaya Tribune*, p. 20. Chairman began his career as apprentice. (1965, April 2). *The Straits Times*, p. 12. Retrieved from NewspaperSG.

57. 'Sinkeh' who became king of dept stores. (1984, August 13). *Singapore Monitor*, p. 10. Retrieved from NewspaperSG. See also: Metro – past, present and into the future. (1982, September 9). *The Business Times*, p. 7. Retrieved from NewspaperSG.

58. Chairman began his career as apprentice. (1965, April 2). *The Straits Times*, p. 12. Retrieved from NewspaperSG.

59. 'Family store' opens in Singapore. (1965, October 30). *The Straits Times*, p. 16; Firm sets up new shop to meet fashion goods demand. (1965, October 30). *The Straits Times*, p. 16. Retrieved from NewspaperSG.

60. Wharton, 2015, p. 22.

61. Ibid., p. 14.

62. Advertisers Association. (1971). *A review of advertising in Singapore and Malaysia during early times.* Singapore: Federal Publications, p. 26. (Call no.: RSING 659.109 ADV)

63. Notices. (1931, January 16). *The Singapore Free Press*, p. 9. Retrieved from NewspaperSG.

64. [Page 16 Advertisements Column 1]. (1940, January 2). *The Straits Times*, p. 16. Retrieved from NewspaperSG.

65. *Who's who in Malaya, 1939*. (1939). Singapore: Fishers Ltd, p. 139. (Call no.: RCLOS 920.9595 WHO-[RFL]); W.J. Warin dies in Singapore. (1950, June 11). *The Straits Times*, p. 9. Retrieved from NewspaperSG.

66. *Who's who in Malaya*, 1939, p. 139.

67. Mainly about Malayans. (1938, December 4). *The Straits Times*, p. 7. Retrieved from NewspaperSG.

68. The rise of Warin Studios: All forms of publicity. (1937, April 27). *The Singapore Free Press*, p. 2. Retrieved from NewspaperSG.

69. *Roda*. (1935, October), pp. 199–203. (Call no.: RUR 369.509595 R)

70. Goerlik, B. (2013). *Incredible Tretchikoff: Life of an artist and adventurer*. London: Art/Books, p. 152. (Call no.: RART 759.968 GOR). *Chinese Girl*, popularly known as *The Green Lady*, portrays a young Chinese woman with a blue-green face dressed in traditional Chinese costume. It sold for almost £1 million at an auction in London in 2013.

Wheels of Change

1. Definition of automobilism in English. English Oxford Living Dictionaries. Retrieved from: https://en.oxforddictionaries.com/definition/automobilism

2. Singapore. Archives and Oral History Department. (1984). *The land transport of Singapore: From early times to the present.* Singapore: Archives and Oral History Department; Educational Publications Bureau Pte Ltd, p. 4. (Call no.: RSING 779.9388095957 LAN)

3. Singapore's first autocar. (1896, August 13). *The Singapore Free Press and Mercantile Advertiser*, p. 2. Retrieved from NewspaperSG.

4. How Singapore has been revolutionised by the modern motor car. (1935, October 8). *The Singapore Free Press and Mercantile Advertiser*, p. 20; An autocar anniversary. (1927, August 13). *The Singapore Free Press and Mercantile Advertiser*, p. 5. Retrieved from NewspaperSG.

5. Singapore's first motor car was a problem. (1958, July 5). *The Straits Times*, p. 9. Retrieved from NewspaperSG.

6. An autocar anniversary. (1927, August 13). *The Singapore Free Press and Mercantile Advertiser*, p. 5. Retrieved from NewspaperSG.

7. Makepeace, W., Brooke, G.E., & Braddell, R.S.J. (Eds.). (1991). *One hundred years of Singapore* (Vol. 2). Singapore: Oxford University Press, p. 364. (Call no.: RSING 959.57 ONE)

8. Mr. Buckley and his coffee machine. (1955, March 13). *The Straits Times*, p. 12. Retrieved from NewspaperSG.

9. Famous 'firsts' of days gone by in S'pore. (1957, November 4). *The Singapore Free Press*, p. 10. Retrieved from NewspaperSG.

10. Makepeace, Brooke, & Braddell, 1991, p. 364.

11. Mr. Buckley and his coffee machine. (1955, March 13). *The Straits Times*, p. 12. Retrieved from NewspaperSG.

12. Yap, J. (2007). *Motoring beyond 100: Celebrating 100 years of the Automobile Association of Singapore.* Singapore: Automobile Association of Singapore, p. 15. (Call no.: RSING 629.2830605957 YAP)

13. Eckermann, E. (2001). *World history of the automobile.* Warrendale, PA: Society of Automative Engineers, p. 25. (Call no.: R 629.22209 ECK)

14. Yap, 2007, p. 3.

15. [Untitled]. (1907, June 6). *The Straits Times*, p. 6. Retrieved from NewspaperSG.

16. Motors & motoring. (1910, May 14). *The Straits Times*, p. 11; The motoring world. (1911, January 6). *The Straits Times*, p. 11; The motoring world. (1928, December 15). *The Straits Times*, p. 18. Retrieved from NewspaperSG.

17. Makepeace, Brooke, & Braddell, 1991, p. 362.

18. Yap, 2007, pp. 53, 58, 73.

19. Laird, P.W. (1996, October). 'The car without a single weakness': Early automobile advertising. *Technology and Culture, 37*(4), 796–812, p. 797. Retrieved from JSTOR via NLB's eResources website: http://www.eresources.nlb.gov.sg

20. Scharchburg, R.P. (1993). *Carriages without horses: J. Frank Duryea and the birth of the American automobile industry.* Warrendale, PA: Society of Automotive Engineers, p. 119. (Call no.: R 338.7629222 SCH)

21. [Page 9 Advertisements Column 1]. (1909, December 24). *The Straits Times*, p. 9. Retrieved from NewspaperSG.

22. Ford Company opens here. (1926, November 23). *The Singapore Free Press and Mercantile Advertiser*, p. 8. Retrieved from NewspaperSG.

23. Ford company in Malaya is 30 years old. (1956, November 9). *The Straits Times*, p. 14. Retrieved from NewspaperSG.

24. Japanese cars to cost more. (1971, October 11). *The Straits Times*, p. 1. Retrieved from NewspaperSG.

25. Taxi-cabs for Singapore. (1910, July 1). *The Singapore Free Press and Mercantile Advertiser*, p. 8. Retrieved from NewspaperSG.

26. [Page 5 Advertisements Column 1]. (1919, April 16). *Malaya Tribune*, p. 5. Retrieved from NewspaperSG.

27. [Page 6 Advertisements Column 3]. (1920, December 21). *The Straits Times*, p. 6. Retrieved from NewspaperSG.

28. [Page 4 Advertisements Column 1]. (1924, September 12). *The Singapore Free Press and Mercantile Advertiser*, p. 4. Retrieved from NewspaperSG.

29. Taximeter Day–Dec. 31. (1953, November 14). *The Singapore Free Press*, p. 5. Retrieved from NewspaperSG.

30. [Untitled]. (1930, May 10). *Malayan Saturday Post*, p. 16. Retrieved from NewspaperSG.

31. Wearne Bros. declare 3 per cent dividend. (1933, December 16). *The Straits Times*, p. 9. Retrieved from NewspaperSG.

32. [Page 16 Advertisements Column 2]. (1933, November 6). *The Straits Times*, p. 16. Retrieved from NewspaperSG.

33. [Page 19 Advertisements Column 1]. (1934, January 15). *The Straits Times*, p. 19. Retrieved from NewspaperSG.

34. [Page 16 Advertisements Column 2]. (1933, November 6). *The Straits Times* , p. 16. Retrieved from NewspaperSG.

35. 700 'pirate' taxis in S'pore. (1946, August 10). *The Singapore Free Press*, p. 1; Police have plan to beat taxi 'pirates'. (1952, January 15). *The Straits Times*, p. 7; Pirate taxis. (1957, May 8). *Singapore Standard*, p. 6; The war against pirate taxis a success. (1962, February 18). *The Straits Times*, p. 16. Retrieved from NewspaperSG.

36. The pirates who are performing a public service. (1962, October 2). *The Straits Times*, p. 10; Special licence urged for transport of pupils. (1965, May 28). *The Straits Times*, p. 4; Pirate taxis: A public service. (1970, October 26). *Singapore Herald*, p. 8. Retrieved from NewspaperSG.

37. 4,000 cabbies want to join NTUC co-op. (1970, August 18). *The Straits Times*, p. 4; 3,800 apply for Comfort's 1,000 taxis. (1970, December 17). *The Straits Times*, p. 7. Retrieved from NewspaperSG.

38. Comfort taxis: A chance for pirate taxi men, too. (1971, January 16). *Singapore Herald*, p. 3; Taximen's chief praises NTUC move to help 'pirates'. (1971, January 18). *The Straits Times*, p. 21. Retrieved from NewspaperSG.

39. Pirate taxis defy ban. (1971, October 12). *The Straits Times*, p. 12; War on pirate taxis goes on. (1972, May 1). *New Nation*, p. 3. Retrieved from NewspaperSG.

That's Entertainment

1. Prospectus for a theatre. (1842, May 19). *The Singapore Free Press and Mercantile Advertiser*, p. 1. Retrieved from NewspaperSG.

2. Yung, S.S., & Chan, K.B. (2003). Leisure, pleasure and consumption: Way of entertaining oneself. In K.B. Chan & C.K. Tong (Eds.), *Past times: A social history of Singapore* (pp. 152–181). Singapore: Times Editions, p. 153. (Call no.: RSING 959.57 PAS-[HIS])

3. Buckley, C.B. (1984). *An anecdotal history of old times in Singapore.* Singapore: Oxford University Press, p. 741. (Call no.: RSING 959.57 BUC-[HIS])

4. [Untitled]. (1833, March 28). *Singapore Chronicle and Commercial Register*, p. 3. Retrieved from NewspaperSG.

5. Makepeace, W., Brooke, G.E., & Braddell, R.J. (Eds.). (1991). *One hundred years of Singapore* (Vol. 2). Singapore: Oxford University Press, pp. 381–383. (Call no.: RSING 959.57 ONE)

6. Makepeace, Brooke, & Braddell, 1991, pp. 381–383.

7. Theatre Royal. (1854, December 8). *The Singapore Free Press and Mercantile Advertiser*, p. 3; [Untitled]. (1856, January 1). *The Straits Times*, p. 4. Retrieved from NewspaperSG.

8. Makepeace, Brooke, & Braddell, 1991, p. 383.

9. Town Hall. (1905, October 2). *Eastern Daily Mail and Straits Morning Advertiser*, p. 3; Burns Concert. (1911, January 14). *The Singapore Free Press and Mercantile Advertiser*, p. 1; [Untitled]. (1924, December 16). *The Straits Times*, p. 8. Retrieved from NewspaperSG.

10. Song, O.S. (1984). *One hundred years' history of the Chinese in Singapore.* Singapore: Oxford University Press, p. 189. (Call no.: RSING 959.57 SON-[HIS])

11. Magic in North Bridge Road. (1935, February 5). *The Straits Times*, p. 13. Retrieved from NewspaperSG.

12. Uhde, J., & Ng Uhde, Y. (2010). *Latent images: Film in Singapore.* Singapore: NUS Press, p. 14. (Call no.: RSING 384.8095957 UHD); The Ripograph. (1897, May 18). *The Singapore Free Press and Mercantile Advertiser (Weekly)*, p. 6. Retrieved from NewspaperSG.

13. Millet, R. (2006). *Singapore cinema.* Singapore: Editions Didier Millet, pp. 16–17. (Call no.: RSING q791.43095957 MIL)

14. The Paris Cinematography. (1904, November 26). *The Straits Times*, p. 3. Retrieved from NewspaperSG.

15. Millet, 2006, pp. 16–17.

16. Fisher, J.S. (1929). Current cinema comments. In J.S. Fisher (Ed.), *British Malayan Annual 1929.* Singapore: Fishers Limited, p. 109. (Microfilm: NL28302)

17. Fisher, 1929, p. 107.

18. Thompson, K., & Bordwell, D. (2010). *Film history: An introduction* (3rd Ed.). Boston; Singapore: McGraw-Hill Higher Education, pp. 202–203. (Call no.: R 791.4309 THO)

19. This refers to the colour-filming system developed by the Technicolour firm.

20. [Untitled]. (1938, September 22). *Morning Tribune*, p. 7. Retrieved from NewspaperSG.

21. Mountain-air climate in Singapore. (1938, July 27). *The Singapore Free Press and Mercantile Advertiser*, p. 4. Retrieved from NewspaperSG.

22. Uhde & Ng Uhde, 2010, pp. 14–30.

23. Barnard, T.P. (2008). The Shaw Brothers' Malay films. In P. Fu (Ed.), *China forever: The Shaw Brothers and diasporic cinema* (pp. 131–153). Urbana: University of Illinois Press, p. 170. (Call no.: RSEA 791.43095125 CHI)

24. 黄爱玲 [Wong, A.L.]. (2009). 前言 [Introduction]. In A.L. Wong (Ed.), 《国泰故事》(增订本) [The Cathay story (Revised Edition)] (pp. 4–9). 香港：香港电影资料馆 [Hong Kong: Hong Kong Film Archive], p. 6. (Call no.: RART Chinese q791.43095125 CAT); Yung, S.S. (2008). Territorialisation and the entertainment industry of the Shaw Brothers in Southeast Asia. In P. Fu (Ed.), *China forever: The Shaw Brothers and diasporic cinema* (pp. 131–153). Urbana: University of Illinois Press, p. 149. (Call no.: RSEA 791.43095125 CHI); Xu, Y.S. [许永顺]. (2015). 新马华文电影, *1927–1965* [Chinese movies in Singapore and Malaysia, 1927–1965]. 新加坡：许永顺工作厅 [Singapore: Xu Yongshun Gongzuoting], p. 13. (Call no.: RSING Chinese 791.4309595 XYS)

25. Wai, S.H. (2014). New Immigrant: On the first locally produced film in Singapore and Malaya. *Journal of Chinese Cinema*, 8(3), 244–258. Retrieved from Taylor & Francis Online.

26. Wong, Y.C., & Tan, K.L. (2004, August). Emergence of a cosmopolitan space for consumption: The New World Amusement Park Singapore (1923–70) in the inter-war years. *Inter-Asia Cultural Studies*, 5(2), 279–304, p. 280. Retrieved from JSTOR via NLB's eResources website: http://eresources.nlb.gov.sg/

27. Tan, B.L. (Interviewer). (1981, November 18). *Oral history interview with Gwee Peng Kwee* [Transcript of recording no. 000128/13/03, p. 23]. Retrieved from National Archives of Singapore website: http://www.nas.gov.sg/archivesonline

28. Wong & Tan, 2004, p. 280.

29. Yung & Chan, 2003, p. 164.

30. Ibid., p. 154.

31. Ibid.

32. Buckley, 1984, p. 216.

Changing Tastes

1. Kong, L., & Sinha, V. (2015). *Food, foodways and foodscapes: Culture, community and consumption in post-colonial Singapore*. Singapore: World Scientific, pp. 222–223. (Call no.: RSING 394.12095957 FOO)

2. Tarulevicz, N. (2013). *Eating her curries and kway: A cultural history of food in Singapore*. Chicago, Illinois: University of Illinois Press, p. 16. (Call no.: RSING 394.12095957 TAR)

3. Perry, J.C. (2017). *Singapore: Unlikely power*. New York, NY: Oxford University Press, p. 69. (Call no.: RSING 330.95957 PER); Turnbull, C.M. (2009). *A history of modern Singapore 1819–2005*. Singapore: NUS Press, p. 93. (Call no.: RSING 959.57 TUR)

4. Goh, C.B. (2013). *Technology and entrepot colonialism in Singapore, 1819–1940*. Singapore: Institute of Southeast Asian Studies, pp. 168–169. (Call no.: RSING 338.064095957 GOH)

5. Local industries. (1897, January 8). *The Straits Times*, p. 3. Retrieved from NewspaperSG.

6. Fu, C., & Yu, J. (2013). *A legend turns 130*. Singapore: Fraser and Neave Limited, pp. 13, 16, 30–31. (Call no.: RSING 338.7663095957 LEG)

7. Framroz celebrates fifty years of progress. (1954, January 10). *Sunday Standard*, p. 5. Retrieved from NewspaperSG.

8. Our aerated water trade. (1932, January 2). *The Singapore Free Press and Mercantile Advertiser*, p. 23. Retrieved from NewspaperSG.

9. Aerated waters. (1925, July 6). *Malaya Tribune*, p. 5. Retrieved from NewspaperSG.

10. Perry, 2017, p. 90.

11. Wong, M. (n.d.). *Singapore: A pineapple canning delight*. Retrieved from National Archives of Singapore website: www.nas.gov.sg/archivesonline/article/singapore-pineapple-canning-delight. Singapore was a staple port that processed and exported primary commodities such as tin from the Malayan hinterland to the rest of the world. As pineapples were cultivated in Singapore as a cash crop, canning technology was used to manufacture canned pineapples, which became a popular export of Singapore.

12. Pilon, M., & Weiler, D. (2011). *The French in Singapore: An illustrated history (1819–today)*. Singapore: Editions Didiet Millet, p. 88. (Call no.: RSING 305.84105957 PIL)

13. The rooster stands for good taste. (1955, October 7). *The Singapore Free Press*, p. 5. Retrieved from NewspaperSG.

14. Materials of proved quality for the building trade. (1936, May 1). *The Singapore Free Press and Mercantile Advertiser*, p. 5. Retrieved from NewspaperSG; Quek, E. (2017, March 26). Three home-grown brands celebrate milestone anniversaries. *The Straits Times*. Retrieved from Factiva via NLB's eResources website: http://eresources.nlb.gov.sg

15. Goh, C.B. (2003). *Serving Singapore: A hundred years of Cold Storage, 1903–2003*. Singapore: Cold Storage, pp. 13, 24. (Call no.: RSING 381.148095957 GOH)

16. Ibid., p. 24; Goh, 2013, p. 171.

17. Goh, 2003, pp. 41–45. Tregonning, K.G. (1967). *The Singapore Cold Storage: 1903–1906*. Singapore: Cold Storage Holdings Ltd, p. vii. (Call no.: RCLOS 664.02852 TRE)

18. Goh, 2003, pp. 24, 41–45, 54, 82; Goh, 2013, p. 187.

19. 'Help-Yourself' service as Fitzpatrick's streamlines. (1949, July 30). *Malaya Tribune*, p. 4; Now shopping in the modern manner comes to Singapore. (1958, August 11). *The Singapore Free Press*, p. 3. Retrieved from NewspaperSG.

20. First super-market in SEA. (1958, August 10). *Sunday Standard*, p. 2. Retrieved from NewspaperSG.

21. Now shopping in the modern manner comes to Singapore. (1958, August 11). *The Singapore Free Press*, p. 3. Retrieved from NewspaperSG.

22. Luk, S. (2014). *Health insurance reforms in Asia*. Abingdon; New York: Routledge, p. 81. (Call no.: RSEA 368.3820095 LUK)

23. Butcher, J.G. (1979). *The British in Malaya, 1880–1941: The social history of a European community in colonial South-east Asia*. Kuala Lumpur; New York: Oxford University Press, p. 68. (Call no.: RSING 301.4512105951033 BUT); Manderson, L. (2002). *Sickness and the state: Health and illness in colonial Malaya, 1870–1940*. New York: Cambridge University Press, p. 75. (Call no.: RSING 362.1095951 MAN)

24. Manderson, 2002, p. 157.

25. Ibid., p. 214.

26. Ibid., pp. 203–204, 214–215.

27. Ibid., pp. 141–142.

28. Europeans believed that the quinine in tonic water could cure malaria. Quinine is bitter-tasting and hence the word '*pahit*' in their 'gin-*pahit*.'

29. Peleggi, M. (2012). The social and material life of colonial hotels: Comfort zones as contact zones in British Colombo and Singapore, ca. 1870–1930. *Journal of Social History*, 6(1), 124–153, p. 138. Retrieved from JSTOR via NLB's eResources website: http://eresources.nlb.gov. sg/

30. A wonderful achievement. (1932, September 30). *The Straits Times*, p. 12; Say 'Tiger' – It's the best beer. (1932, December 20). *The Straits Times*, p. 4. Retrieved from NewspaperSG.

31. Wu, D.Y.H. (1979). *Traditional Chinese concepts of food and medicine in Singapore*. Singapore: Institute of Southeast Asian Studies, pp. 17–19. (Call no.: RSING 641.3 WU)

32. Tobacco industry in Malaya. (1932, January 2). *The Straits Times*, p. 4. Retrieved from NewspaperSG.

A Matter of Style

1. Jayapal, M. (1996). *Old Singapore*. Singapore: Oxford University Press, p. 33. (Call no.: RSING 959.57 JAY-[HIS])

2. Bird, I. (2016). *The Golden Chersonese*. Abingdon, Oxon; New York, NY: Routledge, p. 114. (Call no.: RSING 915.980422 BIR-[TRA])

3. Advertisers Association. (1971). *A review of advertising in Singapore and Malaysia during early times*. Singapore: Federal Publications, p. 4. (Call no.: RSING 659.109 ADV)

4. Frost, M., & Balasingamchow, Y. (2009). *Singapore: A biography*. Singapore: Editions Didier Millet Pte Ltd; National Museum of Singapore, pp. 134–136. (Call no.: RSING 959.57 FRO-[HIS])

5. Bruna, D. (2015). *Fashioning an intimate history of the silhouette*. New Haven & London: Yale University Press, p. 159. (Call no.: RART 746.92 FAS)

6. Hopkins, S. (n.d.). History of men's hats. Retrieved 10 March, 2018, from website: http://fashion-history.lovetoknow.com/fashion-accessories/history-mens-hats

7. Bird, 2016, p. 117.

8. Bleackley, H. (1928). *A tour in Southern Asia (Indo-China, Malaya, Java, Sumatra, and Ceylon, 1925–1926)*. London: John Lane, pp. 127–128. (Call no.: RCLOS 959 BLE-[RFL])

9. Jayapal, 1996, p. 33.

10. De Souza, J., Ong, C., & Rao, T. (2016). *Fashion most wanted: Singapore's top insider secrets from the past five decades*. Straits Times Press, p. 14. (Call no.: RSING 746.92095957 DES)

11. Wallace, A. (2016). *The Malay Archipelago*. London: Penguin Books, p. 18. (Call no.: RSING 915.9804 WAL-[TRA])

12. A *sarong* is a long piece of cloth wrapped around the torso.

13. A six- or nine-yard piece of material that was wrapped around the waist and draped over the shoulder.

14. A lower garment made by draping a single piece of unsewn material around the waist and forming front pleats.

15. National Heritage Board & Fashion Designers Society. (1993). *Costumes through time: Singapore*. Singapore: National Heritage Board; Fashion Designers Society, pp. 12–13, 116. (Call no.: RSING q391.0095957 COS-[CUS])

16. Ibid., pp. 111–118.

17. Ibid., p. 60.

18. A dream comes true. (1958, October 5). *Sunday Standard*, p. 15. Retrieved from NewspaperSG; De Souza, Ong & Rao, 2016, p. 14.

19. Turnbull, C.M. (2009). *A history of modern Singapore, 1819–2005*. NUS Press, p. 284. (Call no.: RSING 959.57 TUR-[HIS]); National Heritage Board & Fashion Designers Society, 1993, p. 7.

20. De Souza, Ong & Rao, 2016, p. 14; *Her World*. (1960). Singapore: Straits Times Press. Retrieved from PublicationSG; National Heritage Board & Fashion Designers Society, 1993, p. 60.

21. Gum, F. (1973). *The artificial face: A history of cosmetics*. Newton Abbot, UK: David & Charles (Holdings) Limited, pp. 65, 129, 131–137, 317. (Call no.: R 391.630942 GUN-[CUS])

22. Corson, R. (1972). *Fashions in makeup: From ancient to modern times*. London: Peter Owen, p. 394. (Call no.: R q391.6309 COR-[CUS]); Gum, 1973, p. 145.

23. Corson, 1972, p. 447; Gum, 1973, pp. 146–151.

24. Corson, 1972, p. 516.

25. Ibid., p. 321; Cox, C., & Widdows, L. (2005). *Hair & fashion*. London: V&A Publications, pp. 20, 48, 51–53. (Call no.: R q391.509 COX-[CUS]); Gum, 1973, p. 146.

26. Song, O.S. (1984). *One hundred years' history of the Chinese in Singapore*. Singapore: Oxford University Press, pp. 51–52. (Call no.: RSING 959.57 SON-[HIS])

27. Bruna, 2015, pp. 177–179.

28. Crash course in Victorian gloves. (2010, September 29). How we do run on. Retrieved from website: http://gwtwscrapbook. blogspot.sg/2010/09/crash-course-in-victorian-gloves.html#. WrMTeOhublU; Walton, G. (2014, June 19). Glove etiquette in the 1800s. *Geri Walton*. Retrieved from website: https://www. geriwalton.com/glove-etiquette/

29. Schneider, S. (2016, June 8). The evolution of neckwear – From scarf to tie and why we wear ties today. *Gentleman's Gazette*. Retrieved from website: https://www.gentlemansgazette.com/ evolution-neckwear-tie-cravat-scarf/

30. Frost & Balasingamchow, 2009, pp. 145–147.

31. Corson, 1972, p. 516.

A Warm Welcome

1. Thomas, M. (2011). *The heritage of hospitality: A history of the Singapore hotel industry*. Singapore: Marshall Cavendish Editions, pp. 12, 14. (Call no.: RSING 338.4764794 HER). High Street used to stretch all the way to present-day St Andrew's Road, near the water. See J.T. Thomson, 1846, *Plan of Singapore town and its adjoining districts*. Retrieved from National Archives of Singapore website: http://www.nas.gov.sg/archivesonline/

2. Thomas, 2011, p. 14

3. Kinloch, C.W. (1852). Singapore hotels. In J. Bastin (Ed.). (1994). *Travellers' Singapore*. Kuala Lumpur; New York: Oxford University Press, p. 71. (Call no.: RSING 959.5705 TRA-[HIS])

4. Train, G.F. (1855). Excursions round Singapore. Ibid., p. 75.

5. New hostel opened. (1917, July 19). *Malaya Tribune*, p. 4. Retrieved from NewspaperSG.

6. Tan, B.L. (Interviewer). (1987, December 8). *Transcript of oral history interview with Ng Seng Mun* [Accession no. 852/10/9], p. 107. Retrieved from National Archives of Singapore website: http://www.nas.gov.sg/archivesonline/

7. 昔日的香格里拉南天走过63年 [The 63 years of the Shangri-La of the past, the Great Southern Hotel]. (1966, January 1). 《联合早报》 [*Lianhe Zaobao*], p. 42. Retrieved from NewspaperSG.

8. Tan, B. L. (Interviewer). (1987, December 8). *Transcript of oral history interview with Ng Seng Mun* [Accession no. 852/10/9], p. 108. Retrieved from National Archives of Singapore website: http://www.nas.gov.sg/archivesonline/. It is unsurprising to find that Chinese hotels and lodging houses offered such services, considering the large number of Chinese migrants arriving in Singapore in the 1920s.

9. 南天酒樓新張廣告 [Advertisement of the opening of Southern Hotel]. (1927, February 15). 《南洋商報》 [*Nanyang Siang Pau*], p. 5. Retrieved from NewspaperSG.

10. Another new hotel built in Singapore. (1953, March 6). *The Straits Times*, p. 10; Boon, G.T. (1953, April 30). Send-off for two new hotels. *The Singapore Free Press*, p. 8; Hammods, K. (1964, February 2). Battle of the big hotels. *The Straits Times*, p. 15. Retrieved from NewspaperSG.

11. Leong-Salobir, C. (2011). *Food culture in colonial Asia: A taste of empire*. Abingdon, Oxon: Routledge, pp. 94–95. (Call no.: RSING 394.12095 LEO); Kennedy, D. (2017). Minds in crisis: Medico-moral theories of disorder in the late colonial world. In H. Fischer-Tiné (Ed.), *Anxieties, fear and panic in colonial settings: Empires on the verge of a nervous breakdown*, pp. 30–31. (Call no.: RSING 325.32 ANX)

12. The Tanjong Katong Hotel. (1884, January 8). *The Straits Times*, p. 2. Retrieved from NewspaperSG.

13. Foran, W.R. (1935). *Malayan symphony*. London: Hutchinson, p. 44. (Microfilm: NL7464)

14. Trips to Katong. (1902, January 17). *The Straits Times*, p. 1. Retrieved from NewspaperSG.

15. The electric tram existed in Singapore from the 1880s to the 1920s. York, F.W., & Phillips, A.R. (1996). *Singapore: A history of its trams trolleybuses and buses*. Surrey: DTS Publishing Limited, pp. 12, 41. (Call no.: RSING q388.41322095957 YOR)

16. Peleggi, M. (2012). The social and material life of colonial hotels: Comfort zones as contact zones in British Colombo and Singapore, ca. 1870–1930. *Journal of Social History*, 46(1), 124–153, p. 136. Retrieved from JSTOR via NLB's eResources website: http://www.eresources.nlb.gov.sg

17. The Oriental Hotel. (1924, January 26). *Malayan Saturday Post*, p. 3. Retrieved from NewspaperSG. Though the concept of the grill room only took off in the 1920s, one of the first grill rooms had been opened in 1898 by Emmerson's Tiffin Rooms. The grill room was hailed as an innovation by the local papers, which also reported that until then there had been "nowhere in town to go for a chop or steak": [Untitled]. (1898, July 7). *The Singapore Free Press and Mercantile Advertiser (Weekly)*, p. 5. Retrieved from NewspaperSG.

18. Raffles new grill. (1923, April 7). *The Straits Times*, p. 10. Retrieved from NewspaperSG.

19. The Europe Hotel had planned to open one in 1921, but the plan fell through: Europe Hotel. (1921, November 5). *The Straits Times*, p. 10. Retrieved from NewspaperSG.

20. S'pore has 10,000 ice-cream eaters daily. (1946, December 23). *Malaya Tribune*, p. 5; [Page 3 Advertisements Column 1]. (1948, March 17). *The Straits Times*, p. 3. Retrieved from NewspaperSG.

21. Lim, S. (1988, July 12). Time runs out for Magnolia Snack Bar. *The Straits Times*, p. 32. Retrieved from NewspaperSG.

22. Tai Tong Restaurant is still around today in the form of Da Dong Restaurant (the Mandarin pronunciation of the Cantonese Tai Tong) on Smith Street.

23. Chua, C.H.J. (Interviewer). (2007, December 17). *Oral history interview with Ow Yong Mun* [Transcript of recording no. 003214/7/5, pp. 173–174]. Retrieved from National Archives of Singapore website: http://www.nas.gov.sg/archivesonline/; Khng, E.M. (1984, July 22). Eating out for breakfast an emerging trend. *The Straits Times*, p. 16. Retrieved from NewspaperSG.

24. [Photograph]. (1935, November 9). *Malaya Tribune*, p. 20; Farewell. (1950, July 27). *Malaya Tribune*, p. 11. Retrieved from NewspaperSG.

25. The ads for Adelphi Hotel cite various dates for the year of its establishment (e.g. 1863), but the hotel was in existence since 1850 at least, when a notice in *The Straits Times* under the title "Adelphi Hotel" announced that a C. Goymour had expanded and moved his hospitality business to larger premises on High Street: Adelphi Hotel. (1850, May 7). *The Straits Times*, p. 7. Retrieved from NewspaperSG.

The Modern Malayan Home

1. The disposal of night soil at Singapore. (1894, January 19). *The Straits Times*, p. 3. Retrieved from NewspaperSG.

2. Staines, V. (1949, May 21). Water is their main problem. *The Singapore Free Press*, p. 4. Retrieved from NewspaperSG.

3. Municipal Council. (1862, June 14). *The Straits Times*, p. 1. Retrieved from NewspaperSG.

4. Energy Market Authority. (n.d.). *Singapore energy story*. Retrieved from www.ema.gov.sg/ourenergystory.aspx

5. Ibid.

6. [TMA advertisement]. (1947, February 23). *The Straits Times*, p. 1. Retrieved from NewspaperSG.

7. Huff, W.G. (2001, May). Entitlements, destitution, and emigration in the 1930s Singapore Great Depression. *The Economic History Review*, 54(2), 290–323, p. 305. Retrieved from JSTOR via NLB's eResources website: http://eresources.nlb.gov. sg/

8. Chua, A.L. (2016) The story of Singapore radio (1924–41). *BiblioAsia*, 12(1). Retrieved from BiblioAsia website: http://www. nlb.gov.sg/biblioasia

9. McDaniel, D.O. (1994). *Broadcasting in the Malay world: Radio, television and video in Brunei, Indonesia, Malaysia, and Singapore*. Norwood, NJ: Ablex Pub., pp. 34–37. (Call no.: RSING 302.2340959 MAC)

10. Chua, 2016.

11. McDaniel, 1994, p. 28.

12. Ibid., pp. 27–28.

13. Chua, 2016.

14. McDaniel, 1994, p. 71.

15. Ibid., p. 72.

16. Fox, B.J. (1990, March). Selling the mechanised household: 70 years of ads in Ladies Home Journal. *Gender and Society, 4*(1), 25–40, pp. 27–28. Retrieved from JSTOR via NLB's eResources website: http://eresources.nlb.gov. sg/

17. Cowan, R.S. (1976, January). The 'Industrial Revolution' in the home: Household technology and social change in the 20th century. *Technology and Culture, 17*(1), 1–23, pp. 9–10. Retrieved from JSTOR via NLB's eResources website: http://eresources.nlb. gov. sg/

18. Fox, 1990, pp. 25–40; Quah, S.R. (1980, July–December). Sex-role socialization in a transitional society. *International Journal of Sociology of the Family, 10*(2), 213–231, pp. 214–215. Retrieved from JSTOR via NLB's eResources website: : http://eresources.nlb. gov. sg/

19. Wong, A.K., & Ko, Y.-C. (1984) Women's work and family life: The case of electronics workers in Singapore [Working paper]. Michigan State University Office of Women in International Development [East Lansing]: Michigan State University. (Call no.: RSING 331.4821381095957 WON); Deyo, F.C., & Chen, P.S.J. (1976). *Female labour force participation and earnings in Singapore*. Clearing House for Social Development in Asia, Bangkok. (Call no.: RSING 331.4095957 DEY); Quah, 1980, p. 221.

20. Interestingly, according to studies on advertising and gender beyond the 1960s, the representation of women in household roles did not necessarily decrease. Instead, brands attempted to diversify the images of families using household items, with men occasionally shown participating in the upkeep of the household, at least from the late '60s onwards.

Treating a Population

1. Lee, Y.K. (2005). *Private practitioners and private hospitals in early Singapore (1819–1872)*. Singapore: [s.n.], p. 490. (Call no.: RCLOS 610.95957 LEE)

2. Lee, Y.K. (1973). *The general hospital in early Singapore (Part II) (1830–1839)*. Singapore: Stamford College Press, p. 519. (Call no.: RCLOS 362.11095957 LEE)

3. Lee, 2005, p. 490.

4. *Singapore almanack and directory*. (1846). Singapore: Straits Times Press, p. 45. (Microfilm: NL 2363)

5. Manderson, L. (1996). *Sickness and the state: Health and illness in colonial Malaya, 1870–1940*. New York: Cambridge University Press, pp. 14, 16, 34. (Call no.: RSING 362.1095951 MAN)

6. Lee, 2005, p. 491.

7. Harper, T.N. (2014). *Histories of health in Southeast Asia: Perspectives on the long twentieth century*. Bloomington, Indianapolis: Indiana University Press, p. 67. (Call no.: RSEA 362.109590904 HIS)

8. A traditional Malay medicine man or healer.

9. A Greco-Arabic traditional system of healing widely practised in South Asia and Central Asia.

10. Manderson, 1996, p. 25.

11. Harper, 2014, p. 67.

12. Manderson, 1996, pp. 34–39.

13. Tong, Y.K., Narayanan, S., & Pradeep, P. (Eds.). (2015). *Caring for our people: 50 years of healthcare in Singapore*. Singapore: MOH Holdings for the Ministry of Health, p. 27. (Call no.: RSING 362.1095957 TON)

14. Parmer, J. (1989). Health and health services in British Malaya in the 1920s. *Modern Asian Studies, 23*(1), 49–71, p. 69. Retrieved from JSTOR via NLB's eResources website: http://www. eresources.nlb.gov.sg

15. Manderson, 1996, p. 14.

16. [Untitled]. (1946, September 11). *The Straits Times*, p. 7. Retrieved from NewspaperSG.

17. Manderson, L. (1996). *Sickness and the state: health and illness in colonial Malaya, 1870–1940*. New York: Cambridge University Press, pp. 201–204. (Call no.: RSING 362.1095951 MAN)

18. Free medical service now welcome in kampongs. (1939, July 9). *The Straits Times*, p. 32. Retrieved from NewspaperSG.

19. Owen, N.G. (Ed.). (1987). *Death and disease in Southeast Asia: Explorations in social, medical and demographic history*. Singapore: Oxford University Press, pp. 257–258. (Call no.: RSING 301.3220959 DEA); Manderson, 1996, p. 54.

20. Hospitals fight against malnutrition. (1938, March 13). *The Straits Times*, p. 32. Retrieved from NewspaperSG; Manderson, 1996, p. 11.

21. Owen, 1987, p. 257.

22. Republic of Singapore. *Medicines (Advertisement and Sale) Act (Chapter 177)*. Retrieved from Health Sciences Authority website: http://www.hsa.gov.sg/content/dam/HSA/HPRG/ Useful_Information_for_Applicants/Legislation/MEDICINES%20 (ADVERTISEMENT%20AND%20SALE)%20ACT.pdf

23. Manderson, 1996, p. 196.

24. Warren, J.F. (1993). *Ah-ku and karayuki-san*. Singapore: Oxford University Press, p. 171. (Call no.: RSING 306.74095957 WAR)

25. Venereal diseases. (1922, November 2). *The Singapore Free Press and Mercantile Advertiser (Weekly)*, p. 277; [Untitled]. (1927, February 9). *The Singapore Free Press and Mercantile Advertiser*, p. 10; Legislative Council. (1926, July 12). *The Straits Times*, p. 10. Retrieved from NewspaperSG.

26. Kandang Kerbau Hospital. (2018). *Hospital milestones*. Retrieved 2018, March 8 from Kandang Kerbau Hospital website: www.kkh. com.sg/AboutUs/Overview

27. St Andrew's Mission Hospital. (2015). *About us*. Retrieved from St Andrew's Mission Hospital website: www.samh.org.sg/about-us

28. Ablution centres were venues that allowed for immediate self-disinfection after sexual intercourse. They were often fitted with sinks, toilets and sanitary products. Some of the earliest centres were set up at Middle Road Hospital, Kreta Ayer Clinic and Joo Chiat Dispensary.

29. Parmer, 1989, p. 60; Hygiene drive. (1945, October 30). *Malaya Tribune*, p. 4; Another ablution centre for Singapore to be built at Bendemeer. (1940, April 27). *Malaya Tribune*, p. 2. Retrieved from NewspaperSG.

30. *Annual departmental report of the Straits Settlements for the year 1926 (Microfilm: NL29302)*. (1928). Singapore: Govt. Print. Off., p. 181.

31. The effectiveness of these measures was questionable, however, as it was not easy to reach working-class sufferers as well as those who were already ill.

32. Manderson, 1996, pp. 201–204.

33. Lee, 2005, pp. 490–491.

34. Trocki, 1990, pp. 117–141.

35. United Nations Office on Drugs and Crime. (1958, January 1). The opium problem in Singapore. *Bulletin on Narcotics*, *IX*(3). Retrieved from United Nations Office on Drugs and Crime website: http://www.unodc.org/unodc/en/data-and-analysis/bulletin/bulletin_1958-01-01_4_page003.html

36. *Annual report of medical department 1926.* (1927). Singapore: Govt. Print. Off., p. 181. (Call no.: RCLOS 362.1095957 ANN-[AR])

Bon Voyage

1. Bastin, J. (1994). Introduction In J. Bastin (Comp.), *Travellers' Singapore: An anthology.* New York: Oxford University Press, pp. xiv–xix. (Call no.: RSING 959.5705 TRA-[HIS])

2. Withey, L. (1997). *Grand tours and Cook's tours: A history of leisure travel 1750 to 1915.* New York: William Morrow and Company, Inc., pp. 268–269. (Call no.: R 910.9 WIT)

3. Withey, 1997, p. 271.

4. Brendon, P. (1991). *Thomas Cook: 150 years of popular tourism.* London: Secker & Warburg, p. 146. (Call no.: R BUS 338.76191)

5. Cook's tour de luxe. (1926, January 29). *The Singapore Free Press and Mercantile Advertiser*, p. 17. Retrieved from NewspaperSG.

6. Malayan outpost: The work of the Malay States Information Agency. (1926, May). *British Malaya*, *1*(1), pp. 27–28. (Microfilm: NL7599)

7. Tan, B. (2010, July). Early tourist guidebooks: The illustrated guide to the Federated Malay States. *BiblioAsia*, pp. 36–37. Retrieved from BiblioAsia website: http://www.nlb.gov.sg/biblioasia

8. Anthony, P.A. (1914). *Federated Malay States Railways: Pamphlet of information for travellers: Tours in the Malay Peninsula.* Federated Malay States Railways, p. 50. (Microfilm: NL29292)

9. Goh, Y.K. (2012). *Where lions fly: 100 years of aviation in Singapore (1911–2011).* Singapore: Straits Times Press, pp. 19–24. (Call no.: RSING 387.7095957 GOH)

10. Bastin, 1994, p. xxi.

11. Stockwell, A.J. (1993). Early tourism in Malaya. In M. Hitchcock, V.T.King & M.J.G. Parnwell (Eds.), *Tourism in South-East Asia.* London: Routledge, pp. 264–265. (Call no.: RSING 338.4791590453 TOU)

12. Crossette, B. (1999). *The great hill stations of Asia.* New York: Basic Books, p. 7. (Call no.: RSEA 950.0943 CRO)

13. Ibid., pp. 3–4.

14. Ibid., p. 8.

15. Withey, 1997, p. 291.

Notes

The image sources for the respective pages are sequenced from top, and left to right.

All newspaper sources were retrieved from NewspaperSG, unless otherwise stated. *The Straits Times Annual* and *Her World* issues were retrieved from PublicationSG, the National Library's legal-deposit collection.

Abbreviations

NSP: Nanyang Siang Pau 《南洋商报》
SFP: The Singapore Free Press and Mercantile Advertiser
ST: The Straits Times
ST Annual: The Straits Times Annual

Introduction

2 Daks, *ST Annual*, 1940, p. 88. **5** Mastheads, *Singapore Chronicle*, 20 Jan 1831; *Lat Pau*, 19 Aug 1887, courtesy of National University of Singapore Libraries; *Jawi Peranakkan*, 28 Mar 1881; *Singai Nesan*, 27 Jun 1887; *Bintang Timor*, 1 Mar 1900. **8** John Little, *ST*, 30 Apr 1927, p. 8. Maison Vogue, *ST*, 8 Apr 1933, p. 18. Roskopf, *Warta Malaya*, 28 Apr 1933, p. 11. Underwood, *Tamil Murasu*, 29 Jun 1937, p. 3. **11** Gordon's, *ST*, 29 Aug 1962, p. 6. **12** Gevaert/Ikoflex, *Nanyang Monthly*, iss. 10, 1 Apr 1958, p. 41. (Call no.: RCLOS 059.951 NM-[HYT]) **13** Whiteaway, Laidlaw & Co., *Souvenir of Singapore*, 1905, [n.p.]. (Microfilm: NL16348) **14** High Street, 1924–1930, courtesy of National Archives of Singapore. **15** Aurora department store, c. 1940, courtesy of National Archives of Singapore. **16** High Street, 1968, George W. Porter Collection, courtesy of National Archives of Singapore. **17** Robinson's, *The Traveller's Guide to Singapore*, 1956, p. 10. (Microfilm: NL31367) **18** Masters, *ST*, 6 Sep 1949, p. 4. Siow Choon Leng, *ST*, 4 Mar 1919, p. 3. **19** Warin Publicity Services, *ST Annual*, 1939, [backcover]. Warin Studios, *Roda*, Oct 1935, p. 200. (Call no.: RUR 369.509595 R)

Wheels of Change

20 Jaguar/Thornycroft, *Handbook of the Automobile Association of Malaya*, 1939, [n.p.]. Retrieved from BookSG. **22** Dunlop, *ST*, 21 May 1923, p. 15. Shell, *Singapore Standard*, 22 Sep 1951, p. 12. Chloride Batteries, *ST*, 15 Dec 1956, p. 22. **23** Sale notice, *ST*, 15 Jan 1906, p. 4. Mr and Mrs G.M. Dare, 1930/31, *British Malaya* (May 1930), p. 190. (Microfilm: NL7601) **24** Morris/Malayan Motors, *A.A.M. News Bulletin*, Nov 1949. Retrieved from PublicationSG. **25** De Dion Bouton/C. Dupire, *ST Annual*, 1907/08. p. 14. (Microfilm 5876). Morris/Malayan Motors, *ST*, 30 Sep 1930, p. 5. **26** Ford/Gadelius, *ST*, 24 Dec 1909, p. 9. Ford, *ST*, 24 Dec 1937, p. 17. Ford Malaya, *A.A.M. News Bulletin*, Nov 1949. Retrieved from PublicationSG. **27** Nissan/Datsun, *ST*, 25 Feb 1958, p. 4. Toyota/Borneo Motors, *ST*, 18 Mar 1969, p. 6. **28** Singapore Motor Taxi Cab, *Malaya Tribune*, 16 Apr 1919, p. 5. Call a Taxi, *ST*, 21 Dec 1920, p. 6. **29** Abrams' Motor Transport, *SFP*, 12 Sep 1924, p. 4. Trojan, *SFP*, 9 Sep 1925, p. 5. Yellow Top Cabs, *ST*, 6 Nov 1933, p. 16. **30** Katz Brothers, *ST*, 29 Aug 1896, p. 1. Rover/Adams-Hewitt, *ST*, 7 Jun 1907, p. 12. De Dion Bouton, *ST*, 7 Sep 1904, p. 1. **31** Ford/Universal Cars, *ST*, 23 Jul 1927, p. 13. Ford Popular, *ST*,

20 Jul 1954, p. 2. Ford cars/trucks, *Malaya Tribune*, 22 Oct 1947, p. 8. Ford Cortina, *ST*, 30 Jul 1969, p. 8. **32** Chevrolet/Borneo Motors, *ST*, 23 Jul 1927, p. 13. Vanguard/Wearne Motors, *SFP*, 13 Aug 1954, p. 14. Graham/Lee Motors, *Malaya Tribune*, 20 Dec 1935, p. 15. **33** Honda, *ST*, 10 Dec 1967, p. 5. Datsun Bluebird, *ST*, 23 May 1966, p. 6. Datsun/Nissan/Tan Chong & Sons Motor, *ST*, 29 Mar 1967, p. 15. **34** Ferodo, *SFP*, 26 Apr 1928, p. 6. Dodge, *ST*, 31 Jan 1921, p. 15. REO/Federated Motors, *British Malayan Annual 1929*, 1929, p. 32. (Microfilm: NL28302). **35** Renault Dauphine, *ST*, 15 Feb 1959, p. 9.

That's Entertainment

36 Capitol, *British Malayan Annual 1929*, p. 20. (Microfilm: NL28302). **38** *The Revenge, Singapore Chronicle and Commercial Register*, 21 Mar 1833, p. 1. **39** Town Hall, 1880s, courtesy of National Archives of Singapore. Victoria Theatre and Victoria Memorial Hall, 1920s, Barry G. and Barbara J. Smith Collection, courtesy of National Archives of Singapore. *Xin Ke, Lat Pau*, 5 Mar 1927, p. 27, courtesy of National University of Singapore Libraries. **40** Star Opera Company and Theatre Royal, courtesy of National Archives of Singapore. Paris Cinematograph, *ST*, 26 Nov 1904, p. 3. **41** Alhambra cinema, c. 1938, Allen Goh Collection, courtesy of National Archives of Singapore. Capitol Theatre, c. 1930, courtesy of National Archives of Singapore. Pavilion Theatre, 1950, Lee Kip Lin Collection. Marlborough Theatre, 1938/39, courtesy of National Museum of Singapore, National Heritage Board. **43** Happy World, 1930s, courtesy of National Museum of Singapore, National Heritage Board. Great World, 1950s, Wong Kwan Collection, courtesy of National Archives of Singapore. Great World archway, 1937, courtesy of National Museum of Singapore, National Heritage Board. **44** Italian circus, *Lat Pau*, 13 Oct 1887, p. 7, courtesy of National University of Singapore Libraries. Hot-air balloons, *Lat Pau*, 17 Mar 1897, p. 7, courtesy of National University of Singapore Libraries. Indian troupe, *Pothujana Mithran*, 22 Mar 1924, p. 5. (Microfilm: A0004279991) **45** Circus, *Lat Pau*, 14 Jun 1900, p. 8, courtesy of National University of Singapore Libraries. Harmston's Circus, *Kabar Selalu*, 27 Mar 1924, p. 2. Beach Road, courtesy of National Archives of Singapore. **46** Town Hall, *SFP*, 8 Sep 1894, p. 2. Chinese opera, *NSP*, 9 Mar 1927, p. 9. Uday Shankar, *Malaya Tribune*, 11 Oct 1935, p. 20. Wayang Kassim, *SFP* 1 Aug 1908, p. 1. **47** Harima Hall, *Lat Pau*, 5 Jun 1918, p. 2, courtesy of National University of Singapore Libraries; *Malaya Tribune*, 5 Jun 1918, p. 3; *Utusan Malayu*, 5 Jun 1918, p. 2. Theatre Royal, *SFP*, 7 Feb 1935, p. 7. Theatre Royal, *Malaya Tribune*, 8 Nov 1935, p. 11. **48** *Leila Majnun, Malaya Tribune*, 24 Mar 1934, p. 10. Marlborough (English), *ST*, 3 Jan 1921, p. 6. Marlborough (Chinese), *NSP*, 28 Jan 1925, p. 10. Various cinema programmes, *ST*, 3 Jan 1921, p. 6. **49** Lion City, *Nanyang Monthly*, Nov 1960, vol. 41, p. 20. (Call no.: RCLOS Chinese 059.951 NM). *Trapeze*/Capitol handbills, National Library collection of movie flyers. (Call no.: RCLOS 791.4361095957 COL) **50** *Adam's Rib, ST*, 19 Jun 1924, p. 6. Mickey Mouse matinee, *ST*, 6 Dec 1934, p. 7. Alhambra/*Baroness, Morning Tribune*, 22 Sep 1938, p. 7. Alhambra/*Broadway Melody, Malaya Tribune*, 2 Jun 1930, p. 6. **51** *Conquering Blood, ST*, 14 Oct 1926, p. 6. *Duke Steps Out, ST*, 7 May 1930, p. 7. *Black Pirate, Malaya Tribune*, 16 Sep 1926, p. 4. *To-night & Every Night, ST*, 18 Jul 1947, p. 6. *Salome, Where She Danced*, 1945–55, & *The Adventures of Ichabod and Mr Toad*, c. 1950, National Library collection of movie flyers. (Call no.: RCLOS 791.4361095957 COL). *Paris Holiday, Nanyang Monthly*, iss. 12, Jun 1958, p. 54. (Call no.: RCLOS Chinese 059.951 NM) **52** Happy Valley, *NSP*, 1 Nov 1930, p. 22. Happy Valley, *ST*, 2 Feb 1924, p. 6. New World, *ST*, 8 Jan 1926, p. 6. **53** Great World, *Xinnanyang nianjian* 《新南洋年鉴》, 1947, p. 甲25, Hsu Yun Tsiao Collection. (Call no.: RCLOS Chinese 959 NYB). Happy World, Singapore Telephone Directory, 1959, p. 221. (Call no.: RDLKL 384.60255957 STB). **54** Great World, *Willis's Singapore Guide*, 1936, p. 66. Retrieved from BookSG. Boxing/New World, *ST*, 24 Dec 1931 p. 7. Great World, *NSP*, 1 Jan 1938, p. 77. **55** Acrobats/Gay World, National Library collection of movie flyers. (Call no.: RCLOS 791.4361095957 COL).

Changing Tastes

56 Riesling, *Menus for Malaya*, 1953, p. 115. (Call no.: RCLOS 642.1 ALL) **58** Fraser & Neave, *ST Annual*, 1907, p. 71. Framroz plant, 1965, Ministry of Information and the Arts Collection, courtesy of National Archives of Singapore. **59** Lee Pineapple, 1935–50, courtesy of National Archives of Singapore. Pineapple canning, 2 Jan 1952, Ministry of Information and the Arts Collection, courtesy of National Archives of Singapore. **60** A. Clouet, *Menus for Malaya*, 1953, p. 28. (Call no.: RCLOS 642.1 ALL). Ayam Brand, *ST*, 26 Jul 1949, p. 7. **61** Cold Storage, *Sunday Tribune*, 24 Jul 1949, p. 5. Fitzpatrick's, *Shops and shopping in Singapore*, 1962, p. 19. Retrieved from BookSG. **62** Ovaltine, *Tamil Murasu*, 8 Feb 1939, p. 1; *ST Annual*, 1936, p. 98. **63** Rowntree's, *ST Annual*, 1937, p. 192. Bovril, *Her World*, 1962, p. 60. Milkmaid, *British Malayan Annual*, 1929, p. 94. Bear Brand, *British Malayan Annual*, 1929, p. 96. (Microfilm: NL28302). **64** *Samsu*, c. 1900, courtesy of National Archives of Singapore. Toddy, *Singapore Standard*, 12 Aug 1951, p. 3. Stengah, *Malaya Tribune*, 29 Feb 1940, p. 13. Tiger, *ST*, 24 Feb 1933, p. 13. **65** 555, *ST Annual*, 1963, p. xv. **66** Katz Brothers, *ST*, 3 Dec 1897, p. 4. Chivers, *ST Annual*, 1940, p. 57. Raisley, *Menus for Malaya*, 1953, p. 40. (Call no.: RCLOS 642.1 ALL). **67** Nescafe, *Menus for Malaya*, 1953, p. 7. Lassie, *Menus for Malaya*, 1953, p. 56. (Call no.: RCLOS 642.1 ALL). Lee's Golden Dew, *Morning Tribune*, 8 Oct 1941, p. 7. Lee Pineapple, *Come to Malaya and Travel by Train*, Apr 1939, p. 8. (Microfilm: NL29343). **68** Framroz, *Willis's Singapore Guide*, 1934, p. 92. (Microfilm: NL30538). Phoenix, *ST Annual*, 1940, p. 106; *The Singapore Cinema Review*, 1933, p. 25. Retrieved from PublicationSG. Roda, Dec 1934, p. 418. (Call no.: RUR 369.509595 R). **69** Red Lion, *ST Annual*, 1961, [backcover]. **70** Lactogen, *ST Annual*, 1937, p. 136. SMA, *Nanyang Monthly*, iss. 15, 1 Sep 1958, p. 33. (Call no.: RCLOS 059.951 NM-[HYT]). Horlicks Milkose, *ST*, 12 Feb 1954, p. 2. **71** Twin Birds, *Theraiyoli*, Nov 1968, p. 2. Retrieved from PublicationSG. Morinaga, *Singapore Herald*, 2 Jan 1940, p. 4. Wei-Yen Mark Tea, *ST*, 2 Aug 1936, p. 6. **72** Cold Storage, 1905, *Souvenir of Singapore*, [n.p.]. (Microfilm: NL16348); *ST Annual*, 1954, p. 112. **73** Fitzpatrick's, *SFP*, 19 Jun 1959, p. 12; *SFP*, 8 May 1959, p. 2. Cold Storage, *ST Annual*, 1956, p. liv. **74** Hall's Wine, *ST*, 2 Jan 1930, p. 21. Black & White, *ST Annual*, 1936, p. 73. 陈李济, *NSP*, 6 Nov 1935, p. 12. Fraser & Neave, *ST*, 6 Sep 1961, p. 1. **75** Tiger Beer, *Warta Malaya*, 2 May 1933, p. 6; *SFP*, 18 Nov 1933, p. 18; *Tamil Murasu*, 27 Mar 1939, p. 1; *ST*, 27 Apr 1940, p. 5. **76** Benson & Hedges, *ST Annual*, 1967, p. 97. Philip Morris, *Menus for Malaya*, 1953, p. 27. (Call no.: RCLOS 642.1 ALL). Garrick, *ST*, 23 Feb 1947, p. 3. 555, *NSP*, 13 Apr 28,

p. 18. **77** Martin's, *ST*, 22 Jun 1947, p. 1. Craven "A", *ST*, 22 Jun 1947, p. 2. Grimault's, *ST*, 23 Aug 1894, p. 4. *Warta Malaya*, 2 Jun 1933, p. 1.

A Matter of Style

78 Bata, *ST Annual*, 1958, p. xxxiii. **80** John Little, *ST*, 25 Jul 1898, p. 2; *ST*, 27 Jan 1902, p. 2. **81** Meakers, *British Malaya*, Feb 1936, p. xv. (Microfilm: NL7602). John Piggott, *British Malaya, Trade and Commerce*, 1914, p. 67, John Koh Collection. (Call no.: RCLOS 381.09595 MAL-[JK]). **82** Hussen and Fakier Saibs, *Singapore Chronicle and Commercial Register*, 19 May 1831, p. 1. Agustine Avizagnet, *Singapore Chronicle and Commercial Register*, 30 Oct 1834, p. 1. Robinson & Co., *ST*, 17 Nov 1928, p. 1. **83** K.A.J. Chotirmall, *ST Annual*, 1936, p. 61. Singer, *Her World*, Jul 1960, p. 52. **84** Shem-el-Nessim, *ST*, 14 Jan 1921, p. 3. Black Prince, *ST*, 30 Jul 1921, p. 1. John Little, *ST*, 16 Sep 1922, p. 8. **85** *Kain pulicat*, *Warta Malaya*, 21 Apr 1933, p. 10. Max Factor, *Fashion*, 9 Jul 1961, p. 24. (Call no.: RCLOS 059.9928 F). Yardley, *Her World*, Jul 1961, p. 5. **86** Crème Simon, *ST*, 11 Feb 1922, p. 2. Lux, *Her World*, Feb 1962, p. 2. **87** Harlene, *ST*, 6 Mar 1893, p. 4. Alpecin, *The Singapore Cinema Review 1937–1938*, 1938, p. 35. Retrieved from PublicationSG. Maison Tani, *Singapore and Malayan Ladies Directory 1937/38*, 1938, p. iii. Retrieved from PublicationSG. **88** Little, Cursetjee and Co., *ST*, 5 Feb 1850, p. 1. Whampoa and Co., *ST*, 5 Feb 1850, p. 1. John Little and Co., *ST*, 15 Jun 1872, p. 5. **89** Robinson and Co., *ST*, 18 Jul 1898, p. 3; *ST*, 6 Aug 1921, p. 1. Aertex/Robinsons, *ST*, 23 Jul 1927, p. 1. **90** Whiteaway, Laidlaw & Co., *ST*, 12 Dec 1901, p. 4; *ST*, 9 Apr 1902, p. 8; *ST*, 14 Dec 1901, p. 4; *ST*, 4 Sep 1913, p. 5. **91** J. Garty, *ST*, 16 Jul 1850, p. 4. Aurora, *Malaya Tribune*, 14 Oct 1938, p. 20. Janilaine, *ST*, 23 Aug 1962, p. 9. H.B. Winter, *ST*, 17 Sep 1927, p. 13. Bajaj Textiles, *SFP*, 3 Feb 1949, p. 3. **92** Whiteaway Laidlaw, *Warta Malaya Singapore*, 22 Apr 1933, p. 13. Kwong Sang Hong, *NSP*, 25 Nov 1935, p. 15. Pond's, *Pond's*, 9 Jul 1961, p. 26. (Call no.: RCLOS 059.9928 F). Casual Corner, 1956, *The traveller's guide to Singapore*, p. 82, John Koh Collection. (Microfilm: NL31367). Antoinette, *SFP*, 22 Dec 1960, p. 12. **93** Longines, *ST Annual*, 1957, p. xx. B.P. de Silva, *ST Annual*, 1936, p. 7. Gian Singh's, *Indian Daily Mail*, 22 Jul 1952, p. 3. **94** Ven-Yusa, *ST*, 11 Feb 1922, p. 3. Palmolive, *ST*, 26 Feb 1926, p. 12. Pond's, *ST*, 21 Jun 1947, p. 9. Max Factor Pan-Cake, *ST*, 22 Jun 1947, p. 5. Endocil, *Her World*, Feb 1964, p. 1. **95** Tata, *Fashion*, 10 Feb 1963, p. 20. (Call no.: RCLOS 059.9928 F). Cuticura, *ST*, 23 Oct 1897, p. 4. Figaro, *NSP*, 15 Sep 1933, p. 10. Gull Bahar, *Warta Malaya*, 13 Jun 1933, p. 15. Anjla, *Tamil Murasu*, 1 Dec 1937, p. 7.

A Warm Welcome

96 Majestic Hotel, *Guangyi dianying huabao* 《光艺电影画报》, 1949, no. 9, [n.p.]. (Call no.: RCLOS Chinese 791.4305 GYDYHB-[AKS]). **98** S. Hallpike board and lodging house, *Singapore Chronicle and Commercial Register*, 19 May 1831, p. 1. London Hotel, *ST*, 29 Apr 1851, p. 3; *The Singapore Almanack and Directory for the year 1855*, 1854, p. [A104]. Retrieved from BookSG. **99** Hotel de l'Europe, *ST Annual*, 1906, p. 27. Raffles Hotel, *ST Annual*, 1906, [n.p.]. **100** YWCA, *Singapore and Malayan Ladies Directory for 1936/37*, [1937], p. 307. (Microfilm: NL25428). Great Southern Hotel, *NSP*, 1 Jan 1937, p. 51. Thong Yit Lodging House, 《新加坡游览指南》 [*Travellers' Guide to Singapore*], 1936, [p. 10]. (Call no.: RCLOS Chinese 915.95704 PXN-

[HYT]). **101** Lion City Hotel, *V.I.P.*, 2(4), 1968, p. 31. Retrieved from PublicationSG. 7th Storey Hotel, *The traveller's guide to Singapore*, 1956, p. 46. (Microfilm: NL31367). Embassy Hotel, *Souvenir of the Singapore Constitution Exposition 1959*, 1959, [n.p.]. (Call no.: RCLOS Chinese q959.57 SOU). **102** Tanjong Katong Hotel, *SFP*, 17 Dec 1891, p. 2. Adelphi Hotel/Sea View Hotel, *ST Annual*, 1955, p. 82. **103** Grove Hotel, *Souvenir of Singapore*, 1905, [n.p.]. (Microfilm: NL16348). Royal Hotel, *ST*, 25 Jan 1910, p. 1. **104** Adelphi Hotel, *SFP*, 13 Feb 1935, p. 1. Southern Hotel, *ST*, 12 Mar 1927, p. 12. Europe Hotel, *SFP*, 20 Sep 1923, p. 1. **105** Cafe Restaurant de Paris, *ST*, 12 Jun 1885, p. 3. Polar Cafe, *Malaya Tribune*, 29 May 1936, p. 7. Café de Luxe, *Willis's Singapore Guide*, 1936, p. 44. Retrieved from BookSG. **106** Magnolia Snack Bar, *ST*, 10 Sep 1966, p. 12. Cold Storage Creameries, *Come to Malaya*, Apr 1939, p. 44. (Microfilm: NL29343). Tong Lee Milk Bar & Confectionery, *ST*, 24 Apr 1960, p. 23. **107** Singapore Airport Hotel, *ST Annual*, 1939, p. 76. Ananda Bhavan, *Indian Daily Mail*, 24 Oct 1956, p. 4. **108** Adelphi Hotel, *SFP*, 16 May 1896, p. 4; *ST Annual*, 1906, [n.p.]; *SFP*, 28 Feb 1958, p. 8. Hotel de la Paix, *ST Annual*, 1906, p. 4. **109** Goodwood Park Hotel, *ST Annual*, 1936, [n.p.]. Raffles Hotel, *ST Annual*, 1938, p. 6; *ST Annual*, 1959, p. vii. **110** The Mansion, *Information for travellers landing at Singapore*, 1911, p. 17. Retrieved from BookSG. Hilltop Guest House, *Morning Tribune*, 9 Nov 1940, p. 11. Sunnyside, *Willis's Singapore Guide*, 1936, p. 36. Retrieved from BookSG. Air View Hotel, 《新加坡游览指南》 [*Travellers' Guide to Singapore*], 1936, p. 54. (Call no.: RCLOS Chinese 915.95704 PXN-[HYT]). Air View Hotel, 1989, courtesy of National Archives of Singapore. **111** Empress Hotel, *NSP*, 29 Nov 1934, p. 10. Majestic Hotel, *Malaya Tribune*, 4 Oct 1949, p. 1. **112** Great Southern Hotel, *Guangyi dianying huabao* 《光艺电影画报》, 1949, no. 9, [n.p.]. (Call no.: RCLOS Chinese 791.4305 GYDYHB-[AKS]). Kam Leng Hotel, *Xinnanyang nianjian* 《新南洋年鉴》 [*New Nanyang Yearbook*], 1947, p. 62, Hsu Yun Tsiao Collection. (Call no.: RCLOS Chinese 959 NYB). Royal Hotel, *SFP*, 31 Dec 1908, p. 1. **113** Katong Rest House, *Guide to Singapore and Spotlight on Malaysia*, 1949, p. 18. (Call no.: RCLOS 959.57 GSSM). Ocean View Sukiyaki House Hotel and Bar, *Singapore Herald*, 19 May 1939, p. 1. Beach House, *Morning Tribune*, 15 Feb 1936, p. 12. Seletar Grange Country Hotel, *SFP*, 25 Aug 1939, p. 4. **114** Happy Restaurant, *NSP*, 1 Jan 1938, p. 63. Islamic Restaurant, *Sunday Standard*, 1 Apr 1951, p. 7. Tai Tong Restaurant, *SFP*, 8 Feb 1950, p. 8. **115** Jubilee Cafe & Restaurant, *V.I.P.*, [1967], no. 9, p. 19. Retrieved from PublicationSG. Singapura Bar & Restaurant, *Diners' Club Magazine*, Apr 1964, p. 10. Retrieved from PublicationSG. Hung Kang Restaurant, *Diners' Club Magazine*, Dec 1964, p. 15. Retrieved from PublicationSG. **116** Café de Luxe, *Singapore Cinema Review*, 1938, p. 7. Retrieved from PublicationSG. G.H. Cafe, *ST Annual*, 1938, p. 172; *Roda*, Nov 1939. (Call no.: RUR 369.509595 R). Little's Café, *ST*, 23 Aug 1947, p. 8. **117** Mont d'Or, *SFP*, 29 Apr 1959, p. 1; *SFP*, 21 Jan 1959, p. 1. Capitol Restaurant and Bar, *ST*, 14 Jun 1937, p. 11. Capitol Milk Bar, *SFP*, 28 Aug 1958, p. 7.

The Modern Malayan Home

118 Osram, *ST Annual*, 1952, p. 8. **120** Gas cooker and Magnet electric cooker, 1927, *The 'Next Meal' cookery book*, [n.p.]. (Call no.: RRARE 641.5 KIN). Municipal gas, *ST Annual*, 1938, p. 64. **121** Hoe Boon Leong, *ST Annual*, 1940, p. 86. **122** Morphy-Richards, *ST Annual*, 1952, p. 114. General Electric, *ST*, 24 Dec 1931. Hoover, *Her World*, Jun 1964, p. 4. **123** Grundig, *ST Annual*, 1961, p. xiv. Emor, *ST*, 20 Sept 1947, p. 2. **124** Marlon Brando at Rediffusion & Broadcast from Rediffusion, c. 1960s, Photograph collection of the National Library. (Call no.: RCLOS 384.540655957 RED). General Electric, *ST Annual*, 1940, p. 98. **125** Kriesler, *Diner's Club Magazine*, Jun 1964, p. 21. Retrieved from PublicationSG. **126** Lux, *Warta Malaya*, 2 May 1933, p. 3. Singer, *FDAWU Magazine*, 1969, p. 62. Retrieved from PublicationSG. Shellane, *Her World*, Sep 1967, p. 46. **127** Kelvinator, *ST Annual*, 1956, p. xx. National, *Her World*, Jun 1962, [inside cover]. **128** City Gas Department, *Menus for Malaya*, 1953, p. 80. (Call no.: RCLOS 642.1 ALL). Mobil Blue Kerosene, *Mastika*, Dec 1956, p. 33. Retrieved from PublicationSG. Shellane, *Her World*, Apr 1965, p. 47. **129** General Electric Company/Osram, *ST Annual*, 1907, p. 106. Lim Yew Chye & Sons, *Malaya Tribune*, 31 Aug 1926, p. 9. Osram, *ST Annual*, 1941, p. 160. Municipal electricity, *Come to Malaya, travel by train*, Apr 1939, p. 20. (Microfilm: NL29243). **130** Kelvinator, *ST Annual*, 1940, p. 80. Nam Kwang & Co., *ST*, 21 Sept 1947, p. 7. Singer, *ST Annual*, 1967, p. 6. **131** United Engineers, *ST Annual*, 1936, p. 119. Solo-Air, *ST Annual*, 1936, p. 46. National, *Her World*, May 1964, [inside cover]. **132** National, *ST Annual*, 1961, p. xxi. **133** TMA, *ST*, 23 Feb 1947, p. 1. Morphy-Richards, *ST Annual*, 1953, p. 14. Singer, *ST Annual*, 1961, p. xi. Sunbeam, *Her World*, Feb 1962, p. 7. **134** Columbia Records, *ST Annual*, 1939, p. 140. Pathé, *ST*, 21 Nov 1947, p. 5. His Master's Voice, *ST*, 23 Aug 1947, p. 9. **135** Edison, *ST*, 2 Jan 1930, p. 1. HMV, *ST Annual*, 1939, p. 102. Philips, *ST Annual*, 1939, p. 58. **136** Radio Electric Company, *ST Annual*, 1936, p. 147. HMV, *ST*, 11 Apr 1950, p. 7. Philips, *ST Annual*, 1966, p. 12. AEG Superhet, *ST Annual*, 1956, p. xviii. **137** *Rediffusion Times*, 29 Oct 1950, 5(5). (Call no.: RCLOS 791.44095957 RT). Mitsubishi, *Her World*, Jan 1966, p. 9.

Treating a Population

138 SevenSeas, *Her World*, Mar 1963, p. 31. **139** Singapore Dispensary, *ST*, 26 Aug 1845, p. 49. **140** Yunani Clinic, *Tamil Murasu*, 1 Dec 1936, p. 2. Unani Medical Hall, *Tamil Murasu*, 5 Jan 1937, p. 4. Tabib H.G. Mustaffa, *Hiboran*, 1 Nov 1951, iss. 272, p. 3. (Call no.: RCLOS Malay 059.9928 H-[UAS]). **141** Ayer's, *ST*, p. 4, 6 Jan 1894. Woodward's, *ST*, 15 May 1926, p. 3. Dr Williams, *ST*, 2 Jan 1930, p. 3. **142** Glaxo, *ST*, 28 Nov 1921, p. 2. Kalzana, *Sunday Tribune*, 26 Mar 1939, p. 13. Mobile dispensaries, 1951, (top) Ministry of Information and the Arts Collection, courtesy of National Archives of Singapore; (bottom) Bukit Panjang Government School Collection, courtesy of National Archives of Singapore. **143** Kharsani, *Fashion*, Singapore, Sep 1961, iss. 397, p. 32. (Call no.: RCLOS 059.9928 F). Vykmin, *SFP*, 2 Oct 1957, p. 2. **144** Trainee nurses, School of Nursing Collection, courtesy of National Archives of Singapore. Saboten, *NSP*, 30 Sep 1940, p. 7. **145** Rezex, *ST*, 25 Dec 1946, p. 8. 万寿果, *NSP*, 10 Oct 1934, p. 8. **146** Campong Glam Dispensary, *ST*, 12 Aug 1845, p. 22. Charles Wilson, *Singapore Chronicle and Commercial Register*, 10 Jul 1834, p. 1. Dr Chew Yit Hong, *Lat Pau*, 23 Jan 1894, p. 7, courtesy of National University of Singapore Libraries. **147** Medical Hall, *Souvenir of Singapore*, 1905, p. 135. The Pharmacy, *Souvenir of Singapore*, 1905, p. 32. (Microfilm: 16348). Western Dispensary, *The Daily Advertiser*, 22 Jan 1891, p. 3. Singapore Dispensary, *The Daily Advertiser*, 1 Dec 1890, p. 4. **148** Listerine, *ST*, 11 Jan 1930, p. 18.

Scott's Emulsion, *ST*, 2 Sep 1933, p. 17. Holloway's Pills, *ST*, 21 Oct 1845, p. 2. Eno, *ST*, 10 May 1890, p. 4. **149** Glaxo, *ST*, 23 Apr 1940, p. 14. Glaxo, *ST*, 14 Feb 1930, p. 22. Woodward's, *ST*, 23 Jan 1926, p. 12. **150** Opium medicine, *NSP*, 1 Oct 1935, p. 2. Xin Tong Xing, *Lat Pau*, 22 Oct 1892, p. 7, courtesy of National University of Singapore Libraries. Pasteur Institute, *SFP*, 15 Oct 1921, p. 2. Minyak Mutiara, *Fashion*, 3 Sep 1961, iss. 395, p. 6. (Call no.: RCLOS 059.9928 F). Tiger Balm, *ST*, 20 Jul 1946, p. 4. Minyak Jasa Kaki Ayam, *Fashion*, 1961, iss. 388, p. 2. (Call no.: RCLOS 059.9928 F). **151** Radion, *ST*, 17 Sep 1927, p. 11. Flit, *ST*, 15 Oct 1932, p. 16. Malario, *Malaya Tribune*, 4 Oct 1937, p. 6. Esanofele, *ST*, 26 Jan 1920, p. 2. **152** Resolve Now, *Tamil Murasu*, 12 Jan 1951, p. 4. Testrones, *ST*, 14 Mar 1947, p. 5. Okasa, *Indian Daily Mail*, 4 Jul 1954, p. 2. Lodhra, *Indian Daily Mail*, 4 Jul 1954, p. 3. Ovarone, *Tamil Murasu*, 7 Jan 1954, p. 3. **153** Feddis, *SFP*, 16 Aug 1960, p. 1. Zinsser, *Berita Harian*, 3 May 1963, p. 5. Vikelp, *Mastika*, Jun 1947, p. 2. Retrieved from PublicationSG. Dr Morse's, *Kabar Slalu*, 3 Apr 1924, p. 4. Kunchi Perkahwinan, *Mastika Filem*, Dec 1962, iss. 6, p. 34. (Call no.: RCLOS Malay 791.43 MF). Vikelp, *NSP*, 1 Mar 1937, p. 20. **154** Gono-ban, *Tamil Murasu*, 27 Mar 1939, p. 2. Maskee, *Tamil Murasu*, 1 Mar 1939, p. 7. 海波药, *NSP*, 20 Jul 1931, p. 4. Herpez, *Hiboran*, 27 Jul 1948, p. 35. (Call no.: RCLOS Malay 059.9928 H-[UAS]). **155** Supplements, *Tamil Murasu*, 19 Aug 1937, p. 10; *Tamil Murasu*, 1 Apr 1939, p. 8. German tonic, *NSP*, 25 Nov 1935, p. 4. Axe Brand, *NSP*, 10 Oct 1934, p. 7.

Bon Voyage

156 Malayan Airways, *ST Annual*, 1958, p. xvii. **158** Thomas Cook's tours, *Cook's tours around the world*, 1909. John Koh Collection. (Call no.: RCLOS 910.9 COO-[JK]). American Express tours, *The American Traveler in the Far East, India and Australiasia*, 1930. (Call no.: RUR 915.04 AME-[TRA]). **159** North German Lloyd, *Een Reis Naar Oost-Azië* [A Journey to East Asia], c. 1920s–30s. John Koh Collection. (Call no.: RCLOS 915.04 EPHE JOH-[JK]). **160** Travel to British Malaya, *British Malaya*, Sep 1936, *11*(5), p. xiv. (Microfilm: NL7602). FMSR, *Come to Malaya and travel by train*, Feb 1938, [cover]. (Microfilm: NL29343). **161** KLM, *ST Annual*, 1937, p. 146. Qantas-BOAC, *The traveller's guide to Singapore*, 1956, [n.p.]. (Microfilm: NL31367). **162** Smoke House Inn, *ST Annual*, 1938, [back cover]. **163** Visit Australia, *ST Annual*, 1936, p. 151. **164** Thomas Cook, *SFP*, 26 Jan 1926, p. 12; *Travellers' Guide to Singapore*《新加坡游览指南》, 1936, Hsu Yun Tsiao Collection, [n.p.]. (Call no.: RCLOS Chinese 915.95704 PXN-[HYT]). Hawaii, *ST*, 23 Jan 1926, p. 4. South Africa, *ST Annual*, 1938, p. 137. **165** KPM to Bali, 1930, John Koh Collection. (Call no.: RCLOS 915.9804 JOH-[JK]). Java, 1910s–20s, John Koh Collection. (Call no.: RCLOS 915.9804 JOH-[JK]). **166** Malayan Information Agency, *British Malaya*, 1936, p. xvii. (Microfilm: NL7602). FMS Railways, *ST Annual*, 1939, p. 92. FMSR cars, *British Malaya*, Aug 1939, [n.p.]. (Microfilm: NL7603). **167** FMSR & Siamese State Railways, *Annual of the East*, 1933, [n.p.]. (Microfilm: NL25739). **168** Cameron Highlands Hotel, *ST*, 1 Aug 1935, p. 1. Grand Hotel Brastagi, *ST*, 17 Jun 1940, p. 7. Smoke House Inn, *ST*, 4 Jan 1940, p. 16. Cameron Highlands Hotel, 4 Jan 1940, p. 1. **169** P&O and B.I., *ST Annual*, 1938, p. 3. N.Y.K. Line, *ST Annual*, 1936, p. 100. **170** North German Lloyd, *Een Reis Naar Oost-Azië* (A Journey to East Asia), c. 1920s–1930s. (Call no.: RCLOS 915.04 EPHE JOH [JK]). **171** Royal Dutch Mails, *ST Annual*, 1937, p. 140. Danish East Asiatic Line, *ST Annual*, 1939, [p. 42]. **172** Qantas, *ST Annual*, 1952, p. 104. Malayan Airways, *ST Annual*, 1960, [p. xvi]. **173** Japan Air Lines, *ST Annual* 1966, [p. 117]. Air-India, *ST Annual* 1957, p. xxi. Garuda, *ST Annual* 1969, [pp. 12–13].

The National Library Board would like to thank Singapore Press Holdings Ltd; the National Museum of Singapore, National Heritage Board; and the National University of Singapore Libraries for allowing the reproduction of their images in this book.

BIBLIOGRAPHY

Books

Advertisers Association. (1971). *A review of advertising in Singapore and Malaysia during early times*. Singapore: Federal Publications. (Call no.: RSING 659.109 ADV)

Ainon Haji Kuntom. (1974). *Malay newspapers, 1876–1973: A historical survey of the literature* [academic exercise]. Pusat Pengajian Ilmu Kemanusiaan, Universiti Sains Malaysia. (Call no.: RSING q079.5951 AIN)

Bastin, J. (Ed.). (1994). *Travellers' Singapore*. Kuala Lumpur; New York: Oxford University Press. (Call no.: RSING 959.5705 TRA-[HIS])

Bhattacharya, J. (2011). *Beyond the myth: Indian business communities in Singapore*. Singapore: Institute of Southeast Asian Studies. (Call no.: RSING 338.708991405957 BHA)

Bird, I. (2016). *The Golden Chersonese*. Abingdon, Oxon; New York, NY: Routledge. (Call no.: RSING 915.980422 BIR-[TRA])

Bleackley, H. (1928). *A tour in Southern Asia (Indo-China, Malaya, Java, Sumatra, and Ceylon, 1925–1926)*. London: John Lane. (Call no.: RCLOS 959 BLE-[RFL])

Brendon, P. (1991). *Thomas Cook: 150 years of popular tourism*. London: Secker & Warburg. (Call no.: R BUS 338.76191)

Bruna, D. (2015). *Fashioning an intimate history of the silhouette*. New Haven & London: Yale University Press. (Call no.: RART 746.92 FAS)

Buckley, C.B. (1984). *An anecdotal history of old times in Singapore*. Singapore: Oxford University Press. (Call no.: RSING 959.57 BUC-[HIS])

Butcher, J.G. (1979). *The British in Malaya, 1880–1941: The social history of a European community in colonial South-east Asia*. Kuala Lumpur; New York: Oxford University Press. (Call no.: RSING 301.4512105951033 BUT)

Chatfield, G.A. (1962). *Shops and shopping in Singapore*. Singapore: Eastern Universities Press. (Call no.: RCLOS 959.51 CHA)

Chen, M.H. (1967). *The early Chinese newspapers of Singapore, 1881–1912*. Singapore: University of Malaya Press. (Call no.: RSING 079.5702 CHE)

Chung, M.K. (2006). *Vintage Singapore*. Singapore: Editions Didier Millet; National Museum of Singapore. (Call no.: RSING 959.57 VIN)

Clarke, B. (2004). *From Grub Street to Fleet Street: An illustrated history of English newspapers to 1899*. Aldershot, UK; Burlington, VT: Ashgate. (Call no.: R 072 CLA)

Corson, R. (1972). *Fashions in makeup: From ancient to modern times*. London: Peter Owen. (Call no.: R q391.6309 COR- [CUS])

Cox, C., & Widdows, L. (2005). *Hair & fashion*. London: V&A Publications. (Call no.: R q391.509 COX-[CUS])

Crossette, B. (1999). *The great hill stations of Asia*. New York: Basic Books. (Call no.: RSEA 950.0943 CRO)

De Souza, J., Ong, C., & Rao, T. (2016). *Fashion most wanted: Singapore's top insider secrets from the past five decades*. Singapore: Straits Times Press. (Call no.: RSING 746.92095957 DES)

Deyo, F.C., & Chen, P.S.J. (1976). *Female labour force participation and earnings in Singapore*. Clearing House for Social Development in Asia, Bangkok. (Call no.: RSING 331.4095957 DEY)

Eckermann, E. (2001). *World history of the automobile*. Warrendale, PA: Society of Automotive Engineers. (Call no.: R 629.22209 ECK)

Fischer-Tiné, H. (Ed.), *Anxieties, fear and panic in colonial settings: Empires on the verge of a nervous breakdown*. (Call no.: RSING 325.32 ANX)

Foran, W.R. (1935). *Malayan symphony*. London: Hutchinson. (Microfilm: NL7464)

Frost, M., & Balasingamchow, Y. (2009). *Singapore: A biography*. Singapore: Editions Didier Millet Pte Ltd; National Museum of Singapore. (Call no.: RSING 959.57 FRO-[HIS])

Fu, C., & Yu, J. (2013). *A legend turns 130*. Singapore: Fraser and Neave Limited. (Call no.: RSING 338.7663095957 LEG)

Fu, P. (Ed.), *China forever: The Shaw Brothers and diasporic cinema*. Urbana, IL: University of Illinois Press, p. 170. (Call no.: RSEA 791.43095125 CHI)

George, C. (Ed.). (1995). *150 years of newspapers: The Straits Times July 15, 1845–1995*. Singapore: Singapore Press Holdings. (Call no.: RSING 079.5957 ONE)

Goerlik, B. (2013). *Incredible Tretchikoff: Life of an artist and adventurer*. London: Art/Books, p. 152. (Call no.: RART 759.968 GOR)

Goh, C.B. (2003). *Serving Singapore: A hundred years of Cold Storage, 1903–2003*. Singapore: Cold Storage. (Call no.: RSING 381.148095957 GOH)

Goh, C.B. (2013). *Technology and entrepot colonialism in Singapore, 1819–1940*. Singapore: Institute of Southeast Asian Studies. (Call no.: RSING 338.064095957 GOH)

Goh, Y.K. (2012). *Where lions fly: 100 years of aviation in Singapore (1911–2011)*. Singapore: Straits Times Press. (Call no.: RSING 387.7095957 GOH)

Gum, F. (1973). *The artificial face: A history of cosmetics*. Newton Abbot, UK: David & Charles (Holdings) Limited. (Call no.: R 391.630942 GUN-[CUS])

Harper, T.N. (2014). *Histories of health in Southeast Asia: Perspectives on the long twentieth century*. Bloomington, Indianapolis: Indiana University Press. (Call no.: RSEA 362.109590904 HIS)

Hiroshi, S., & Hitoshi, H. (1999). *Japan and Singapore in the world economy: Japan's economic advance into Singapore 1870–1965*. Abingdon, UK; New York: Routledge. (Call no.: RSING 337.5205957 SHI)

Jayapal, M. (1996). *Old Singapore*. Singapore: Oxford University Press. (Call no.: RSING 959.57 JAY-[HIS])

Kong, L., & Sinha, V. (2015). *Food, foodways and foodscapes: Culture, community and consumption in post-colonial Singapore*. Singapore: World Scientific. (Call no.: RSING 394.12095957 FOO)

Kuo, E.C.Y. (1980). The sociolinguistic situation in Singapore: Unity in diversity. In E.A. Afendras & E.C.Y. Kuo (Eds.), *Language and society in Singapore*. Singapore: Singapore University Press. (Call no.: RSING 409.5957 LAN)

Kuo, H.-Y. (2104). *Networks beyond empires: Chinese business and nationalism in the Hong Kong-Singapore corridor, 1914–1941*. Leiden & Boston: Brill. (Call no.: RSING 338.8895109041 KUO)

Latha d/o Sinasamy. (1999/2000). *Tamil Malar: Voice of the Tamil community (1964–1980)* [BA Honours Thesis]. Singapore: National University of Singapore. (Call no.: RSING 079.5957 SIN)

Lee, Y.K. (1973). *The general hospital in early Singapore (Part II) (1830–1839)*. Singapore: Stamford College Press. (Call no.: RCLOS 362.11095957 LEE)

Lee, Y.K. (2005). *Private practitioners and private hospitals in early Singapore (1819–1872)*. Singapore: [s.n.]. (Call no.: RCLOS 610.95957 LEE)

Leong-Salobir, C. (2011). *Food culture in colonial Asia: A taste of empire*. Abingdon, Oxon: Routledge. (Call no.: RSING 394.12095 LEO)

Luk, S. (2014). *Health insurance reforms in Asia*. Abingdon; New York: Routledge. (Call no.: RSEA 368.3820095 LUK)

Makepeace, W., Brooke, G.E., & Braddell, R.S.J. (Eds.). (1991). *One hundred years of Singapore* (Vols. 1–2). Singapore: Oxford University Press. (Call no.: RSING 959.57 ONE-[HIS])

Manderson, L. (2002). *Sickness and the state: Health and illness in colonial Malaya, 1870–1940*. New York: Cambridge University Press. (Call no.: RSING 362.1095951 MAN)

Marina Samad. (1972, January). Early Malay journalism: Jawi Peranakan and the first Malay newspapers. *Leader, Malaysian Journalism Review*. (Call no.: RSEA 079.5957 MAR)

McDaniel, D.O. (1994). *Broadcasting in the Malay world: Radio, television and video in Brunei, Indonesia, Malaysia, and Singapore*. Norwood, NJ: Ablex Pub. (Call no.: RSING 302.2340959 MAC)

Millet, R. (2006). *Singapore Cinema*. Singapore: Editions Didier Millet. (Call no.: RSING q791.43095957 MIL)

National Heritage Board. (2012). *Kampong Glam: A heritage trail*. Singapore: National Heritage Board, pp. 23, 33. (Call no.: RSING 599.2 KAM)

National Heritage Board & Fashion Designers Society. (1993). *Costumes through time: Singapore*. Singapore: National Heritage Board; Fashion Designers Society. (Call no.: RSING q391.0095957 COS-[CUS])

Owen, N.G. (Ed.). (1987). *Death and disease in Southeast Asia: Explorations in social, medical and demographic history*. Singapore: Oxford University Press. (Call no.: RSING 301.3220959 DEA)

Perry, J.C. (2017). *Singapore: Unlikely power*. New York, NY: Oxford University Press. (Call no.: RSING 330.95957 PER)

Pillai, G., & Kesavapany, K. (Eds.), *50 years of Indian community in Singapore*. Singapore; Hackensack, NJ; London: World Scientific. (Call no.: RSING 305.89141105957 FIF)

Pilon, M., & Weiler, D. (2011). *The French in Singapore: An illustrated history (1819–today)*. Singapore: Editions Didiet Millet. (Call no.: RSING 305.84105957 PIL)

Proudfoot, I. (1994) *The print threshold in Malaysia* [Working Paper 88]. The Centre of Southeast Asian Studies, Monash University. (Call no.: RSEA 070.509595 PRO)

Rai, R. (2014). *Indians in Singapore, 1819–1945: Diaspora in the colonial port city*. New Delhi: Oxford University Press. (Call no.: RSING 909.049141105957 RAI)

Rimmer, P.J., & Dick, H.W. (2009). *The city in Southeast Asia: Patterns, processes and policy*. Singapore: NUS Press. (Call no.: RSING 307.76.0959 RIM)

Scharchburg, R.P. (1993). *Carriages without horses: J. Frank Duryea and the birth of the American automobile industry*. Warrendale, PA: Society of Automative Engineers. (Call no.: R 338.7629222 SCH)

Sidhu, R.S. (2017). *Singapore's early Sikh pioneers: Origins, settlement, contributions and institutions*. Singapore: Central Sikh Gurdwara Board. (Call no.: RSING 305.8914205957 SID)

Singapore. Archives and Oral History Department. (1984). *The land transport of Singapore: from early times to the present*. Singapore: Archives and Oral History Department; Educational Publications Bureau Pte Ltd. (Call no.: RSING 779.9388095957 LAN)

Song, O.S. (1984). *One hundred years' history of the Chinese in Singapore*. Singapore: Oxford University Press. (Call no.: RSING 959.57 SON-[HIS])

Stockwell, A.J. (1993). Early tourism in Malaya. In M. Hitchcock, V.T. King & M.J.G. Parnwell (Eds.), *Tourism in South-East Asia*. London: Routledge. (Call no.: RSING 338.4791590453 TOU)

Tarulevicz, N. (2013). *Eating her curries and kway: A cultural history of food in Singapore*. Chicago, Illinois: University of Illinois Press, p. 16. (Call no.: RSING 394.12095957 TAR)

Thomas, M. (2011). *The heritage of hospitality: A history of the Singapore hotel industry*. Singapore: Marshall Cavendish Editions. (Call no.: RSING 338.4764794 HER)

Thompson, K., & Bordwell, D. (2010). *Film history: An introduction* (3rd Ed.). Boston; Singapore: McGraw-Hill Higher Education. (Call no.: 791.4309 THO)

Tong, Y.K., Narayanan, S., & Pradeep, P. (Eds.). (2015). *Caring for our people: 50 years of healthcare in Singapore*. Singapore: MOH Holdings for the Ministry of Health. (Call no.: RSING 362.1095957 TON)

Tregonning, K.G. (1967). *The Singapore Cold Storage: 1903–1906*. Singapore: Cold Storage Holdings Ltd. (Call no.: RCLOS 664.02852 TRE)

Turnbull, C.M. (2009). *A history of Singapore, 1819–2005*. Singapore: NUS Press. (Call no.: RSING 959.57 TUR-[HIS])

Uhde, J., & Ng Uhde, Y. (2010). *Latent images: Film in Singapore*. Singapore: NUS Press. (Call no.: RSING 791.43095957 UHD)

Wallace, A. (2016). *The Malay Archipelago*. London: Penguin Books. (Call no.: RSING 915.9804 WAL-[TRA])

Warren, J.F. (1993). *Ah-ku and karayuki-san*. Singapore: Oxford University Press. (Call no.: RSING 306.74095957 WAR)

Wharton, C. (2015). *Advertising: Critical approaches*. Abingdon, UK; New York: Routledge. (Call no.: 659.1 WA-[BIZ])

Who's who in Malaya, 1939. (1939). Singapore: Fishers Ltd. (Call no.: RCLOS 920.9595 WHO-[RFL])

Williams, K. (2010). *Read all about it!: A history of the British newspaper*. Abingdon, UK; New York: Routledge. (Call no.: R 072.09 WIL)

Withey, L. (1997). *Grand tours and Cook's tours: A history of leisure travel 1750 to 1915*. New York: William Morrow and Company, Inc. (Call no.: R 910.9 WIT)

Wong, A.L. [黄爱玲] (Ed.), 《国泰故事》（增订本）[The Cathay story (Revised Edition)]. 香港：香港电影资料馆 [Hong Kong: Hong Kong Film Archive]. (Call no.: RART Chinese q791.43095125 CAT)

Wu, D.Y.H. (1979). *Traditional Chinese concepts of food and medicine in Singapore*. Singapore: Institute of Southeast Asian Studies. (Call no.: RSING 641.3 WU)

Xu, Y.S. [许永顺]. (2015). 新马华文电影，1927–1965 [Chinese movies in Singapore and Malaysia, 1927–1965]. 新加坡：许永顺工作厅 [Singapore: Xu Yongshun Gongzuoting]. (Call no.: RSING Chinese 791.4309595 XYS)

Yap, J. (2007). *Motoring beyond 100: Celebrating 100 years of the Automobile Association of Singapore*. Singapore: Automobile Association of Singapore. (Call no.: RSING 629.2830605957 YAP)

York, F.W., & Phillips, A.R. (1996). *Singapore: A history of its trams trolleybuses and buses*. Surrey: DTS Publishing Limited. (Call no.: RSING q388.41322095957 YOR)

Yung, S.S., & Chan, K.B. (2003). Leisure, pleasure and consumption: Way of entertaining oneself. In K.B. Chan & C.K. Tong (Eds.), *Past times: A social history of Singapore* (pp. 152– 181). Singapore: Times Editions. (Call no.: RSING 959.57 PAS-[HIS])

Articles

Chan W.K.K. (1996). Personal styles, cultural values and management: The Sincere and Wing On companies in Shanghai and Hong Kong, 1900–1941. *Business History Review, 70*(2). Retrieved from JSTOR via NLB's eResources website: http://www. eresources.nlb.gov.sg

Cowan, R.S. (1976, January). The 'Industrial Revolution' in the home: Household technology and social change in the 20th century. *Technology and Culture, 17*(1), pp. 1–23. Retrieved from JSTOR via NLB's eResources website: http://eresources.nlb.gov. sg/

Fox, B.J. (1990, March). Selling the mechanised household: 70 years of ads in Ladies Home Journal. *Gender and Society, 4*(1), pp. 25–40. Retrieved from JSTOR via NLB's eResources website: http:// eresources.nlb.gov. sg/

Gibson-Hill, C.A. (1953). The Singapore Chronicle (1824–37). *Journal of the Malayan Branch of the Royal Asiatic Society, 26*(2), p. 176. Retrieved from JSTOR via NLB's eResources website: http://www. eresources.nlb.gov.sg

Huff, W.G. (2001, May). Entitlements, destitution, and emigration in the 1930s Singapore Great Depression. *The Economic History Review, 54*(2), pp. 290–323. Retrieved from JSTOR via NLB's eResources website: http://eresources.nlb.gov. sg/

Laird, P.W. (1996, October). 'The car without a single weakness': Early automobile advertising. *Technology and Culture, 37*(4), 796–812. Retrieved from JSTOR via NLB's eResources website: http://www. eresources.nlb.gov.sg

Parmer, J. (1989). Health and health services in British Malaya in the 1920s. *Modern Asian Studies, 23*(1), 49–71. Retrieved from JSTOR via NLB's eResources website: http://www. eresources.nlb.gov.sg

Peleggi, M. (2012). The social and material life of colonial hotels: Comfort zones as contact zones in British Colombo and Singapore, ca. 1870–1930. *Journal of Social History, 6*(1), 124–153. Retrieved from JSTOR via NLB's eResources website: http:// eresources.nlb.gov. sg/

Quah, S.R. (1980, July–December). Sex-role socialization in a transitional society. *International Journal of Sociology of the Family, 10*(2), 213–231. Retrieved from JSTOR via NLB's eResources website: http://eresources.nlb.gov. sg/

Wai, S.H. (2014). New Immigrant: On the first locally produced film in Singapore and Malaya. *Journal of Chinese Cinema, 8*(3), 244–258. Retrieved from Taylor & Francis Online.

Wong, A.K., & Ko, Y.-C. (1984). Women's work and family life: The case of electronics workers in Singapore [Working paper]. Michigan State University Office of Women in International Development [East Lansing]: Michigan State University. (Call no.: RSING 331.4821381095957 WON)

Wong, Y.C., & Tan, K.L. (2004, August). Emergence of a cosmopolitan space for consumption: The New World Amusement Park Singapore (1923–70) in the inter-war years. *Inter-Asia Cultural Studies, 5*(2), 279–304. Retrieved from JSTOR via NLB's eResources website: http://eresources.nlb.gov. sg/

Periodicals

Annual departmental report of the Straits Settlements for the year 1926. (1928). Singapore: Govt. Print. Off., p. 181. (Microfilm: NL29302)

Annual report of medical department 1926. (1927). Singapore: Govt. Print. Off., p. 181. (Call no.: RCLOS 362.1095957 ANN-[AR])

British Malayan Annual 1929. Singapore: Fishers Limited. (Microfilm: NL28302)

Roda. (1935, October). (Call no.: RUR 369.509595 R)

Her World. (1960). Singapore: Straits Times Press. Retrieved from PublicationSG.

British Malaya. (1926, May). *1*(1). London: Association of British Malaya. (Microfilm: NL7599)

Singapore almanack and directory. (1846). Singapore: Straits Times Press. (Microfilm: NL2363)

Newspaper Articles

(All retrieved from NewspaperSG unless otherwise stated)

南天酒樓新張廣告 [Advertisement of the opening of Southern Hotel]. (1927, February 15). 《 南洋商报 》 [Nanyang Siang Pau], p. 5.

昔日的香格里拉南天走过63年 [The 63 years of the Shangri-La of the past, the Great Southern Hotel]. (1966, January 1). 《联合早报》 [Lianhe Zaobao], p. 42.

[Page 2 Advertisements Column 3]. (1845, September 2). *The Straits Times*, p. 2.

[Page 4 Advertisements Column 1]. (1858, October 28). *The Singapore Free Press and Mercantile Advertiser*, p. 4.

[Page 16 Advertisements Column 1]. (1940, January 2). *The Straits Times*, p. 16.

[Page 7 Advertisements Column 1]. (1979, July 23). *The Straits Times*, p. 7.

[Photograph]. (1935, November 9). *Malaya Tribune*, p. 20.

[Untitled]. (1927, February 9). *The Singapore Free Press and Mercantile Advertiser*, p. 10.

700 'pirate' taxis in S'pore. (1946, August 10). *The Singapore Free Press*, p. 1.

3,800 apply for Comfort's 1,000 taxis. (1970, December 17). *The Straits Times*, p. 7.

4,000 cabbies want to join NTUC co-op. (1970, August 18). *The Straits Times*, p. 4.

A dream comes true. (1958, October 5). *Sunday Standard*, p. 15.

A wonderful achievement. (1932, September 30). *The Straits Times*, p. 12.

Adelphi Hotel. (1850, May 7). *The Straits Times*, p. 7.

Aerated waters. (1925, July 6). *Malaya Tribune*, p. 5.

An autocar anniversary. (1927, August 13). *The Singapore Free Press and Mercantile Advertiser*, p. 5.

Another ablution centre for Singapore to be built at Bendemeer. (1940, April 27). *Malaya Tribune*, p. 2.

Another new hotel built in Singapore. (1953, March 6). *The Straits Times*, p. 10.

Bata's new premises. (1940, June 26). *Malaya Tribune*, p. 4.

Big new Singapore store. (1938, July 24). *The Straits Times*, p. 1.

Boon, G.T. (1953, April 30). Send-off for two new hotels. *The Singapore Free Press*, p. 8.

Burns Concert. (1911, January 14). *The Singapore Free Press and Mercantile Advertiser*, p. 1.

Chairman began his career as apprentice. (1965, April 2). *The Straits Times*, p. 12.

Comfort taxis: A chance for pirate taxi men, too. (1971, January 16). *Singapore Herald*, p. 3.

Cook's tour de luxe. (1926, January 29). *The Singapore Free Press and Mercantile Advertiser*, p. 17.

Europe Hotel. (1921, November 5). *The Straits Times*, p. 10.

'Family store' opens in Singapore. (1965, October 30). *The Straits Times*, p. 16.

Farewell. (1950, July 27). *Malaya Tribune*, p. 11.

Firm sets up new shop to meet fashion goods demand. (1965, October 30). *The Straits Times*, p. 16.

First super-market in SEA. (1958, August 10). *Sunday Standard*, p. 2.

Ford Company opens here. (1926, November 23). *The Singapore Free Press and Mercantile Advertiser*, p. 8.

Ford company in Malaya is 30 years old. (1956, November 9). *The Straits Times*, p. 14.

Framroz celebrates fifty years of progress. (1954, January 10). *Sunday Standard*, p. 5.

Free medical service now welcome in kampongs. (1939, July 9). *The Straits Times*, p. 32.

'Help-yourself' service as Fitzpatrick's streamlines. (1949, July 30). *Malaya Tribune*, p. 4.

Hammods, K. (1964, February 2). Battle of the big hotels. *The Straits Times*, p. 15.

Hygiene drive. (1945, October 30). *Malaya Tribune*, p. 4.

Hospitals fight against malnutrition. (1938, March 13). *The Straits Times*, p. 32.

How Singapore has been revolutionised by the modern motor car. (1935, October 8). *The Singapore Free Press and Mercantile Advertiser*, p. 20.

James, J. (2001, April 26). High life on High Street. *The Straits Times*, p. 8.

Japanese cars to cost more. (1971, October 11). *The Straits Times*, p.1.

Kaur, M. (1981, September 11). Memory lane. *The Straits Times*, p. 13.

Khng, E.M. (1984, July 22). Eating out for breakfast an emerging trend. *The Straits Times*, p. 16.

Legislative Council. (1926, July 12). *The Straits Times*, p. 10.

Lim, S. (1988, July 12). Time runs out for Magnolia Snack Bar. *The Straits Times*, p. 32.

Local industries. (1897, January 8). *The Straits Times*, p. 3.

Magic in North Bridge Road. (1935, February 5). *The Straits Times*, p.13.

Materials of proved quality for the building trade. (1936, May 1). *The Singapore Free Press and Mercantile Advertiser*, p. 5.

Mainly about Malayans. (1938, December 4). *The Straits Times*, p. 7.

Men's shop opens in S'pore today. (1971, April 2). *The Straits Times*, p. 16.

Metro – past, present and into the future. (1982, September 9). *The Business Times*, p. 7.

Motors & motoring. (1910, May 14). *The Straits Times*, p. 11.

Mountain-air climate in Singapore. (1938, July 27). *The Singapore Free Press and Mercantile Advertiser*, p. 4.

Mr. Buckley and his coffee machine. (1955, March 13). *The Straits Times*, p. 12.

Municipal Council. (1862, June 14). *The Straits Times*, p. 1.

New hostel opened. (1917, July 19). *Malaya Tribune*, p. 4.

Notices. (1931, January 16). *The Singapore Free Press*, p. 9.

Now shopping in the modern manner comes to Singapore. (1958, August 11). *The Singapore Free Press*, p. 3.

Our aerated water trade. (1932, January 2). *The Singapore Free Press and Mercantile Advertiser*, p. 23.

Pirate taxis. (1957, May 8). *Singapore Standard*, p. 6.

Pirate taxis: A public service. (1970, October 26). *Singapore Herald*, p. 8.

Pirate taxis defy ban. (1971, October 12). *The Straits Times*, p. 12

Police have plan to beat taxi 'pirates'. (1952, January 15). *The Straits Times*, p. 7.

Prospectus for a theatre. (1842, May 19). *The Singapore Free Press and Mercantile Advertiser*, p. 1.

Quek, E. (2017, March 26). Three home-grown brands celebrate milestone anniversaries. *The Straits Times*. Retrieved from Factiva via NLB's eResources website: http://eresources.nlb.gov.sg

Raffles new grill. (1923, April 7). *The Straits Times*, p. 10.

Ran, S. (1985, April 23). High Street – on the road to new life. *The Straits Times*, p. 1.

S'pore has 10,000 ice-cream eaters daily. (1946, December 23). *Malaya Tribune*, p. 5.

Say 'Tiger' – It's the best beer. (1932, December 20). *The Straits Times*, p. 4.

Singapore new department store opens. (1938, October 14). *Malaya Tribune*, p. 20.

Singapore's first autocar. (1896, August 13). *The Singapore Free Press and Mercantile Advertiser*, p. 2.

Singapore's first motor car was a problem. (1958, July 5). *The Straits Times*, p. 9.

'Sinkeh' who became king of dept stores. (1984, August 13). *Singapore Monitor*, p. 10.

Special licence urged for transport of pupils. (1965, May 28). *The Straits Times*, p. 4.

Staines, V. (1949, May 21). Water is their main problem. *The Singapore Free Press*, p. 4.

Taxi-cabs for Singapore. (1910, July 1). *The Singapore Free Press and Mercantile Advertiser*, p. 8.

Taximen's chief praises NTUC move to help 'pirates'. (1971, January 18). *The Straits Times*, p. 21.

Taximeter Day–Dec. 31. (1953, November 14). *The Singapore Free Press*, p. 5.

The disposal of night soil at Singapore. (1894, January 19). *The Straits Times*, p. 3.

The motoring world. (1911, January 6). *The Straits Times*, p. 11.

The motoring world. (1928, December 15). *The Straits Times*, p. 18.

The Paris Cinematograph. (1904, November 26). *The Straits Times*, p. 3.

The Ripograph. (1897, May 18). *The Singapore Free Press and Mercantile Advertiser (Weekly)*, p. 6.

The rise of Warin Studios: All forms of publicity. (1937, April 27). *The Singapore Free Press*, p. 2.

The rooster stands for good taste. (1955, October 7). *The Singapore Free Press*, p. 5.

The Tanjong Katong Hotel. (1884, January 8). *The Straits Times*, p. 2.

The Oriental Hotel. (1924, January 26). *Malayan Saturday Post*, p. 3.

The war against pirate taxis a success. (1962, February 18). *The Straits Times*, p. 16.

The pirates who are performing a public service. (1962, October 2). *The Straits Times*, p. 10.

Theatre Royal. (1854, December 8). *The Singapore Free Press and Mercantile Advertiser*, p. 3.

Tobacco industry in Malaya. (1932, January 2). *The Straits Times*, p. 4.

Town Hall. (1905, October 2). *Eastern Daily Mail and Straits Morning Advertiser*, p. 3.

Trips to Katong. (1902, January 17). *The Straits Times*, p. 1.

Venereal diseases. (1922, November 2). *The Singapore Free Press and Mercantile Advertiser (Weekly)*, p. 277.

W.J. Warin dies in Singapore. (1950, June 11). *The Straits Times*, p. 9.

War on pirate taxis goes on. (1972, May 1). *New Nation*, p. 3.

Wearne Bros. declare 3 per cent dividend. (1933, December 16). *The Straits Times*, p. 9.

Where to shop in Singapore: No. III, High Street. (1939, May 3). *The Singapore Free Press and Mercantile Advertiser*, p. 12.

Websites

Chia, J.Y.J., & Nor-Afidah Adb Rahman. (2007). Old racecourse (Farrer Park). *Singapore Infopedia*. Retrieved from Singapore Infopedia website: http://www.eresources.nlb.gov.sg/infopedia

Chia, J.Y.J., & Tay, S. (2016). John Little. *Singapore Infopedia*. Retrieved from Singapore Infopedia website: http://eresources.nlb.gov.sg/infopedia/

Chua, A.L. (2016). The story of Singapore radio (1924–41). *BiblioAsia*, 12(1). Retrieved from BiblioAsia website: http://www. nlb.gov.sg/biblioasia

Crash course in Victorian gloves. (2010, September 29). How we do run on. Retrieved from website: http://gwtwscrapbook. blogspot. sg/2010/09/crash-course-in-victorian-gloves.html#. WrMTeOhubIU

Davison, J. (2014). Swan & Maclaren: Pioneers of Modernist architecture. *BiblioAsia*, 13(2). Retrieved from BiblioAsia website: http://www.nlb.gov.sg/biblioasia/2017/07/06/ swan-maclaren-pioneers-of-modernist-architecture/

Definition of automobilism in English. English Oxford Living Dictionaries. Retrieved from: https://en.oxforddictionaries.com/ definition/ automobilism

Energy Market Authority. (n.d.). *Singapore energy story*. Retrieved from www.ema.gov.sg/ourenergystory.aspx

Faris Joraimi. (2017, January 29). Wardah. *s/pores*, 15. Retrieved from s/pores website: http://s-pores.com/2017/01/wardah-by-faris-joraimi

Fernandez, W. (Ed.), *Living history: 170 years of the Straits Times* [ebook]. Retrieved from The Straits Times website: http://graphics. straitstimes.com/STI/STIMEDIA/ebooks/Living-History.pdf

Hopkins, S. (n.d.). *History of men's hats*. Retrieved 10 March, 2018, from website: http://fashion-history.lovetoknow.com/fashion-accessories/history-mens-hats

Hudd, S. (2017). London Missionary Society in Singapore. *Singapore Infopedia*. Retrieved from Singapore Infopedia website: http:// eresources.nlb.gov.sg/ infopedia/

Jay Gee Group. (n.d.) *Milestones*. Retrieved from Jay Gee Group website: http://jaygee.com.sg/corporate-milestones/

Kandang Kerbau Hospital. (2018). *Hospital milestones*. Retrieved 2018, March 8 from Kandang Kerbau Hospital website: www.kkh. com.sg/AboutUs/Overview

Mazelan Anuar. (2016, January 26). The first newspaper. *BiblioAsia*, 11(4). Retrieved from BiblioAsia website: http://www.nlb.gov.sg/ biblioasia/

National Library Board. (2014). King George VI Dock opens. *HistorySG*. Retrieved from HistorySG website: http://eresources. nlb.gov.sg/ history/

National Library Board. (2014). Robinson's department store is established. *HistorySG*. Retrieved from HistorySG website: http:// eresources.nlb.gov.sg/history/

Nor-Afidah Abd Rahman. (2004). Echigoya. *Singapore Infopedia*. Retrieved from Singapore Infopedia website: http://eresources. nlb.gov.sg/infopedia/

Republic of Singapore. *Medicines (Advertisement and Sale) Act (Chapter 177)*. Retrieved from Health Sciences Authority website: http://www.hsa.gov.sg/content/dam/HSA/HPRG/ Useful_Information_for_Applicants/Legislation/MEDICINES%20 (ADVERTISEMENT%20AND%20SALE)%20ACT.pdf

Schneider, S. (2016, June 8). The evolution of neckwear – From scarf to tie and why we wear ties today. *Gentleman's Gazette*. Retrieved from website: https://www.gentlemansgazette.com/ evolution-neckwear-tie-cravat-scarf/

St Andrew's Mission Hospital. (2015). *About us*. Retrieved from St Andrew's Mission Hospital website: www.samh.org.sg/about-us

Tan, B. (2010, July). Early tourist guidebooks: The illustrated guide to the Federated Malay States. *BiblioAsia*. Retrieved from BiblioAsia website: http://www.nlb.gov.sg/biblioasia

Tan, L.G. (2014). Charting multilingualism in Singapore: From the nineteenth century to the present [Final-year project]. Singapore: Nanyang Technological University. Retrieved from Nanyang Technological University website: http://www.soh.ntu. edu. sg/Programmes/linguistics/Undergraduate%20Programme/ Documents/Good%20Sample%20FYP%20Reports/AY2014/Tan%20 Lijia%20Gloria.pdf

United Nations Office on Drugs and Crime. (1958, January 1). The opium problem in Singapore. *Bulletin on Narcotics*, IX(3). Retrieved from United Nations Office on Drugs and Crime website: http://www.unodc.org/unodc/en/data-and-analysis/ bulletin/ bulletin_1958-01-01_4_page003.html

Walton, G. (2014, June 19). Glove etiquette in the 1800s. *Geri Walton*. Retrieved from website: https://www. geriwalton.com/glove-etiquette/

Wong, M. (n.d.). *Singapore: A pineapple canning delight*. Retrieved from National Archives of Singapore website: www. nas.gov.sg/ archivesonline/article/singapore-pineapple-canning-delight

Oral History Interviews

(All retrieved from National Archives of Singapore website: http://www.nas.gov.sg/archivesonline)

Chew, D. (Interviewer). (1985). *Oral history interview with Girishchandra Kothari* [Accession no. 549/23]. Retrieved from National Archives of Singapore website: http://www.nas.gov.sg/archivesonline/

Chua, C.H.J. (Interviewer). (2007). *Oral history interview with Ow Yong Mun* [Accession no. 3214/7/]. Retrieved from National Archives of Singapore website: http://www.nas.gov.sg/archivesonline/

Lim, H.S. (Interviewer). (1981). *Oral history interview with Rajabali Jumabhoy* [Accession no. 74/37]. Retrieved from National Archives of Singapore website: http://www.nas.gov.sg/archivesonline/

Tan, B.L. (Interviewer). (1981). *Oral history interview with Gwee Peng Kwee* [Accession no. 128/13]. Retrieved from National Archives of Singapore website: http://www.nas.gov.sg/archivesonline

Tan, B.L. (Interviewer). (1987). *Transcript of oral history interview with Ng Seng Mun* [Accession no. 852/10]. Retrieved from National Archives of Singapore website: http://www.nas.gov.sg/archivesonline

Map and Ephemera

Thomson, J.T. (1846). *Plan of Singapore Town and its adjoining districts.* Retrieved from National Archives of Singapore website: http://www.nas.gov.sg/ archivesonline/

Anthony, P.A. (1914). *Federated Malay States Railways: Pamphlet of information for travellers: Tours in the Malay Peninsula.* Federated Malay States Railways. (Microfilm: NL29292)

Akshata Patkar

Assistant Manager
Content & Services (Research)
National Library
Akshata conducts research into public policy and current affairs, and has a keen interest in cultural studies.

Chung Sang Hong

Assistant Director
Exhibitions & Curation
National Library
Sang Hong is the lead curator of the exhibition, *Selling Dreams: Early Advertising in Singapore*. He is interested in the social history of early Singapore.

Fiona Lim

Associate Librarian
Singapore & Southeast Asia
National Library
Fiona is interested in space, history, time, memory and power, as well as the interactions between them. She is currently researching on the penal system in colonial Singapore.

Georgina Wong

Assistant Curator
Exhibitions & Curation
National Library
Georgina is the co-curator of the exhibition, *Selling Dreams: Early Advertising in Singapore*. Her research interests include historical architecture and decorative art history.

Goh Yu Mei

Librarian
Literary Arts
National Library
Yu Mei works with the Chinese arts and literary collection and her research interest lies in the interaction between society and Chinese literature.

Liviniyah P.

Associate Librarian
Singapore & Southeast Asia
National Library
Liviniyah's responsibilities at the National Library include managing and developing the content and collection on Singapore and Southeast Asia, particularly with regard to the Indian community.

Mazelan Anuar

Senior Librarian
Singapore & Southeast Asia
National Library
Mazelan's research interests are in early Singapore Malay publications and digital librarianship. He is involved in managing the National Library's Malay-language collection as well as NewspaperSG. He is a safe driver who drives the reliable and boring Toyota Wish.

Nadirah Norruddin

Associate Librarian
Singapore & Southeast Asia
National Library
Nadirah's main responsibility is managing and developing the Singapore and Southeast Asia collection. Her research interest lies in the customs and traditions of the Malay world.

Yu-Mei Balasingamchow

Writer
Yu-Mei is the co-author of *Singapore: A Biography* (2009) and co-editor of *In Transit: An Anthology from Singapore on Airports and Air Travel* (2016). She works on history, art and culture projects and has curated exhibitions for the National Museum of Singapore and the National Archives of Singapore. She also writes fiction. Her website is http://www.toomanythoughts.org